The
BIBLE
and
SPIRITUAL
LIFE

The
BIBLE
and
SPIRITUAL
LIFE

A. T. Pierson

Kingsley Press

Shoals, Indiana

The Bible and Spiritual Life

Published by Kingsley Press
PO Box 973
Shoals, IN 47581
USA

Tel. (800) 971-7985
www.kingsleypress.com
E-mail: sales@kingsleypress.com

ISBN: 978-1-937428-40-2 (paperback)
ISBN: 978-1-937428-41-9 (ebook)

First published in 1908 by The Baker and Taylor Co.

First Kingsley Press edition 2014

Contents

Contents

Introduction

Each link in a chain is complete in itself; but in order to make a chain, the links must overlap, otherwise there is no continuity.

The addresses which are reproduced in this book are meant to continue and complete the two series of "Exeter Hall Lectures" which preceded: *The Living Oracles of God* and *The Bible and Spiritual Criticism*; and the overlapping or partial repetition is necessary to indicate and ensure connection and continuity in the treatment of the larger theme.

The main object of the initial course was to show that the Word of God is its own evidence of its divine inspiration; that the vital breath of the living God makes it a living book and its utterances his living oracles. The second course aimed to show that, as the Bible is a spiritual book, appealing to the spiritual man rather than the merely intellectual, it demands in the reader spiritual senses and a spiritual frame, a receptive, verifying faculty, moral and spiritual harmony with its author, if its deeper truths are to be unveiled and understood.

In the present and concluding series the aim is to show and illustrate the fact that, for all the cravings and crises of man's moral and spiritual life, this book of God is the exact provision, satisfaction and guide; that only he who, having made man, knows what is in man, could have made a book which so anticipates and answers all the needs of his higher nature.

Arthur T. Pierson
1127 Dean St., Brooklyn, N. Y.

Chapter 1

The Bible as God's Book

The book and its divine author must have a vital relation if the Bible is to be man's book in the highest sense of perfect adaptation to all his spiritual needs.

As it becomes us to lay a biblical foundation for all teaching which concerns the Word of God, each chapter will begin with a few leading texts which may serve to hint the lines of thought to be followed, and serve as a basis for the treatment of each subject.

First of all, four of its grand utterances may constitute the basis of all that follows—a general groundwork for the specific treatment of successive chapters.

For ever, O Lord, thy word is settled in Heaven (Ps. 119:89).

This was Luther's maxim, inscribed on the walls of his chamber and embroidered on his robe. It means that the Word of God is established in heaven—far above and beyond the reach of all disturbing causes, as the stars are beyond the reach of man's watering pot, and cannot be quenched by the ocean spray.

Thou hast magnified thy word above all thy name (Ps. 138:2).

This suggests that, beyond all other previous manifestations of the divine character and will, his written word revealed him. This was affirmed, of course, before the incarnation of God in Christ, the living Word, had furnished its final revelation of God.

Buy the truth and sell it not (Prov. 23:23).

Briefly this bids us give any price to get the truth, but take no price to part with it.

These are the true sayings of God (Rev. 19:9).

A comprehensive and grand description of the whole content and character of the Holy Scriptures, repeated and amplified in the first words of the epilogue to this closing apocalypse: "These sayings are faithful and true" (22:6).

Before we descend to man's level, it may be well to glance at the fitness of the Bible to represent its divine author himself. Does it befit the "spiritual life" of *God?* If so, we shall be the more assured in advance of its correspondence and adaptation to man as his creature.

More surely than the crown shows the king, the perfect work proves the skilled workman. Giotto revealed himself to a stranger by drawing a perfect circle at a stroke, and Mendelssohn to the keeper of the organ in Strasbourg Cathedral by the way he made that organ speak.

Three psalms, 1, 19, 119, extol the Word of God. The first, as making the devout reader prosperous and fruitful; the hundred and nineteenth, as adapted to all the varied experiences of a believer. But the nineteenth shows the law of the Lord as the mirror of its maker. The psalm is divided into three parts—the first and second exactly correspond—the first represents the *material* universe as the mirror of his *natural* attributes; the second shows the *written law or Scripture* as the mirror of his *moral* attributes. The dome of the firmament with its sun and stars aflame with his power, wisdom and eternity; but his Word is a grander firmament in which his glory as a moral being shines as in constellations of suns.

Here we touch the crown of all arguments for the divine origin of the Bible—the supreme evidence and apologetic: It is such a book as *befits a divine author and such as he only could produce.* This is a fact that has never been properly weighed, but, when once clearly seen, it takes out of court all further inquiry—the case is closed. There is one witness whose testimony is so conclusive and irrefutable that to call any other would be an insult to the intelligence and integrity of judge and jury, and that witness is the Bible itself. Only the atheistic fool, who can study the mechanism celestial and say there is *no God,* can search the Scriptures and say they are the work of *man,* for they present another celestial mechanism still more inexplicable without a divine designer.

In showing how this book of God harmonizes with the whole nature and life of its author, again we recall the beautiful tradition, connected with the Westminster Assembly of 1643, that, when it was needful to frame an answer to that august question, "What is God?" Rev. George Gillespie, one of the four Scottish commissioners, and the youngest member of the assembly, being asked to lead in prayer for divine guidance, began with a sentence that was unanimously adopted as the best possible answer:

"O God, who art a spirit, infinite, eternal and unchangeable, in thy being, wisdom, power, holiness, justice, goodness and truth."

Taking this sentence as an outline portrait of the divine being, the correspondence of the Word of God with the features here drawn is marvelously complete. Let us put them side by side.

God Is	The Word of God
A spirit,	Deals with spiritual verities;
Infinite,	Transcends all bounds of time and space;
Eternal,	Illumines the past, present and future;
Unchangeable;	Teaches immutable laws and principles;
In his being,	Is the mirror of divine personality;
Wisdom,	Reflects his omniscience, and foresight;
Power,	His omnipotence and miracle working;
Holiness,	His perfection of moral character;
Justice,	His absolute rectitude in administration;
Goodness,	His benevolence and beneficence;
Truth.	His infinite veracity and fidelity.

This hasty glance suffices to show how the best definition of God that man has perhaps ever framed finds in the Bible an exact reflection of all the elements believed to enter into the most complete and exalted conception of the divine character and personality.

There are a few passages of Scripture which may add further confirmation to this proof that in his Word, God is wondrously revealed.

Hear, O Israel, Jehovah, our God, is One Jehovah (Deut. 6:4).

This is meant to be conspicuous. These words form the beginning of the SHAMA ("Hear") of the Jewish services, and belong to the daily morning and evening office. Indeed, they have been termed the "Jewish Creed." Their expression in the Hebrew is singular in terseness and force: "Jehovah, our Elohim, Jehovah one." If they are differently construed, it is owing to their very dignity, majesty and brevity. They contain far more than a mere statement of the unity of God as opposed to polytheism; or of the supremacy of the revelation made to his chosen people as opposed to all pretended manifestations of his will and essence. Here is a majestic assertion that Jehovah God is absolutely and alone THE GOD, beyond causation or competition, sovereign and undisputed. The last letters of the first and last words of this verse are, in the original, *majascula*, i.e., written larger than the ordinary size, and these two *majascula* form together a word signifying "*witness*," ("Ed" Josh. 22:34), construed by the Jewish commentators as highly significant, importing that this utterance is a witness for the faith, or that God is challenged as a witness to the sincerity and correctness of him who utters it.

This is therefore one of the marked sentences of the Old Testament and deserves to be written in large capitals. It asserts in the divine being a peculiar *unity*—the unity of solitariness, of inapproachable perfection, of absolute independence of another and of consistency with himself. It suggests also the unity of perfect symmetry and beauty to which nothing can be added, from which nothing can be subtracted.

If the Bible is God's book, we shall find in it a corresponding unity. It will reveal a certain solitariness, standing alone amid all other books as having a character of its own; it will be complete in itself, and exhibit symmetry of proportion and evidence of a divine plan and purpose, forbidding all addition or subtraction.

The pyramid of Cheops is still, as of old, one of the Seven Wonders of the World. It seems to have been built mainly as a royal sepulcher, but having also astronomical and scientific ends, for the structure is carefully oriented, its sides facing the cardinal points and the angle of its entrances pointing to the north star. It took from twenty to thirty years to complete and employed at a time a hundred thousand workmen; and as there were four relays of workmen a year, millions must have helped to build it. Yet there was but one proper architect, however many workmen.

The Word of God is a massive pyramid which it took centuries to build, and it has not only outlived millions of other books, but rises solitary above all other monuments of literature. It is marked by a peculiar unity of purpose and of structure. It is supremely the book of salvation. Whatever subordinate ends it serves, its lines all converge in one point. Its capstone, like its cornerstone, is the Lord Jesus Christ, who alone can complete and crown it.

Aside from this, in every part it exhibits unity of character and design. It has a symmetry, unaccountable except as, behind all the forty human writers and more than sixty books, one architectural mind planned it and carried the plan to completion. Its proportions, like those of an ideal structure, are mathematical, and show a mathematical mind. However many human pens contributed to its contents, there must have been some ONE, independent of the bounds of time and space, and above the reach of all that changes, who is its original, responsible author.

A chart (No. 1) accompanies this chapter, which, however rude and crude as a drawing, and without pretensions as a work of art, is meant to present to the eye this conception of the structural unity of the English Bible. It shows the five books of the Pentateuch like basal blocks, surmounted by the twelve minor books of history from Joshua to Esther; then the five poetic books, from Job to Solomon's Song; then the five major prophetic, and the twelve minor prophetic books; above these the five historical books—the New Testament Pentateuch; and above these the twenty-one epistles, with the Apocalypse crowning the whole as a dome.[1]

The recurrence of certain numbers in this structural arrangement is very noticeable, such, for example, as *five*, which reappears at four points conspicuously. But we shall find the same number in individual books, as in the five sacrifices or offerings in Leviticus, the five books which the Jews call the Pentateuch of the Psalms,[2] and where they trace in the psalm which opens each division, a likeness to the successive books of Moses. Again we see this fivefold arrangement in Job's five trials, in Solomon's five experiments in Ecclesiastes, and in the five parts of the book of Proverbs. There are also five epistle writers of the New Testament, Paul, James, Peter, John and Jude, and as many great themes which they especially represent, such as faith, hope, love, good works, and the perils of apostasy.

This mathematical law pervading the book is at least a hint of the mathematical mind of the author, who reveals the same regard to the symmetry of number and form in the material universe. The planetary and stellar worlds Kepler found to obey the strictest mathematical laws, fixed proportions existing between their respective sizes, orbits, and distances from the sun and from each other. In botany, mineralogy, vegetable and animal structure, there is the same universal law of mathematical arrangement and proportion; so that the natural inference is that since the creator of nature is the author of the Bible, similar marks of his mind will appear in both.

While referring to the numerical structure and mathematical peculiarities of the Bible, it may be well to add that no less a man than Rev.

---

1   Compare *The Bible and Spiritual Criticism*, chapter 8.
2   Psalms 1–12; 13–72; 73–89; 90–106; 107–150.

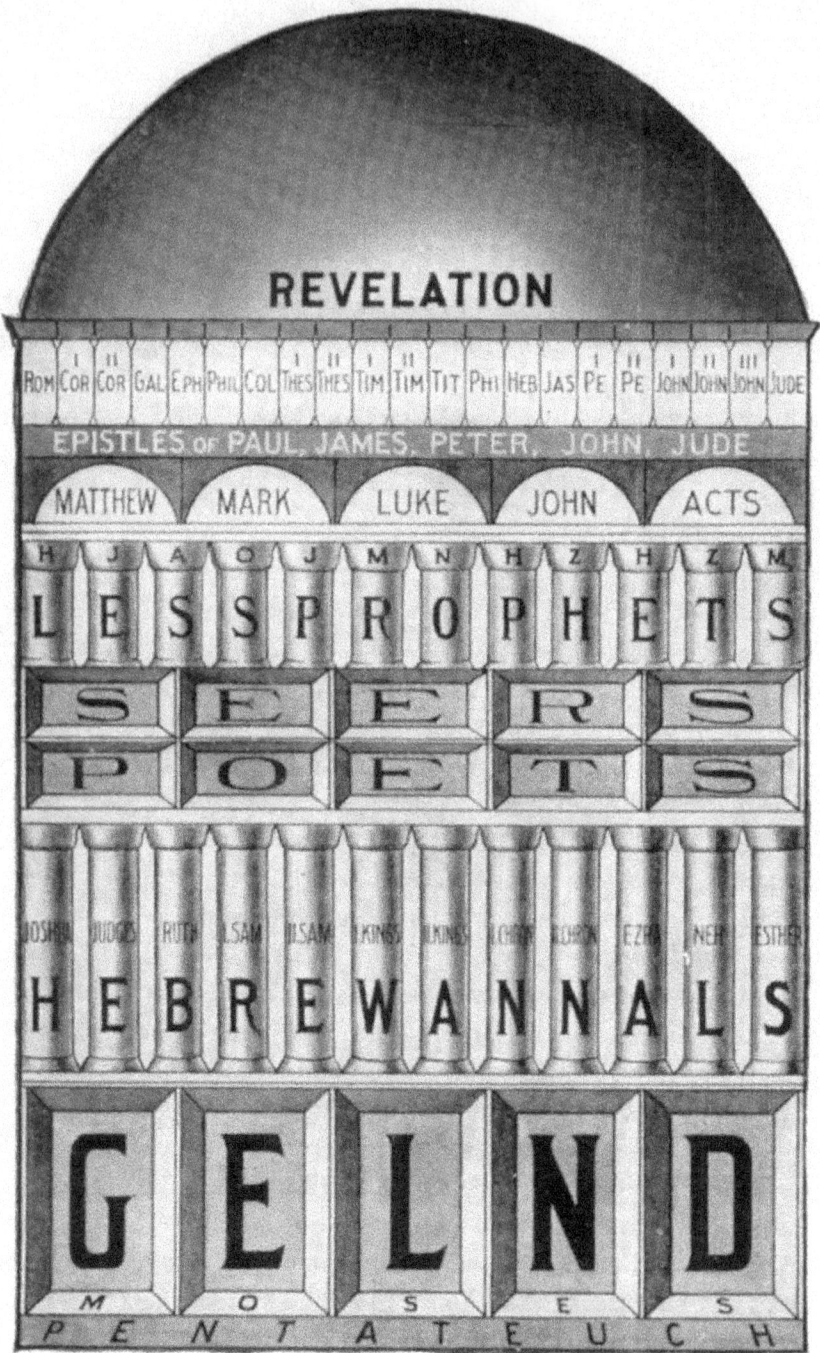

1. The Bible as a structure

Edward Hayes Plumptre, M. A., Professor of Divinity in King's College, London, and Examining Chaplain to the bishop of Gloucester and Bristol, after a most careful and scholarly examination of the numbers and proportions of the tabernacle writes thus:

> Dimensions also had their meaning. Difficult as it may be to feel sure that we have the key to the enigma, there can be but little doubt that the older religious systems of the world did attach a mysterious significance to each separate number, that the training of Moses must have made that transparently clear to him which to us is almost impenetrably dark.

It may be useful, he adds, to exhibit briefly the chief thoughts which have been connected with the numbers that are most prominent in the language of symbolism.

The following are his equivalents:

ONE—The Godhead, eternity, life, creative force, the sun, man.

Two—Matter, time, death, receptive capacity, the moon, woman.

THREE—As a number or in the triangle, the universe in connection with God, the absolute in itself, the unconditioned, God.

FOUR—The number or in the square or cube, conditioned existence, the world as created, divine order, revelation.

SEVEN—As the sum of three and four, the union of the world and God, rest, as in the Sabbath, peace, blessing, purification.

TEN—As the sum of 1 + 2 + 3 + 4, completeness moral and physical, perfection.

FIVE—Perfection half attained, incompleteness.

TWELVE—The multiple of 3 × 4, the signs of the Zodiac, the cycle of the seasons, in Israel the ideal number of the people, of the covenant of God with them.

The symbol, the perfect cube of the holy of holies, the constant recurrence of the numbers 4 and 10, may well be accepted as symbolizing order, stability, perfection. The symbol reappears in the apocalypse. There the heavenly Jerusalem is described in words which absolutely exclude the literalism which has sometimes been blindly applied to it, as a city four square, 12,000 furlongs (1,500 English miles) in length, breadth and height (Rev. 21:16).

Mathematics pertains to eternal truth, for we cannot imagine any system of things where two and two do not equal four, or the three interior angles of a triangle do not together equal two rectangles. We must conclude therefore that the same God is behind nature and Scripture.

Far more important is the moral structure of the Bible. In the first words of the first book we read: "In the beginning, God;" and this is the keynote to all that follows. God is the universal starting point for truth, authority, worship, obedience, knowledge and duty. There are at least seven grand ideas around which all this system of truth centralizes and crystallizes, such as the ideas of:

1. God, one, supreme, incomparable, incomprehensible, eternal.
2. Man, his creation, and originally in his image and likeness.
3. Sin, making man and God aliens by destroying all unity.
4. God-Man, the representative incarnation of God in sinless man.
5. Man reconciled to God, in the God-Man restored to harmony.
6. God in man, by the Holy Spirit imparting the divine nature.
7. God over man, finally restored to supremacy as sovereign.

This is very imperfect as an outline, but it serves to suggest a wide territory for thought and study. Bengel said that some twenty words so pervade Scripture that to master their meaning is to unlock its hidden chambers. So, about these seven central ideas, we may arrange all the moral and spiritual contents of this divine book. How is it conceivable that such unity of substance in the book can be accounted for except by one infinite teacher? Manifestly it was impossible for the scores of human contributors to its contents to confer, and combine their efforts so as to preserve this substantial agreement in their standards of truth and duty. This unity of Scripture, despite all the natural and human hindrances, thus appears from every point of view, in that mystery of *form* which is both inclusive and exclusive, admitting only what is helpful to that unity of plan but embracing all that conduces to it.

This we account one of the foremost proofs of the superhuman origin of Scripture. For example, the grand object in view is to reveal God to man so as to draw man into vital and loving relation with God. Hence, the book deals with God as man's creator and rightful ruler; with man, as his creature and rightful subject; with man as alien from God; and with God, as necessarily hostile to man as a sinner, because of his own essential hatred of sin; with the God-Man as the personal medium and mediator for God's approach to man and man's to God; with man as in him reconciled to God, making possible God's harmony with man. Then it reveals God as dwelling in man by his Holy Spirit, and finally ruling over redeemed man in a heavenly kingdom. Thus, from first to last, the truth and history advance steadily to the consummation.

Some careful readers think they see this orderly arrangement even in the *minutiae* of the Word of God, so that nothing is out of place; and discover so many details in which a systematic plan is revealed that there seems danger of fanciful inventions taking the place of discoveries. But, after making all allowance for such possible extremes, it still remains true that every new advance in the reverent and prayerful study of this book is attended with a new advance in appreciation of its contents. To him who, as in the Yosemite Valley, gets the true "Inspiration Point" from which to command a view of the whole, every part of the book is seen to bear a harmonious relation to every other, and all together to constitute a unique revelation of God.

God might naturally be jealous of his own inspired word, and, as he turneth the hearts of men whithersoever he will, we may expect that, as a pilot holds the helm of his vessel through all the vicissitudes of wind and wave, the divine author would guard his book, controlling historic events with reference to its completeness and determining the order in which book after book should find its way into the canon. The careful student of the *English* Bible cannot but observe that in so many cases the order of the books is inseparable from the *progress of doctrine*, that, although it is not exactly the order of arrangement of the Hebrew and Greek originals, the author seems by his providence to have guided even in this canonical arrangement of the English version.

As a matter of convenience, the *English Bible* has been made the basis of the chart on the structure of the Word of God, partly because this is the version that is actually in the hands of English readers, and partly because we believe that God had a purpose in permitting this version to assume its present form. Notwithstanding the violation of the *chronological* order, a *logical* order is followed that can hardly be accidental or fortuitous. God must have foreseen that the English Bible, as we have it, would become the model for most of the translations into other languages; and it is a singular fact that such is the case in the five hundred such translations now extant. Hence the order of books, as they appear in this English version, as he foresaw, becomes the fixed arrangement for the nations of the world. Is it too much to believe therefore that, for reasons of his own, this order was allowed to displace the chronological, and also the order of the original Hebrew canon of the Old Testament, as most adapted to the general purpose for which the complete Bible is designed? We feel confident that a providential control is to be traced

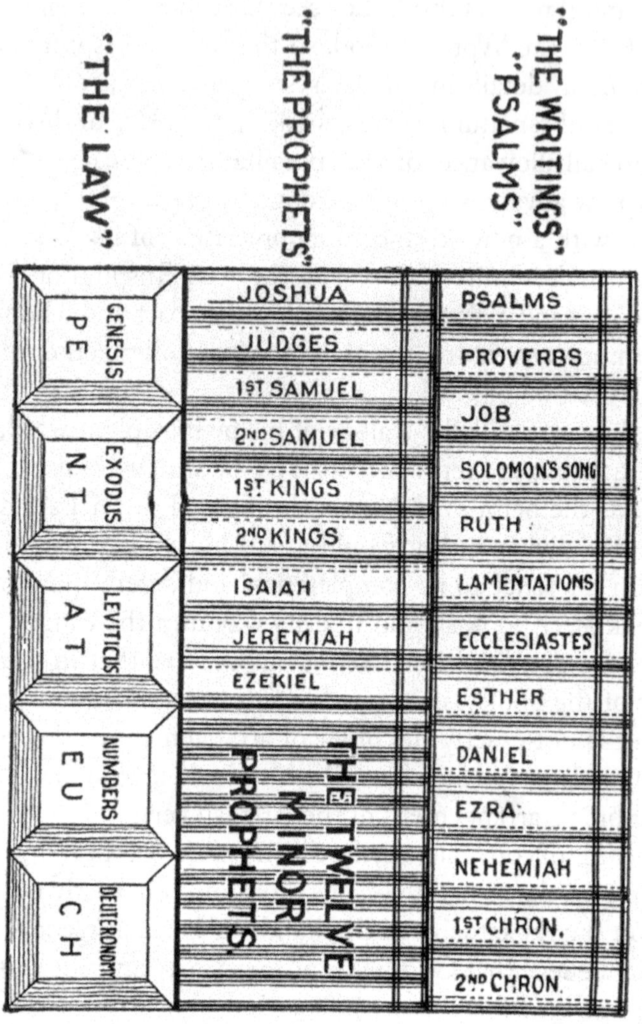

"THE LAW"
"THE PROPHETS"
"THE WRITINGS"
"PSALMS"
PE
NT
AT
EU
CH
GENESIS
EXODUS
LEVITICUS
NUMBERS
DEUTERONOMY
JOSHUA
JUDGES
1ST SAMUEL
2ND SAMUEL
1ST KINGS
2ND KINGS
ISAIAH
JEREMIAH
EZEKIEL
THE TWELVE MINOR PROPHETS.
PSALMS
PROVERBS
JOB
SOLOMON'S SONG
RUTH
LAMENTATIONS
ECCLESIASTES
ESTHER
DANIEL
EZRA
NEHEMIAH
1ST CHRON.
2ND CHRON.

2. Structure of Hebrew Old Testament

in the determination of this latest arrangement. It may be interesting, however, for students of Scripture to compare the chronological arrangement, and that of the Hebrew Old Testament with that of the Word of God as we have it, and hence we add a second diagram showing the books in this order, following the arrangement of the Hebrew Scriptures in the Old Testament, as the Jews had them, arranged as the "Law," the "Prophets," and the sacred "writings" (Diagram 2).

The correspondence of the Two Testaments is itself a fascinating field of research, which has been treated with singular success by such men as Adolph Saphir, in his *Divine Unity of the Scripture*. There is a Hebrew and a Greek portion; the old is preparatory, typical, prophetical; the new is supplemental, experimental, final. The old is patent in the new, while the new is latent in the old. In the former God the Father is conspicuous, the Son appearing only in forecast, and the Spirit in occasional and official manifestations; in the new, the Son and Spirit come into such prominence that this new revelation of God almost fills the horizon of view. The Old Testament reminds of the ark, floating over waters of judgment and saving a chosen few; the new, of the emergence of that few to re-people and subdue the earth. In the old, the great thought is separation, preservation, conservation; in the new, dissemination, promulgation, evangelization. The old covenant aimed to keep God's people faithful to him by keeping them apart from other peoples; but the new covenant sends them out into the midst of all nations that they may win men to him. In hundreds of particulars the contrast is obvious, while it is as plain that the two Testaments belong as halves to one whole, and neither can be complete in itself. The oak may displace the acorn, but it grows out of it and must find root in the grave of the acorn, and will die if it is removed from that burial place of the seed, or is cut off from its roots in the original germ. If the Old Testament has developed to majestic beauty and completeness in the New, it is still true that the germinal suggestions of all New Testament truth lie in the Old Testament soil. Even what has undergone change has elements of permanence, for it is only the figurative passing into the literal; prophecy fulfilling in history, forecast merging into actual event, one jot or tittle in no wise passing from the law till all is fulfilled in the gospel.

The Bible, as the book of God, may be expected, as has been said in brief already, to be the mirror of his attributes. It is obvious that the great God could not produce a book, even through human agency, without leaving upon it some unmistakable marks of his own divinity, somewhat as Michaelangelo, in his famous cartoons, which were drawn by pupils from his designs, shows everywhere the traces of his hand, not only in grandeur of conception, but in details of form and color, where his own brush has supplemented and completed their work.

There are certain attributes of God which are inseparable from his being and of which we think instinctively when God is mentioned or suggested, such as his *eternity, omniscience, sovereignty, infinity, omnipotence.*

He is the one being who passes all finite *bounds*—bounds of time in his eternal existence—bounds of finite knowledge in omniscience—bounds of human power in omnipotence—bounds of human control in sovereignty.

The most careless examination of this book shows us that for once we have in hand a volume that, more than any other, deals in eternal things—more than that, which is singularly indifferent to human limitations of *time*. In the Word of God, past, present and future are all in a sense *one*. Even in the use of tenses of verbs, the future is described in the language of the *present* or even the *past*. In the fifty-third chapter of Isaiah the sufferings of Christ are outlined, eight hundred years before his birth; yet, from the tenses it is impossible to discover whether the prophet is portraying present facts or facts of past time.

> He *hath* no form nor comeliness.
> He *is* despised and rejected of men.
> He *hath* borne our griefs and carried our sorrows.
> He *was* oppressed and he was afflicted.

Indeed, so prominent are these present and past tenses that we could not be sure that a future Messiah is referred to, but for the definite statements in the New Testament where this language is quoted and applied to the Lord Jesus Christ, from which we learn "these things said Isaiah when he saw his glory and spake of him" (John 12:41).

Assuming that God is the author of the book, all this is plain. He is the I AM to whom all past and future events are present; as Dr. Watts wrote:

> Eternity with all its years
> Stands present in thy view,
> To thee there's nothing old appears—
> Great God, there's nothing new.

Or as we might say, with more fullness of expression,

> Eternity transcends all finite bounds of time.
> Knows nothing of duration, with successive years;
> Before thy vision, panoramic and sublime,
> Past, present, future, at one glance appears;
> Unnumbered cycles pass before thy view;
> The new is as the old, the old is as the new.

This thought it is impossible to express properly, because it is impossible to think it adequately, and human words are but the body of human thought, its incarnation. But one can understand, if God speaks through man, how he will use man's imperfect language in a new and strange way that is to man contradictory and paradoxical. One can understand also how it is that an inspired prophet is a *seer*—one who *sees* what is beyond man's vision. He looks back into a pre-historical past, like Moses, and pictures a creative process which could not be described by a human observer, because it had no such observer, for it antedated man's creation. Or the seer looks forward into a future that has not only no history but as yet no *reality*, alike without observer and as yet without occurrence, and describes it even in detail with as much accuracy and certainty as though he were narrating what is actually taking place before his eyes.

And so, likewise, the inspired seer sees the present, past and future in their relations mutually, because he sees through God's eyes. "When the prophet foretells the future, he presents the future in the light of the present; when he admonishes or reproves, he presents the present in the light of the future."[3]

The perfection of God implies also his *immutability*. "I am Jehovah! I change not." He cannot change for the better, for that implies present imperfection, and possible improvement; he cannot change for the worse, since that implies degeneration. He is "the same yesterday and today and forever."

His book therefore mirrors this unchanging immutability. It abounds in changeless elements. Number enters largely into its very structure

---

3 Alfred Edersheim.

because number belongs to what is eternal. Two things belong to the unchangeable—mathematics and morals. As we cannot conceive a material system where mathematical truths do not rule, we cannot imagine a *moral* system, anywhere, in which a lie is as right as truth, where selfishness is as beautiful as benevolence and where virtue and vice are equally worthy of honor. Hence again we find the Word of God embodying the immutable—an unchanging ethical system. The Ten Commandments were written by the finger of God upon tables of stone, to indicate that they were changeless and eternal principles of life. Wax tablets were commonly used for transient records, but how easily can their records be erased, or, to use a Bible word, "blotted out," simply by inverting the stylus and passing its flat blade where the point had gone.

The *omniscience* of God is thus reflected in biblical forecasts of the future.

Biblical predictions stand that fourfold test which makes all imposture impossible: remoteness of time, minuteness of detail, novelty of combination and mystery of contradiction. According to the laws of compound probability, the more than three hundred and thirty particulars, recorded in the Old Testament, and in their complete form in the hands of the Jews both in the Hebrew and Septuagint versions hundreds of years before the birth of Christ, concerning the Messiah, must have had an inspired origin. A master mathematician, calculating the problem of probabilities, makes the chances of accidental fulfillment or coincidence, over a million multiplied into itself fifteen times—against one![4]

These are only the predictions concerning *Christ*; but these constitute but half of the complete body of biblical prediction. Here are six hundred particular items of forecast, scattered over from ten to twenty centuries, presenting combinations wholly without historic precedent or parallel, and often couched in paradoxes so inexplicably contradictory that they were enigmas even to the prophet himself, unexplained until events solved the mystery. And, as constructive design proves one original and supreme planner and builder, far above all human workmen, so the supernatural vision of the seers compels us to admit a higher intelligence than man's. Omniscience alone can account for such an insight and foresight. Reason is overwhelmed by the proofs of the superhuman origin of the Word of God. Granting the Bible to be a divine product, it befits the author. It reflects not only his unity, infinity, eternity, immutability, but also his knowledge. It is such a book as befits an omniscient God.

---

4   His exact statement is 13.367 followed by 97 digits, against one.

As we shall consider further on, there are evidences that the Bible is a divine book which demand *spiritual sympathy* with God to perceive and receive; a like nature with himself being the verifying faculty, the subjective response to the objective proof. But there are other forms of evidence which address the natural man and need only a candid mind, like an open eye, to feel their force, and are manifestly meant to satisfy honest inquiry and furnish a reasonable answer for our faith.

To one of these, emphatic reference has been made in the fact of *constructive design*. In the structure of the Bible as a whole we detect a certain unity and symmetry, system and plan, that preclude the possibility of its production by a human author.

To another of these forms of evidence we are now turning attention, namely *predictive prophecy*, which is itself alone sufficient to accredit the Bible as superhuman.

This is a much neglected department of evidence. The ancient prophets being not only teachers, but *seers*, had supernatural vision, and it was not only predictive, but retrospective; they looked backward as well as forward, and thus commanded the whole horizon of history past and future. The divine author puts such peculiar value and emphasis on this supernatural vision of past and future as an evidence of inspiration, that in the prophecies of Isaiah alone he seven times challenges any false and idolatrous faith or cult of the world to produce any other seers like unto his, who can show "former things" or "latter things"; whose vision reaches back to ages before history began, or forward to ages not yet historic.

This subject of predictive prophecy has had fuller treatment in the preceding series of these Bible lectures.[5] But a summary of the argument may not be out of place in this connection, especially as two charts are now added to exhibit this system of inspired prediction to the eye. The indisputable evidence afforded by prophecy is not appreciated at its full value. It alone would, if mastered, make candid intellectual doubt impossible.

Diagram 3 represents the *concentric circles of prophecy*. The outside circle, the predictions of Noah as to the general history of the race, its three primeval streams, the Semitic, Japhetic and Hamitic; the next circle, the several nationalities that both geographically and historically are associated with the Jews; then yet inside, the Jews themselves, their predictions

---

5 *The Living Oracles of God*, chapters 4, 5, and 6; *The Bible and Spiritual Criticism*, chapter 9.

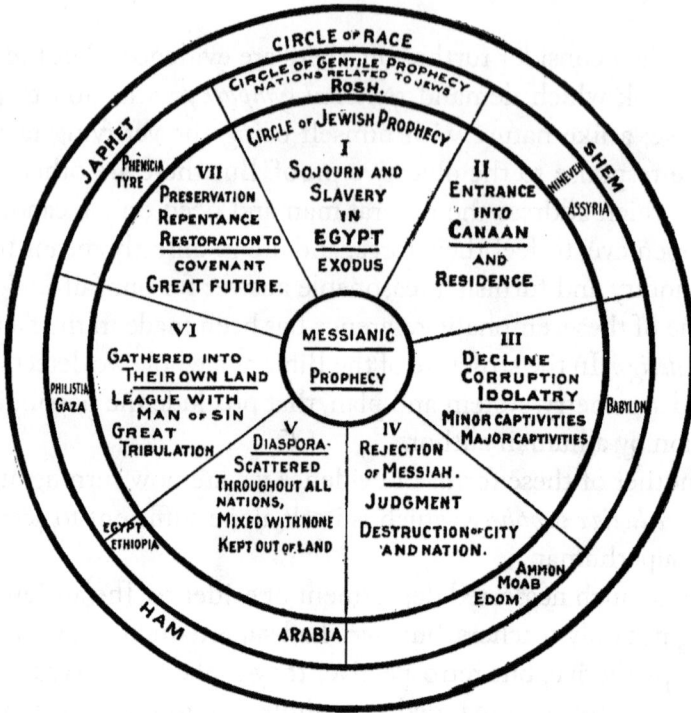

CIRCLE OF RACE
CIRCLE OF GENTILE PROPHECY
NATIONS RELATED TO JEWS
ROSH.
CIRCLE OF JEWISH PROPHECY

JAPHET
SHEM

PHENICIA
TYRE
NINEVEH
ASSYRIA

VII
PRESERVATION
REPENTANCE
RESTORATION TO
COVENANT
GREAT FUTURE.

I
SOJOURN AND
SLAVERY
IN
EGYPT
EXODUS

II
ENTRANCE
INTO
CANAAN
AND
RESIDENCE

MESSIANIC
PROPHECY

VI
GATHERED INTO
THEIR OWN LAND
LEAGUE WITH
MAN OF SIN
GREAT
TRIBULATION

V
DIASPORA-
SCATTERED
THROUGHOUT ALL
NATIONS,
MIXED WITH NONE
KEPT OUT OF LAND

IV
REJECTION
OF MESSIAH.
JUDGMENT
DESTRUCTION OF CITY
AND NATION.

III
DECLINE
CORRUPTION
IDOLATRY
MINOR CAPTIVITIES
MAJOR CAPTIVITIES

PHILISTIA
GAZA
BABYLON

EGYPT
ETHIOPIA
AMMON
MOAB
EDOM

HAM
ARABIA

3. The concentric circles of prophecy

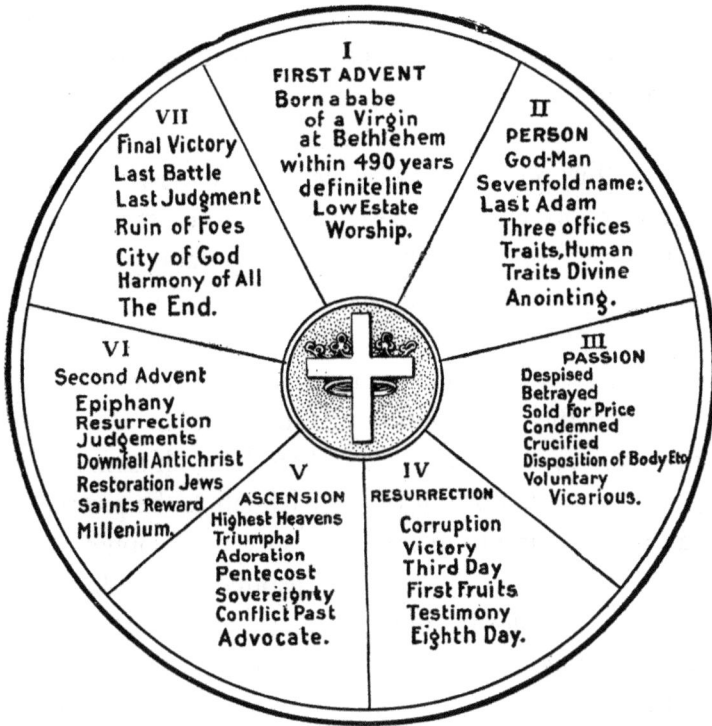

4. Messianic prophecy

being for convenience in seven sections; and the innermost circle, the prophecies about Christ, which are represented more fully on diagram 4 which again is divided into seven sections.

The theme, thus presented in visible form, is inexhaustible. Noah, in about forty words (Genesis 9:25–27) briefly forecast the whole course of human history. Then subsequent prophets, notably those belonging to the so-called prophetic era from the days of David to Malachi, foretold the doom of the various nations that were historically interlinked with the Jews. With even greater particularity Moses foresaw and his successors amplified the whole future of God's chosen people; and, most important of all, from Genesis 3:15, where Jehovah himself is the prophetic speaker, and the portrait of the Messiah as the promised seed of the woman is drawn in outline, prophet succeeds prophet until there is no longer any "open vision," each, as an inspired artist, adding some new detail of drawing or coloring, until the majestic portrait is complete.

Beside arguments of this class, which address the reason, and may be called the *rational* proofs, there is another class which appeal to the heart, and may be called the *experimental.* These depend upon the voice and verdict of *experience.* This proof is subjective rather than objective, and takes its point of view from within rather than from without. Many of the features of the Word of God may be seen from without, by the mere observer, as one may study the stately form and proportions of a cathedral; but there are other attractions visible only after one enters, like the combinations and colors of some exquisite rose window which need the sunlight shining through, to be revealed in all their patterns and hues. These appeal not to the mere *observer* but to the *believer.*

To this class of evidences only experiment can introduce. It is a humiliating fact, declared in the Word of God itself, that even "the princes of this world,"[6] cannot discern these spiritual beauties, because they do not take their stand within. Here is a whole hemisphere of scripture truth that, to the natural man, is an Apocrypha—hidden, until faith, leading to obedience and begetting experience, makes it an Apocalypse—revealed. Divine illumination must assist the natural powers. Only he who willeth to do his will knoweth this teaching,[7] and hence the psalmist's prayer,

---

6 1 Cor. 2.
7 John 7:17.

"open—unveil—thou mine eyes that I may behold wondrous things out of thy Law."[8]

To this class of proofs we are now to turn almost exclusive attention, in the chapters that remain. Our Lord declares that obedience not only precedes this higher knowledge but is itself the organ of such higher revelation, so that only when and so far as we obey, do we or can we know the doctrine. Even the teacher must "do" as well as "teach" if he is to reach the highest competency for his work of instruction, testing for himself the truth, and seeking to be all he would have others be. No parrot-like repetitions of these grand precepts will suffice; we must be not only messengers but witnesses. To him that knows by experience there comes a subtle power of testimony, which, like the perfume of a flower, however indescribable, is unmistakable, and carries an authority which is close akin to inspiration itself. Such a witness can reverently say, with his Master, "We speak that we do know and testify that we have seen." It is such personal witness, born of experience, that is sometimes practically resistless. In the breaking up of a Siberian winter, not even the return of the sun after the long night suffices to unloose the icy bonds, until the soft south wind breathes its charm, and then nature is freed from her wintry fetters. It is when the gospel message has incarnated itself in a believer's character and life that it melts hard hearts and sets prisoners free. Even supernatural light itself may fail to subdue and transform, until that subtler influence of love is exercised and finds response. Then light, love and life together bathe our being as in the beams of the sun of righteousness, and lo, the winter is past, and the reign of death is over and gone.

Here then we leave this part of our theme, already more fully treated in the volumes which precede. But, before closing this chapter it may be well to state briefly and succinctly a few leading reasons for our unshakable conviction and confidence in the Bible, as God's inspired and infallible book.

1. Its unity of structure, numerically and arithmetically, ethically and organically.

2. Its divine insight and foresight, the whole system of retrospective and predictive prophecy, with its general and specific forecasts of the future, and especially the Messiah.

---

8 Ps. 119:18.

3. Its philosophy of history—its unfolding of God's plan of the ages, revealing a redemptive purpose carried out in divine performance.

4. Its moral structure—meant as a guide to man, his counterpart and counselor, and self-interpreting.

5. Its matchless example of the perfect man, in whom all prophetic lines converge, and all examples and models of human excellence find their prototype.

6. Its survival as a living book amid the wreck and ruin of ancient literature, having both an indestructible vitality and a life-giving power.

7. Its regenerating and saving power; its triumphs over the individual and in the community, in every age and clime.

Philosophers insist on their doctrine of the *adequate hypothesis:* that if any supposition, being applied to the mystery of facts, proves an adequate solution and accounts for them all, it may be accepted as the truth. And we are sure that the key that unlocks what no other can is the key that was made and meant for the lock. Without this one solution—that God's mind and hand are behind the Bible—the book is a hopeless enigma. With this key in hand, every closed door is unlocked and the chambers of mystery become chambers of revelation.

Chapter 2

The Bible as Man's Book

If the Bible befits its divine author, does it equally befit the human reader?

Again we begin by laying a scriptural platform for our discussion:

Have not I written thee excellent things in counsels and knowledge? That I might make thee know the certainty of the words of truth, that thou mightest answer the words of truth to them that send unto thee (Prov. 22:20–21).

Thy word is a lamp unto my feet and a light unto my path (Ps. 119:105).

Thou hast the words of eternal life (John 6:68).

Eye hath not seen, nor ear heard, neither have entered into the heart of man, the things which God hath prepared for them that love him: but God hath revealed them unto us by his Spirit (1 Cor. 2:9–10).

These four texts may serve to teach progressive truth: first, that God has given words of supreme wisdom that we might attain unto certainty for ourselves, and help others to certainty by giving an intelligent and rational answer to those who inquire after knowledge. Then, that in his Word, we have a guide book for daily and hourly direction. To the obedient, it is a lamp to the feet, for the next step; and, as we go forward like a man carrying a lantern, it casts light upon the path ahead as we need it. Moreover, within the compass of the Holy Scriptures are found the words of Christ, the secrets of eternal life; and here the Holy Spirit is actually working, to illumine both his own book and the reverent and obedient reader.

"'Order is heaven's first law'; and the second is like unto it: that everything serves an end. This is the sum of all science. These are the two mites, even all that she hath, which she throws into the treasury of the Lord, and, as she does so in faith, Eternal Wisdom looks on and commends the deed."[9]

---

9 *Typical Forms in Creation*, Dr. James McCosh, p. 30.

A kindred truth in the spiritual sphere we seek now to express and enforce. In the inspired Word of God is exhibited a divine order. It is a cosmos of orderly arrangement and symmetrical proportion, not a chaos of confusion, with contradictory teaching and irreconcilable inconsistency. But, beside order, there is adaptation. Everything has an end, and serves a definite purpose. What that grand end is and how the divine volume, in every part, answers to its mission, it will be the one supreme aim to exhibit and illustrate.

More specifically, this book of God is pre-eminently the book of man. It is God's message to man—written with omniscient knowledge of man's nature and need, with infinite wisdom as to the best way to meet all man's problems, and with perfect love to assure a sympathetic and gracious ministry to his fallen condition. Hence we may expect to find not only that everything in this book serves an end in man, but that everything in man is served by something in the book.

This we account a wonderful feature in this most wonderful book: that it exactly *finds* man's deepest need and as exactly *fits* into it. It pierces to the mysterious realm—the dividing asunder of soul and body.

The adaptation of the Bible to man's needs and nature is part of its perfection, yet it explains what some account its imperfection.

This is a proper point in our discussion to remove some of the stumbling blocks of misconception. We are wont to associate imperfection with everything human. If, therefore, there be in the Bible a necessary human element, how can it be an absolutely perfect book?

In 2 Timothy 3:16, all Scripture is said to be "God-inbreathed," and the reference seems to be to man's creation, when God made man out of the dust of the ground, and inbreathed the breath of lives (original), and man became a living soul. Here is a compound product: a body of earth and a breath of God. Somewhat so, God made the body of his Word out of earthly elements, human letters and language, words and sentences, but inbreathed his Holy Spirit, so that the book became a living book.

As to perfection, there are two kinds, absolute and relative: absolute perfection admits no possible improvement in any direction; relative perfection is that of perfect adaptation to a purposed end. When the perfection of God's Word is affirmed, we are not competent to say whether or not he could have made a more perfect book in itself, but the determinative question is whether he could have better fitted it for its end, in reaching and teaching men.

This distinction is vital to our understanding of the subject. The Creator, it is conceivable, might have made a more magnificent world than this—as Shakespeare expresses it, "of one entire and perfect chrysolite"—radiant with rainbow hues, a crystal sphere of light; but such a globe would have been unfit for man's habitation and home, relatively imperfect because absolutely perfect. He might make a more beautiful member than the hand, perhaps, but part of its beauty lies in its manifold uses, made with equal fitness to hold the poet's pen, the artist's pencil, the sculptor's chisel, or the mechanic's tool, to dig a ditch or play a harp, to lift a weight or press another hand in love. It is very doubtful if God ever made anything more perfect for its purpose.

So, we may conceive a book, spoken into being, glorious like himself, and in a heavenly dialect, untouched by any finite hand, human or angelic, and by its divine luster repelling finite approach, like the scroll in the hand of him who sat upon the throne in apocalyptic vision. But who on earth could have read it or even stood before such a book! Its absolute perfection would only unfit it for human uses, and, even if man could have read it, he could not have understood it. Therefore God, in making a book for man, used men to write it, and human language as the medium of expression. If it lacks absolute perfection, it is in order to its relative perfection as man's counselor and guide.

Another stumbling block is found in "inspiration" which even intelligent people often mistake to mean that every statement in the Bible has God's sanction. There are obviously a thousand utterances and actions recorded in God's word that carry no approval, and some of which are expressly condemned. In this case, inspiration covers the accuracy of the narrative but not the approval of the word or deed. Even *verbal* inspiration means only that, in the composition of the book, the Spirit of God so controlled, as that the language used by the writers should convey the divine meaning and not pervert it, for careless expression sometimes does injustice to a grand conception, and a wrong word may obscure or even obstruct a thought. We need to think of inspiration in a *threefold* aspect: first, where it guarantees the truth of the record only, not the sentiment expressed, as when the Devil tempted Eve; second, where it approves a motive or act, because it was according to the light then enjoyed, though not conformed to the highest ideals, or perfectly accordant with the will of God as afterwards revealed. Solomon seems to have gathered many of his proverbs from uninspired sources, and they are embodied in this divine book, because, so far as they go, they are wise though they do not reveal the highest wisdom, and are partly meant to show that even the best of human sages cannot show unto us the way of salvation. David, in zeal for God, told Nathan of his purpose to build a house for the Lord, and Nathan bade him "go on, for the Lord is with thee." Had we no further record, we should gather that the whole matter had the Lord's approval. But we are expressly told that he forbade David to carry out his design. He comforted him, however, by approving his motive: "it was well that it was thine heart."

There is, however, a higher sanction of inspiration. Whenever it covers a direct "*thus saith the Lord*," the whole narrative, with all its contents, carries the divine sanction, and every word spoken or act done is by his authority. The careful reader of God's Word must, therefore, learn to discriminate. He must draw proper lines of demarcation between narratives of the sayings and doings of fallible men with all their mistakes and errors, which, like the forty years' unbelief and disobedience of Israel in the desert, are written for our learning and admonition; and the authoritative utterances of God, whether in his own person or through inspired prophets and historians and teachers. The whole contents of the Bible, as we believe, carry a divine *authority*, but not every sentiment found therein carries a divine *approval*—a distinction which needs only to be once drawn to be seen and accepted.

We are now prepared to pursue our main inquiry: is the Bible divinely fitted to be man's book, the lamp to his feet, the light to his path? Is there any important problem, pertaining to our temporal or spiritual life and well being, for which we can find here no excellent words of counsel and knowledge?

In examining this adaptation to human wants, we begin with the individual man, and afterwards advance to consider its fitness for the regulation of man in his collective capacity, in the family, church and state.

In the natural world we have seen the two grand arguments for an intelligent and personal creator to be *order* and *design;* all being articulated together in an orderly system, and everything serving a distinct and definite end. In the Word of God and throughout it similar laws prevail: all the contents, however apparently disjointed, belonging to a perfectly organic order and system, and everything being appointed to, and fitted for, a specific purpose. The more exhaustive the study of details, the more sublimely perfect does this adaptation appear; and all that follows is meant to illustrate this fact, that the book which thus befits God as its author, equally befits man as its reader.

Here the two famous sayings of Coleridge and Hallam recur to mind, that the book of God is equally the book of man because it *finds* him as no other does in his deepest being, and *fits* all the strange crooks and corners of his peculiar individual life.

As, at the beginning of the first chapter, the question, "What is God?" found a grand answer in the Westminster Catechism, so, at the outset of this discussion of the Bible, as *man's* book, we may similarly ask, what is *man?* and may follow the lines of the previous definition in contrasting man and God.

Man is a created being, embracing body, soul and spirit, finite, temporal and mortal, one who is born and dies; mutable, subject to constant change in himself and his surroundings; prone to folly, and ignorant, weak and impotent, a sinner by nature and habit; naturally unrighteous and unjust, selfish and malevolent, deceiving and being deceived.

To every aspect of his character and condition the Word of God is marvelously fitted.

1. As a created being, it introduces him to his *creator*, acquaints him with his relations to him, and his duty and obligation toward him.

2. As a complex being, here he is taught the relations of spirit, soul and body; how the spirit may be indwelt by God's Holy Spirit and rule the soul, and through the soul, the body; the whole man thus brought into subjection to God, and the lower nature to the higher.

3. As a finite being, the Word of God teaches man his comparative littleness in God's sight, his limited faculties, and inculcates humility and dependence on infinite resources.

4. As a creature of time, born to die, the Bible teaches him to make life here the vestibule to life beyond, and use the temporal with reference to the eternal, assuring him that the gift of God is eternal life through Jesus Christ our Lord.

5. As a being subject to change, here is revealed how all changes for the better may be secured, and for the worse, avoided; and how all changes of surroundings and experience may serve to discipline and chasten the spirit for a future and changeless existence in a perfect state.

6. As to one who is ignorant and unwise, the Bible reveals the higher certainties of knowledge, and imparts wisdom from above for every crisis, laws of heaven for life on earth.

7. As to one who is weak and impotent, it reveals divine strength as made perfect in weakness and shows us how to link impotence to omnipotence.

8. As a sinner, it unfolds to him a way of salvation, so complete that it assures us of deliverance from the penalty, power and presence of sin; and so simple in its terms as to be available to all who need salvation and will accept it as God's gift.

9. As one who is unrighteous and unjust it gives to man a perfect code of law and presents a perfect example of both faultless obedience and beauty of character.

10. As a being who lacks goodness, it teaches him unrivaled lessons of unselfish love, and an example of self-oblivion and self-sacrifice absolutely without a parallel.

11. As one who is prone to untruth and insincerity, this book teaches the lips to utter and the heart to love truth and honesty, and magnifies childlike simplicity and guilelessness.

Thus at every point of our definition we find the Word of God exactly suited to man's nature and need.

There is a story of a magic mirror in which every man saw himself reflected, not as in an ordinary glass, but a historical reflection, where his whole history, outer and inner, was revealed at a glance. Many were the long journeys which curiosity prompted men and women to make from far-off corners of the earth to see themselves in that magic reflector.

That magic mirror is the Bible. In its pages each man may see his moral and spiritual history revealed, his secret thoughts and desires and aims, so that it has more than once happened that a heathen reader coming into contact with the Word of God has actually suspected the missionaries of the fraud of trying to palm off as an ancient book some description of heathenism as they had seen it themselves.

But the Bible is not only a mirror; it is also a mold of character. It shows us what we are, that it may shape us as we ought to be. Hence (in Romans 6:18) we read of those who were once "servants of sin," but who have from the heart yielded themselves to that mold of doctrine, or teaching, into which they had been delivered, as is the true meaning and rendering of that significant verse. What a sign of a divine book, that it should exhibit our real inmost character as sinners, exposing all our follies and faults, analyzing our motives and impulses, not to make us despair, but to lead us to hope; and the same word that at one moment mirrors our depravity and makes us shudder at the self-revelation, at another moment becomes the matrix or mold in which we take a new form according to godliness!

More even than this, the Bible is milk and meat for the growth of the disciple—milk for the babe—food which has passed through another's digestion and can be easily assimilated—and strong meat for the man who knows how to meditate, which is the way spiritually to masticate the food. This precious book contains the simplest truths for the little child, that require no developed understanding to receive and appropriate. For example, the seven words which describe the way of becoming a disciple: "look," "hear," "take," "taste," "come," "choose," "trust"—is there any little child who cannot understand them? And they all mean "to receive." The eye receives by looking; the ear, by hearing; the hand, by taking; the mouth, by tasting, etc. A little child who knows enough to take the hand of a strong man to lead him in the dark, or to give up a heavy load to a strong arm to carry for him, knows enough to bring the burden of sin to Jesus and trust him to lead and guide him.

There are other truths, so deep, high, grand, that the greatest and wisest may spend life in searching and never fully find out all their meaning. There is a great sea of love in God that even angels have never sounded; and so as we grow we find truth that needs all our powers to master, and repays all study and laborious search.

Blessed is he who, like a tree planted by the rivers of waters, takes up the teaching of God's Word and transforms it into holy living.

The fitness of the Bible for man is manifold. Taking it as a whole, we first notice that there are *two* Testaments, together constituting one book, and singularly fitted to each other and to human need.

The Old Testament, characteristically a book of *law and promise*, presents to sinful man a perfect moral code, the effect of which is mainly to show how far he falls short of it; becoming practically, not so much mold of his character and conduct as the mirror of his sin and guilt. Side by side with this, however, is a promise and forecast of redemption—of a ransomer—a Second Man and Last Adam, in whom in God's mysterious way salvation shall come to the sinner and a new righteousness. All this is marvelously set forth in a kind of visible, spectacular parable that we call ceremonial law, and a singular structure, called the "tabernacle of meeting"—so that, before the eye as well as ear the great leading facts

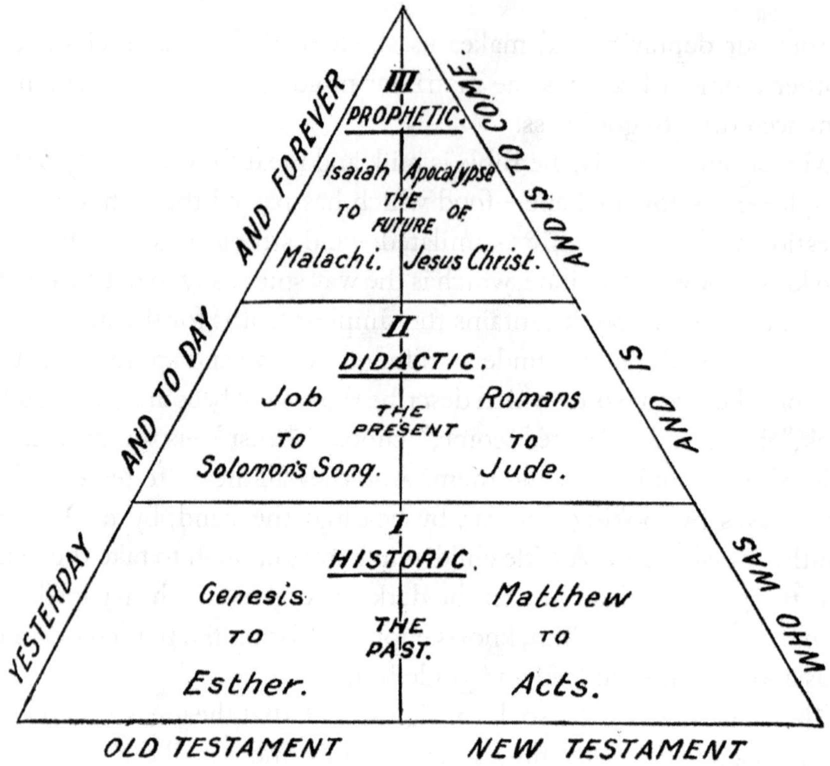
III
PROPHETIC.
Isaiah
TO
Malachi.
THE
FUTURE
Apocalypse
OF
Jesus Christ.
II
DIDACTIC.
Job
TO
Solomon's Song.
THE
PRESENT
Romans
TO
Jude.
I
HISTORIC.
Genesis
TO
Esther.
THE
PAST.
Matthew
TO
Acts.
YESTERDAY
AND TO DAY
AND FOREVER
WHO WAS
AND IS
AND IS TO COME.
OLD TESTAMENT
NEW TESTAMENT

5. Threefold division of both testaments

and truths of this redemption by blood were exhibited in a series of scenes, sacrifices, fasts and festivals; and in a regular order year by year.

Then the New Testament, as characteristically, is a book of grace displayed and promise fulfilled. What was exhibited in a legal standard unattainable by sinful man is there exemplified in a perfect life—and what was forecast in prophecy and pictorial rites and forms is now, without such a parable, exhibited in the actual death and resurrection of the Lamb of God, Christ our Passover slain for us. Thus the curiosity and inquiry, stimulated by the Old Testament, is met and answered by the plain facts and explicit teachings of the New.

Then each Testament is in three parts more or less marked: each begins with a historical portion, followed by a practical, ethical and experimental section; and concludes with an apocalyptic or prophetical part. The five books of the Pentateuch and the twelve that follow form the historical, in the Old Testament; the poetical books, the ethical and the prophecies from Isaiah to Malachi, the prophetical. The five historical books that begin the New Testament correspond to the Pentateuch, and the Revelation to the prophetical, and all the epistles, from Romans to Jude, form the ethical and practical division. Of course these divisions overlap, as prophecies and precepts are found scattered through the historical and conversely; still, the lines of division are clear.

Here is a marked fitness both as to God and man. For the historical befits him who was; the ethical, him who is, and the prophetical, him who is to come; while these three parts supply to man a knowledge of the past, a guide for the present, and a forecast of the future.[10]

The completeness and progress of biblical teaching is continually exhibiting itself to the careful reader.

Take as an example the five *poetical* books known as devotional and experimental. They form a distinct division and department in our English Bible, and it is astonishing how complete they are and how together they leave out nothing and yet embrace nothing not needful to completeness. Man has morally and spiritually five imperative needs: he has to experience adversity and he needs compensation and consolation. He has to meet a variety of experiences and needs a universal refuge. He has to solve countless moral problems and needs a key to unlock them. He meets many forms of disappointment and needs a satisfying portion. He has to confront the snares of the world and needs a spiritual presence.

---

10 See diagram 5.

These five wants are successfully and successively met in these five books. In Job we have a man encountering a fivefold mystery of suffering and finding comfort and final deliverance in a vision of God. In Psalms we have every variety of heart history, with God interpreting and giving the soul satisfaction. In Proverbs, human wisdom utters its voice and shows how far it can go, and the need it cannot supply met by the wisdom from above. In Ecclesiastes every experiment is made to find in this world something beside vanity and vexation of spirit, but only heavenly verities are found to give symmetry to character and conduct. Then in Solomon's Song the believer feels the mighty attractive force of this world, but finally turns from all else to find happiness in the invisible God and the unseen. Thus all soul cravings are met, and when these five books have been studied, the soul of man finds all great perplexities solved.

Take again the five books of major prophecy.

Nothing in the future interests the believer as does the whole career of the Messiah and its relation to his redeemed people. The Word of God teaches that it begins in humiliation and suffering and ends in glory—and that between the cross and crown lie, in church history, two great periods—one of decline and another of restoration for the people of God. Isaiah portrays his sufferings and death especially and their first fruits; Daniel particularly emphasizes the final triumph of the King; and Jeremiah and Ezekiel are respectively the prophets of declension and restoration.

The five books of the New Testament form by themselves a complete historical introduction not only to the New Testament, but to the life of faith.

In Ezekiel's vision of "the glory of the Lord" (chapter 9), he sees a complex creature with four heads—those of a lion, calf, man and eagle, and the whole pervaded by the invisible, all-controlling Spirit.

Whether designed or not, these first five books singularly correspond to that vision. Matthew presents our Lord as the lion of the tribe of Judah; Mark, as the sacrificial calf; Luke, as the man among men; John, as the eagle, soaring to heavenly heights and gazing, unblinded at the sun itself; and in the Acts, we see the spirit of life moving in all the complex mechanism of Christian life and church enterprise. This correspondence can scarcely be due to chance coincidence. It hints the deeper unity of the Two Testaments. It shows how even prophetic visions wait for New Testament explanations and unveilings.

But, more than this, there is here as elsewhere a progress of doctrine. Matthew addresses the Hebrew mind, for it was of first consequence to link Old Testament prediction to New Testament fulfillment. Mark follows, writing specially for the Roman, showing the power of Christ to save and his obedience unto death. Luke, addressing the Greek, presents him as the ideal of virtue and beauty, the perfect man; hence the pathetic touches that reveal his sympathy and compassion (7; 15; 19; etc.). John follows with the vindication of his deity.

In the Acts, we have a sort of biography of the Holy Spirit, corresponding to the Gospel records, and showing how, over a similar period of about one-third of a century, the Spirit was the presiding presence and controlling personality in primitive church assemblies.[11]

Surely no one can fail to see a divine design and order here. Thus in these first five books of the New Testament our Lord is successively presented as the fulfillment of prophecy, the miracle worker, the perfect Son of Man and the perfect Son of God; miraculously born of a virgin, miraculously working among men, miraculously exhibiting the perfection of humanity and miraculously manifesting the perfection of deity; then in the Acts of the Apostles as revealing himself in his last and in some respects most important manifestation, as still living and working, "doing and teaching" among men, in the undying life of the Spirit of God.

The five prominent epistle writers of the New Testament, Paul, Peter, James, John and Jude, each stand particularly for *one* great theme—Paul, for faith; Peter, hope; John, love; James, good works; Jude adds a solemn warning against apostasy which is destructive alike to faith, hope, love and good works.

It is noticeable that there are seven church letters—counting two as one when addressed to the same church—Romans to Thessalonians;

Then three *personal* epistles follow, to Timothy, Titus, Philemon;

Then three Jewish epistles, Hebrews, James and Peter;

Then the Epistles of John, and Jude, having a particular value and purpose as written after the tide of apostasy set in.

If these groups be examined the most remarkable *completeness* and *order* is noticeable.

The seven church epistles, though not in the order of *production*, are in the order of *instruction*—an order, not historical but logical—showing

11 *Acts of the Holy Spirit*, A. T. Pierson.

how all the great experiences of their divine head are representative experiences of all the members: death, burial and resurrection, in Romans;
the inbreathing of the Holy Spirit as the spirit of life, Corinthians; the
holy forty days' walk, Galatians; the ascension to the heavenlies, Ephesians; the compensating joy, Philippians; the session at God's right hand,
Colossians; the coming in glory, Thessalonians.

As to the Hebrew epistles, three things were especially precious to
the Hebrew people:

Their history as a peculiar redeemed people, under Moses, Aaron, etc.;
their peculiar privilege as repositories of the law and oracles of God; and
their entrance into and possession of the land, their peculiar inheritance.

In the Epistle to the Hebrews we have the typical fulfillment of the
first; in the Epistle of James the revelation of a higher heavenly law and
wisdom; in the Epistles of Peter, the pilgrimage to another heavenly
inheritance.

The Epistles of John and Jude complete the body of ethical and practical truth. John and Jude both wrote after the apostasy had begun; and
hence their writings have a special value and pertinence for the church
during the whole dispensation. Here we find the emphatic warning
against errors in doctrine and practice which had then appeared and
have ever since been more or less prominent; and here we shall find the
particular teaching meant to guide the believer as to meeting the world,
the flesh and the Devil, as the threefold foes of his spiritual life.

It is no accident that these epistles come *last* and complete the whole
body of this ethical and practical teaching. Anywhere else they would be
out of place.

A prominent spiritual teacher, lately departed, gave as almost his last
word to survivors, "Brethren, do not neglect the ministry of John." Why
this emphasis on John's writings? As another has said, this can be seen
only by the careful study of the order in which, so far as the dates can
be known, the books of the New Testament were given. "The church is
seen in *order* up to about A.D. 65. This is marked in 1 Timothy and Titus.
Bishops or elders, and deacons, are officially recognized. What change
had taken place in about a year may be seen by reading 2 Timothy, 2 Peter
and Jude. The church, as a testimony of God on earth, had already failed.
Deceivers and corrupters had crept in and for a time inspiration had
ceased; as generally supposed for about twenty years. For all those years
declension had rolled on. Then the Holy Ghost spake by John. He spake

of the church only as that which had failed on earth, and to be judged (Rev. 2, 3). One assembly is selected and described in the epistles, but an entirely new order had been established there, one person taking authority. This was so opposed to the true principles of the church of God, that this man refused even the apostle John. We are left in no uncertainty whether God, by his aged servant John, approved or disapproved of this new order which, I doubt not, had then become general.[12]

The complete teaching of the epistles may be briefly summarized, thus: The *Church* Epistles: The Believer's union with Christ:

My righteousness by faith is he.—Romans.

His Holy Spirit dwells in me.—Corinthians.

In him my daily walk on earth.—Galatians.

In him my hidden life in heaven.—Ephesians.

In him, for every present loss, eternal future gain is given.—Philippians.

In him, my seat is on the throne.—Colossians.

And he will come to claim his own.—Thessalonians.

The *Hebrew* Epistles: Christ, foreshadowed in the Old Testament:

God's pilgrims, now dispersed abroad.

Have found, in Christ, Messiah, God.—Hebrews.

New wisdom, coming from above.—James.

Their true inheritance of love.—Peter.

The *General* Epistles: The warning against apostasy:

Love not the world; its charms decay;

Yield not to fleshly lusts, and Satan's sway.—John.

Keep in God's love, his Word obey,

In Hope, look forward to Christ's "day."—Jude.

Twelve conspicuous symbols are chosen in the Word of God to represent its uses and the range and scope of its application to all human need. We may class them under seven divisions.

1. The *mirror*, to show us ourselves as we are and may be (James 1:25).

2. The *laver*, to wash away our sins and our defilement (Eph. 5:26).

3. The *lamp and light*, to guide us in the right way (Ps. 119:105).

4. The *milk, bread, strong meat and honey*, affording sustenance and satisfaction to the believer at all stages of spiritual development (Heb. 5:12–14; Ps. 19:10, etc.).

5. The fine *gold*, to enrich us with heavenly treasure (Ps. 19:10).

---

12 *Incidents of Gospel Work*, Charles Stanley, 135–142

6. The *fire, hammer, sword*, to be used in the warfare of life (Jer. 23:29; Heb. 4:12; Eph. 6:17).

7. The *seed*, to beget souls in God's image, and to plant harvest fields for GOD (James 1:18; 1 Peter 1:23; Matt. 13).

Another remarkable proof of this divine and perfect adaptation of the Bible to man is that it is *self-unlocking*. In reading and studying other great books one has need of a library of reference; otherwise they cannot be understood. Lexicons, scientific treatises, histories and biographies, encyclopedias, all must be at hand. The first lines of *Paradise Lost* reveal a wealth of learning that demands hours of study to master. But the simplest and most unlettered man by searching the Word itself, comparing the two Testaments, one book with another, and one passage with another, finds all that it is needful to understand, made plain; so that oftentimes to the most unlearned in man's eyes this book is no longer a sealed book.

What would be the results on individual and collective life if the Bible was our law?

John Adams, afterwards President of the United States, wrote thus when a young man:

> Suppose a nation in some distant region should take the Bible for their only law book, and every member should regulate his conduct by the precepts there exhibited! Every member would be obliged, in conscience, to temperance and frugality and industry; to justice and charity towards his fellow-men, and to piety, love, and reverence towards Almighty God. In this commonwealth no man would impair his health by gluttony, drunkenness, or lust; no man would sacrifice his most precious time to cards or any other trifling and mean amusement; no man would steal, or lie, or in any way defraud his neighbor, but would live in peace and good will with all men; no man would blaspheme his maker or profane his worship; but a rational, a manly, a sincere and unaffected piety and devotion would reign in all hearts. What a Utopia, what a paradise would this region be!"[13]

---

13 *Works of John Adams*, vol 2, pp. 6 and 7.

Chapter 3

The Problem of the Family

On this, one of the gravest of questions, the teaching of the Word is unusually full and explicit, and may be grouped under four heads:
1. The divine origin, institution, ideal and object of marriage in Eden;
2. The scriptural laws and limitations governing marital selection;
3. The prenatal influences that should shape the character of offspring;
4. The proper administration of household law, life, and habits.
Under each of these groups, a few representative passages may be chosen.

1.

The Lord God caused a deep sleep to fall upon Adam and he slept: and he took one of his ribs, and closed up the flesh instead thereof: and the rib which the Lord God had taken from man, made he a woman, and brought her unto the man; and Adam said, this is now bone of my bones, and flesh of my flesh: she shall be called woman because she was taken out of man. Therefore shall a man leave his father and his mother, and shall cleave unto his wife: and they shall be one flesh (Gen. 2:21–24).

2.

Thou shalt not take a wife unto my son of the daughters of the Canaanites among whom I dwell: but thou shalt go unto my country, and to my kindred, and take a wife unto my son Isaac (Gen. 24:3-4).

She is at liberty to be married to whom she will—only in the Lord (1 Cor. 7:39).

3.

Lo, children *are* an heritage of the Lord; *and* the fruit of the womb *is his* reward (Ps. 127:3).

For this child I prayed; and the Lord hath given me my petition which I asked of him, therefore also I have lent him to the Lord; as long as he liveth he shall be lent to the Lord. And he worshiped the Lord there (1 Sam. 1:27–28).

The unfeigned faith that is in thee, which dwelt first in thy grandmother Lois, and thy mother Eunice (2 Tim. 1:5).

In those days also saw I Jews *that* had married wives of Ashdod, of Ammon, *and* of Moab, and their children spake half in the speech of Ashdod, and could not speak in the Jews' language, but according to the language of each people (Neh. 13:23–24).

4.

"I know him, that he will command his children and his household after him, and they shall keep the way of the Lord, to do justice and judgment; that the Lord may bring upon Abraham that which he hath spoken of him" (Gen. 18:19).

"I will judge his house for ever for the iniquity which he knoweth; because his sons made themselves vile, and he restrained them not" (1 Sam. 3:13).

"Adonijah the son of Haggith exalted himself, saying, I will be king; and he prepared him chariots and horsemen and fifty men to run before him, and his father had not displeased him at any time in saying, Why hast thou done so?" (1 Kings 1:5, 6).

"Hear, O Israel: The Lord our God *is* one Lord. And thou shalt love the Lord thy God with all thine heart, and with all thy soul, and with all thy might. And these words, which I command thee this day, shall be in thine heart. And thou shalt teach them diligently unto thy children, and shalt talk of them when thou sittest in thine house, and when thou walkest by the way, and when thou liest down, and when thou risest up. And thou shalt bind them for a sign upon thine hand, and they shall be as frontlets between thine eyes. And thou shalt write them upon the posts of thy house, and on thy gates" (Deut. 6:4–9).

"Continue thou in the things which thou hast learned and hast been assured of, knowing of whom thou has learned *them*. And that from a child thou hast known the holy scriptures, which are able to make thee wise unto salvation through faith which is in Christ Jesus" (2 Tim. 3:14–15).

"Children, obey your parents in the Lord, for this is right. Honor thy father and mother (which is the first commandment with promise), that it may be well with thee, and thou mayest live long on the earth. And, ye fathers, provoke not your children to wrath, but bring them up in the nature and admonition of the Lord" (Eph. 6:1–4).

These important Scripture quotations serve to indicate the rich veins of biblical teaching that reward the careful student. We are here led back to the Edenic origin of marriage and the family, and confronted with the divine ideal. Then we are reminded of the fundamental importance of choosing for such life partnership only such as are fitted to enter into it in God's faith and fear. Then the question of offspring is put before us, and the fact that prenatal influences in the parental character and life predispose to good or evil; and finally that children are to be carefully and prayerfully taught and trained in all godly habits.

Here the cardinal points of the whole subject are definitely fixed, so that all minor details which fall within the whole circle of the horizon of the theme may from them be readily determined; somewhat as a traveler in an unknown country, when once he has with accuracy settled the four points of the compass, may with but little difficulty calculate and measure all intermediate angles of direction. No candid Scripture student need, with such clear leading as to essentials, long hesitate as to the lesser problems and perplexities arising in family life. But the moment that, in any of these great particulars, we depart from or disregard the divine pattern, we are like those who lose their way and at every step are in danger of plunging into deeper darkness and difficulty.

To begin at the beginning then, *marriage is a divine institution*, and this especially stamps it with *dignity and sanctity*. God's crowning creative act was the making of woman. At the close of each creative day, it is formally recorded that "God saw what he had made, that it was good." But, when Adam was made, it is explicitly recorded that "God saw that it was *not* good, that the man should be alone." As to man the creative work lacked completeness, until, as all animals and even plants had their mates, there should be found for Adam also an help, meet for him—his counterpart and companion. Not till this want was met did God see the work of the last creative day also to be good.

This is the first great Scripture lesson on family life, and it should be well learned. Two relics of Edenic life, alone, survive the fall: the *Sabbath*, and *marriage*, and they must be somehow fundamental to Edenic ideals. The former teaches man not only to hallow one seventh of time as sacred to God, but to consecrate *all* time. The weekly recurrence of the day of rest is a frequent reminder of God's right to our time as the setting apart of the tithe reminded of his proprietorship in all things and of our stewardship. Before one Sabbath had ceased to exercise its restraint and constraint, the approach of another renewed the hallowing influence. The latter, the divine institution of marriage, teaches that the ideal state of both man and woman is not in separation but in union, that each is meant and fitted for the other; and that God's ideal is such union, based on a pure and holy love, enduring for life, exclusive of all rivalry or other partnership, and incapable of alienation or unfaithfulness because it is a union in the Lord—a holy wedlock of soul and spirit in mutual sympathy and affection.

This is a proper place to correct a current and erroneous conception of the narrative in Genesis.

"And the LORD God said, *It is not* good that the man should be alone; I will make him an help, meet for him." God saw that man could not reach an *ideal state* in solitude. Quite apart from the *peopling* of the earth, there was the question of man's own need and welfare. "And God said, I will make him an help, meet for him."

Observe this is not a compound word—help-meet. This may seem a small matter, but in part, upon a mistaken and mischievous conception of this text, has been built up a system of domestic tyranny and injustice that lasted for ages, on one hand developing in the man marital despotism, and on the other, wifely subjection and servitude, and the degradation of woman.

What God *did* say was, literally, "*one, over against him,*" that is his *counterpart*, correspondent, his other half. No superiority on his part, nor inferiority on her part, is necessarily implied. There is indeed a marital headship, entrusted to the husband and emphasized in the New Testament as well as the Old; but it is a headship not to be held in willfulness or selfishness, nor exercised in arbitrary authority but in unselfish devotion, provision and protection, leadership and love. "The husband is head of the wife even as Christ is the head of the church."

The practical inference, too often gathered from the record in Genesis, is that man was created as woman's lord and master—his imperial majesty, the man, to be lord of creation; and woman—God's last and best creative product, to be, if not his lackey, at best his servant, to bow at his feet, wait on him, do his bidding, without any way or will of her own, to sink alike her individuality and independence in his pleasure and caprice. And, under the sanction of this perverted notion, woman has been degraded for centuries and millennia into a slave of man's despotism, a victim of his tyranny, and even a tool of his passions, when God meant her to be his companion and equal, his helper and counselor. The historic outcome of such perversion has been a long history of social wrong—polygamy with its harem and seraglio; domestic and social seclusion and exclusion, with its zenana; capricious divorce with its companion and consequence—adulterous unions, and a whole brood of kindred curses and crimes.

Man is no doubt in some respects superior to woman, in capacity for leadership, active and aggressive enterprise; and he has proved historically to surpass her in inventive genius and public achievement. But he is also inferior in heart qualities, in moral intuition, in affectional depth, in emotional sensibility, in capacity for suffering and sacrifice. Each has proficiencies and deficiencies. What one has, the other lacks, and conversely. Comparisons are often invidious because unfair. When things are not *alike* each must be looked at apart from the other; and so man and woman must be studied, in order to understand how each is, in a higher sense a part of the other, or rather a part of the perfect whole.

We all know what a triumph of invention is the achromatic lens. The varying degrees of refraction, producing all the colors of the rainbow on the double convex lens, interfered fatally with astronomic and microscopic observation. Hall and Dolland discovered the mode of constructing lenses, free from chromatic dispersion, by using two lenses of two different kinds of glass, crown and flint glass, closely joined together. God, in infinite wisdom, saw that by intimately uniting the man and the woman, in a partnership of love so closely that they ceased to be longer twain and became one flesh, the deficiencies of each could so be met by the proficiencies of the other that the *unit* would be as near as possible a perfect humanity and it is this which is so finely expressed in the original story of creation.

There is no doubt that in a true marriage each party helps the other equally. The Earl of Shaftesbury quaintly said, that if the Pope had been married he would have soon discovered that he was not infallible!

Inasmuch as God saw that for the man to be alone was not good, those who venture to hold and teach any other doctrine or philosophy join issue with God.

This does not imply a universal rule that every man and woman is obligated to enter matrimonial ranks; for there may be the highest motives, both prudential and pious, for abiding alone—sufficient reasons for celibacy, physical and moral, domestic and social. But a single life should be regarded and treated as abnormal and exceptional, rather than ideal. Any teaching that leads men and women to think of the marriage bond as the sign of bondage, and the sacrifice of all independence; to construe wifehood and motherhood as drudgery, and interference with woman's higher destiny; any tendency of society to cultivate celibacy as more desirable, preferable and honorable, or to substitute anything else for marriage and home, not only invades God's order, but opens the door to nameless crimes and threatens the very foundations of society.

Those who watch the signs of the times must see certain alarming signals at different points of the horizon like the lightning flashes that hint the coming storm.

Among these threatening forecasts of disaster, none is more perilous than the doctrine of *marital affinity*. It teaches that every man and woman has some special inborn or inbred fitness for some other, and the great secret of happiness is to find one's counterpart; and that this is so important that, if unsuccessful at first, another experiment is the only resort with hope of a better result. This is the theory put into as delicate language as its viciousness permits; and of all the perils that menace domestic and social life, none is more serious. Even if for the moment considered as a possible remedy for some existing evils, it introduces more than it relieves. It encourages hasty and ill-assorted marriages in suggesting a ready cure for marital blunders and mistakes. It justifies capricious divorce, separating husband and wife for causes absolutely disallowed by Scripture, and so fosters nuptial discord and unrest, by justifying the sundering of sacred ties on the ground of supposed incompatibility of mind and temper, or some caprice of fancy that some new connection would be more acceptable and agreeable.

God who instituted marriage made it a life bond, a partnership between one man and one woman, the most intimate known to humanity—the twain becoming one flesh—a partnership whose only sanction is love, and whose only dissolution is by death, or by that other death of love through the allowance of a rival love that by its very existence destroys the previous and purer bond.

In making the tie thus permanent, he evinced his perfect wisdom. He foresaw that the easier the dissolution of the bond, the less motive for forbearance and mutual and resolute effort to promote agreement and harmony. He would have all who take such a step, count the cost and understand that it is irrevocable, so that they may enter into wedlock "soberly, advisedly and in the fear of God."

Notwithstanding these plain Scriptural teachings and their abundant vindication in human experience, a bill was presented before the legislature of the state of Colorado, intended to provide for and legalize trial marriages, and authorizing a marriage contract "for a limited term, not less than three, nor more than ten years, and for any term of years between these terms of three and ten."

> If, after six months of any limited marriage contract have expired, should said parties desire, they may appear before the said officer, if alive and in office, and if not, before any other proper officer, and, delivering up the limited contract aforesaid, may make another and new contract, which shall in all cases be a contract for life, and not for another term of years.

Not only so, but a woman of prominence has lately published a book in which are suggested, if not advocated, such experimental marriages, as a possible solution to existing estrangements in married life. Meanwhile, in one of the worst criminal trials on record, the disgusting details of fashionable debauchery and adultery have been unblushingly paraded in print, and respectable women clamored for entrance into the courtroom, showing how public sentiment finds in marital infidelities a carcass upon which to feed as with the voracity of a vulture.

Another sign of the low level of ideas of marriage is seen in the matches of *convenience* that so largely displace the wedlock of love, turning into sacrilege what ought to be a sacrament. How shocking is it that human beings should barter virtue for a price, paid in money, title, or social rank, dignifying by the name of marriage, what in God's vocabulary bears quite a different designation, and allowing mercantile motives to crowd aside moral considerations!

All this reminds us that the best is always capable of being perverted to the worst; and, as the inverted images in water project as deep downward as the objects reflected rise upward, so what God designs as the highest blessing may become by human perversity the greatest curse.

Moreover, all marital crimes are *mutual*. Some sins are individual; they involve others as suffering victims, but not participators. Not so here. Whatever involves the family in ruin by such unlawful relations implies participation in crime and guilt. Nor must it be forgotten what fearful harvests of sin and crime come by geometrical progression from such sowing to the flesh. What ultimate possibilities of good or evil lie germinally in every family! Jacob entered Egypt with seventy souls; at the Exodus they had multiplied over eight thousand five hundred times. In the light of such considerations as these must our studies be conducted into the problem of the family.

We cannot lay too heavy stress on the Scripture idea and ideal of the family, because nothing is just now in greater peril. The same tidal wave of practical infidelity that is beating wildly against the Gibraltar of Holy Scripture is actually sweeping away the whole fabric of marriage with all that it involves in the family and home.

Rev. Dr. Charles H. Parkhurst, of New York, a mighty agitator for both political and moral or ethical reform, has recently thundered out a noble remonstrance against modern laxity in the whole notion and practice as to the family life. He is not opposed to progress, but believes some progress is backward. He accepts the ramification of fresh branches and the unfolding of new blossoms, but he stands by the truth and swears by the root, and believes that there are some things "so inherently true that they will continue to be true till eternity ends and God dies."

The family is one of the few institutions that has an unchanging ideal in the mind of God and Word of God, and no hand of man *can* improve it, and God never will alter it. It belongs to a sinless Eden and partakes of the perfect moral order that antedates sin and the fall. It partakes of God's immutability and the solidity and stability of his eternity. Man is not to attempt with his crowbar to loosen and lift the everlasting mountains or even question what God has settled. God's ideal of family life is something stable that does not crawl about on legs or wander about on wheels. Any club life or hotel life that displaces home life is a curse to the community. What upsets home is sacrilegious; it profanes a sanctuary. What breaks up the unity of home life is ruinous to church and state—"for the unit of society it substitutes a lot of vulgar fractions."

What wonder if, about marriage with such issues hanging upon it, restrictions are placed. Believers are left at liberty to marry whom they will, "*only in the Lord.*" That sacred phrase, one of the mystic symbols of the New Testament, must not be construed to mean, "only with a fellow believer or a church member." Throughout the Epistles, it means a *sphere of life*, an element in which we live and move and have our being. Believing on Christ we so enter into his life as to be identified with him; and henceforth what cannot be done in him is not to be done at all. A union in the Lord is not only one approved and appointed of him, but *constituted in him*, as the sphere of its sanctity, authority, activity, fertility. Each party, by faith one with the Lord, in him by love becomes one with the other. Such a union not only bars out an ungodly, unbelieving partner, but makes impossible wedlock between a spiritual, and a nominal, carnal disciple, leading those who truly live in Christ to demand in a companion similar devotion to him.

The writer recalls an instance of a young woman, brought to Christ under his ministry, who, while herself alien from God, had pledged herself to an infidel, but who came for counsel, declaring that she could not marry such a man, because she was "already the bride of Christ" and it would be infidelity to him; and she pleaded with God to show her the way to an honorable release from a pledge that had become abhorrent to her.

Issues so vast, not only for the parties themselves, but for generations to come, hang on godly marriages, that it seems strange that any true disciple can even entertain the thought of such union with another who is not in hearty spiritual accord, however in sympathy in lesser things.

The precepts of the Levitical code typically hint the principles explicitly laid down in the New Testament.

"Be not unequally yoked together with unbelievers" (2 Cor. 6:14) unmistakably points back to the precept, "Thou shalt not plow with an ox and an ass together" (Deut. 22:10). One was an unclean beast, never laid on God's altar; the other clean and a sacrificial victim. God would not have under one yoke, harnessed to one plow, two animals of such different class, thereby hinting that a believer and servant of God he would not have closely yoked up with an unbeliever and servant of Satan.

When we read, "Thou shalt not let thy cattle gender with a diverse kind" (Lev. 19:19) and find the Hebrews forbidden even to mix woolen and linen in a garment, or sow a field with mixed seed, we cannot but see another hint as to the impropriety of mismatched marriages.

God's original ideal then must be kept before us: One man and one woman, mutually in sympathy, intellectually, morally and religiously, united in a partnership whose association is more intimate and tender, perfect and permanent than any other, displacing even filial and fraternal ties, so that a man shall leave father and mother and cleave unto his wife, they being no more twain, but one flesh, losing almost individuality and duality in a higher and sacred mutuality and unity.

It must also be borne in mind that God's ultimate object in marriage is *offspring*. To our first parents, while yet in a sinless Eden, he said, "be fruitful and multiply, and replenish the earth and subdue it"—multiplication of the higher forms of intelligence and life in order to subjugation of the lower, that the material and animal creation should be ruled by man, by brain rather than brawn, by intelligence and integrity rather than brute force.

Here is a goal indeed—increase and multiplication, not in money or material possessions, but in humanity itself, an investment of the capital of character for the sake of a like interest, character—profit and property realized in offspring bearing the parental likeness. Man being made in God's image, multiplying reflections and reproductions of that image. Here is a business that trades in *being*, subduing lower forms of life by propagating the higher!

The natural increase of the family is itself a problem of grand importance.

Few appreciate the immense opportunity and responsibility involved in such natural and normal growth. Nature hints that wedlock shall not take place before physical maturity, or what is known as majority—say about twenty-one years of age. Curiously, in the healthy body, the years of fruitfulness average another equal period, and if children are given only once in three years it allows an average of seven to a normal family life. Allowing for average mortality this would make possible a rate of increase that seems incredible. It has been estimated that, were there now no more families on earth than emerged from the ark, and each family multiplying its numbers but fourfold every forty years, in less than six hundred years, at this rate of geometrical progression, the earth might have as large a population as now. It was similar numerical calculations to these that led Malthus to fear that, in time, the earth could not sustain its own inhabitants. He observed that while the race increased by geometrical progression, the increase of agricultural products, taking into account waste, etc., was only in arithmetical ratio, and hence population would soon surpass the means of subsistence. So it would be, but for the ravages of pestilence, famine, disease and war. But Malthus thought further checks should be put upon the increase of the race, by preventive measures, such as forbidding marriage until a proper age, with physical fitness and capacity to support a family. The poor law reform of 1834 was one fruit of his researches, and many economists who did not accept his estimates were influenced by his ideas.

All other problems concerning marriage therefore are outranked in importance by the question, how may we secure generations of upright and godly offspring?

Three facts face us: first, in thousands of Christian families there are unconverted children, some of whom are profligate; again, unless there is a reasonable ground of confidence that children will be godly, it is presumption, if not crime, to dare parenthood; and, yet again, God's command that parents shall "bring up children in the nurture and admonition of the Lord" implies the possibility and ability, for every commandment is an enablement. If God says I *ought*, he implies I *can*.

Remarkable contrasts exist in family history extending through generations, which cannot be wholly accounted for by natural causes, and seem to confirm and illustrate God's own words:

"I the LORD thy God am a jealous God, visiting the iniquity of the fathers upon the children unto the third and fourth generation of them that hate me; and showing mercy unto thousands of them that love me, and keep my commandments."

Jonathan Edwards was the son of a most godly sire. His father was a preacher and before him his mother's father. Some pains have been taken to trace the history of the descendants of this singularly separated man. More than four hundred of them have been thus traced, and they include fourteen college presidents and one hundred professors; one hundred of them have been ministers of the gospel, missionaries and theological teachers. More than a hundred of them lawyers and judges. Out of the whole number sixty have adorned the medical calling and as many more known as authors of high rank, or editors of journals. In fact almost every conspicuous American industry has had as its promoters one or more of the offspring of the Edwards stock since the remote ancestor was married in the closing half of the seventeenth century.

On the contrary, there has been careful search into the history of one criminal family known as the Jukes, and it is equally conspicuous as a long record of pauperism and profligacy, imbecility and insanity. Twelve hundred descendants have been traced of this prolific family tree. Four hundred of these were physically self-wrecked; three hundred and ten professional paupers, one hundred and thirty convicted criminals, sixty habitual thieves and pickpockets, and seven murderers; while out of the whole twelve hundred only twenty ever learned a trade, and of these half of them owed it to prison discipline.

The author has been greatly interested in a letter from a remote relative who has taken pains to trace to some extent the children of our common ancestry. He writes:

> The Pooles and Piersons are the descendants of Hannah Standwick, born in the seventeenth century, about the middle, at Broadway County, Somerset, who married George Poole, of the same place. The second son of Mr. Poole's nephew, Joel Standwick, was a pre-eminently holy man; and one characteristic of his family prayers, and I believe of such as were offered in public (although prayer meetings were a comparative rarity in those days), was his never failing to intercede for *unborn* generations, especially among his own kin. Now I may add that the result is very significant. I know hardly one in all the families which have the Standwick blood, and I knew them extensively, who is or was an irreligious person; nearly all were professors of religion, while many, if not the bulk of them, have adorned the gospel they were not ashamed to confess, and many have served as ministers and office bearers both in Britain and in the States.

All these principles which demand a godly union in wedlock have tenfold force when it is remembered that the *marital* relation is bound up with the *parental*. Either party may be left by the death of the other to the sole charge of a family of children, and what if in the surviving parent there be no root principles of piety to germinate in godly nurture and admonition, Scripture teaching and prayer habits!

The Word of God counsels that where such alliance has been formed before conversion, the believer shall seek with intense earnestness to save the other. But to those as yet only contemplating wedlock, there is no doubt that the Spirit's counsel and command are rather to abide alone than enter into such a union without the basis of a godly fellowship.[14]

Only those whose long experience gives them a lofty point of view can appreciate the reasons for such emphatic Scripture teachings. When all outward charms fade and worldly advantages fail; when age comes on and youth and beauty flee; when health and wealth are gone; when a

14 "The Sincerity of the Marriage Tie."

family has been reared and character is beyond parental shaping; when crises throng where nothing can avail but a love whose corner stone is piety; then in the review is seen the immense importance of having made a right choice, and that, next to the espousal of Christ as Savior, stands a godly marital union. How many, at a dying bed or open grave, with a broken heart, bewail the mistakes that can never be undone. There comes an hour when riches, rank, personal attractions and even intellectual culture become apples of Sodom, turning to ashes when there is need of a comfort and consolation that only such love can supply as has grown ripe on the Tree of Life!

If godliness in offspring can be assured at all, the most vital condition is a *holy parental character.*

The whole teaching of the Bible implies a definite aim and purpose in the Christian parent to bear and rear offspring *for God*. Hence that remarkable language, "children are an heritage of the Lord; and the fruit of the womb is his reward" (Ps. 132:3).

God counts them as his inheritance and as the reward of his toil as though in procreation when it is what it ought to be the creator is claiming his own, both by right of creative power and gracious covenant.

This suggests that even the right to assume parenthood may rest on *covenant relations* with God. For how can anyone not in covenant with him form the holy partnership wherein a disciple undertakes to bear and rear, nurse and nurture, train and develop children for *God!* How would such a sacred conception of wedlock and such a holy purpose in wedlock lift all marital and parental relations to a wholly new plane! And how could it fail to ennoble the whole character of offspring!

Nothing is more indisputable than the *prenatal influences* that mold offspring, reaching back especially to the *mother's* whole attitude of mind and heart, as well as body, her attitude becoming in her unborn child an *aptitude*. Hannah prayed for Samuel, and from the time of that prayer he was lent to the Lord in advance. Had that nothing to do with the character and career of that child in whom the open prophetic vision was restored after a long silence? In Timothy, Paul traced a faith that dwelt first in the mother Eunice and back of her in the grandmother Lois. Here is something which comes near to being a *hereditary faith!*

The character of the parents *must*, in some degree, and may in a very large degree, be reproduced in offspring. "Adam begat a son after his own likeness (Gen. 5:3), after his image" (comp. 1:26). If attributes are not inherited, *aptitudes* are—dispositions, tastes and tendencies toward good or evil. And it is impossible to say either how much evil may be the legacy of parent to child or how much good. If some children go astray, as soon as they be born speaking lies, there was on the contrary a Samuel that from his birth was given to the Lord, and a John that from his mother's womb was filled with the Holy Ghost—instances left on record to remind us of parental possibilities.

Hence the family is the supreme problem: it is the mold of the individual, the norm of society, alike of church and state, and the factor of the future. Catharine Booth felt so intensely the responsibility of motherhood that she boldly said to God, "I will not have a godless child!" Can we imagine God as indifferent to a vow, which showed at once such godly determination and such trust in him as one who had called her to the sacred office and function of maternity! Not much risk of such a household falling into the category of the families that call not on thy name (Jer. 10:25). It was this modified heredity of character that led Dr. Bushnell to the bold position that every child should be trained as presumptively a child of God and an heir of heaven.[15] Certainly thousands of children of believers have been born with aptitudes so markedly religious that they have grown up Christians, without any conscious and definite change such as is called conversion.

There is also great need of *authority* in the family.

Godly restraint is a necessary factor in every well-regulated home. Gladstone has connected with all the weak concessions to a child's caprices, whereby willfulness and selfishness are so often encouraged, the telling phrase—"depraved accommodations."

Children are the heritage of the Lord

By an exhaustive study of the parentage of every person born since the Reformation whose name appears in the British *Dictionary of National Biography*, Bishop Weldon has compiled some interesting facts and figures as to the sons of ministers of the gospel. In *The Nineteenth Century* he points out that among those who had attained distinction in various departments of the national life, 1,270 were the sons of ministers, 510 the sons of lawyers, and 350, of doctors. "It is to be set down to the honor of ministerial homes," says *The Presbyterian* (Toronto), "that no other

---

15 *Christian Nurture*, Horace Bushnell.

source has made so large a contribution to the learning, energy and honor of Great Britain."

Similar facts were long ago ascertained by the careful investigations of Dr. Wm. B. Sprague, who wrote his voluminous *Annals of the American Pulpit*. But such encouraging family records are even more abundant in the history of *missionaries*. Witness the remarkable family of John Scudder, the missionary physician of Ceylon, whose nine children were all missionaries in Southern India, and the missionary blood did not run out in the second generation. We know no better examples of the heredity of aptitudes for duty and service than in missionary families, another illustration of which is now before us in the Labaree family and many more like them of our own day—such as Hudson Taylor's, Dr. Grattan Guinness's, whose names are synonyms of missionary heroism. May this not be one way of God's reward and recognition of missionary consecration?

*Pre*natal aptitudes, however, must be developed by *post*natal nurture. Hence the injunction to train up our children "in the nurture and admonition of the Lord."

What *is* this nurture?

It means, first of all, making the *supreme aim of all family life, household piety*, everything else being subordinated thereto.

This implies *authority*—pre-eminently the proper reign of law. "I know him that he will command his children and his household after him," etc. There can be no Christian *nurture* without household government—*authority* supported by *penalty*. The command, "honor thy father and thy mother," stands first in the second table—the leading place, as the command, "thou shalt have no other gods before me," stands in the first, and for a reason. It heads the second table because for some years of the child's life the parent stands to him in the place of God—all the God he knows. If he is taught to love and obey his earthly father, it is both easy and natural, when the idea of a Father in heaven dawns on his consciousness, for him to transfer love and obedience to the higher authority. But, if the child habitually rebels against the human parent, it is most natural that when he comes to know there is a God, he should transfer to him his lawlessness.

In this matter of family life, neither husband nor wife can throw on the other all the responsibility for the religious character of the home. It is a very conspicuous fact that men are, as a rule, far less religious than women. Dr. John Hall said that many men in his congregation were only "brothers-in-law"—their wives being church members, but they not. And there is a lesson in the merchant's dream, who thought he was refused entrance to heaven, as himself a stranger at the gates; and, when he apologized for his neglect of sacred things, saying that he attended to worldly things and his wife went to church and prayer meeting for both, the answer was, "Well, your wife has *gone in for you both!*"

This "nurture and admonition of the Lord" is both negative and positive. In Colossians 3:21 Paul says: "Provoke not your children to anger," and adds, "lest they be discouraged." They may be excited and enraged in various ways, such as by hastiness of temper, by punishing instead of correcting, by indulging a severity of spirit instead of kindness and love, by threatenings which it is not intended to execute, and promises it is not meant to perform. Rash actions and angry words may provoke to wrath and discourage all efforts at obedience or, worse still, lead to studied habits of deceit, doing wrong on the sly or hiding wrong when done; thus changing entirely the field of effort, so that, instead of trying to obey, the one endeavor will be to avoid the excessive anger and punishment which even petty offenses excite.

The positive side of this precept is, "bring them up in the nurture and admonition of the Lord"—that is, such education and discipline as is required by God, and such as God himself administers as a father to his children. We are to study his fatherly corrections and educative measures if we would learn how children should be treated. The Greek word—*paideia*—manifestly includes all family and relative duties, such as love, respect, obedience to parents; all doctrines and duties, moralities and self-denials, owed in church life; and even those honest trades and honorable professional callings which make a child a respectable, self-supporting and helpful member of society, for, as the Jewish maxim reads, "he who teaches his son no trade, teaches him to steal." This word is very inclusive—it embraces all that a child ought to be taught to make him understand and be able to discharge his duties in the family, church and state.

But discipline in its proper sense (*nouthesia*) must accompany such education. This is the right disposing of the mind or *nous*, training it to right habits of thought, and noble resolve—this teaches self-restraint, moral control. Such discipline alone can make education effective for good, for it teaches how to turn education to a good purpose. To be well informed is good, but to be well controlled is better. An ideal family training aims at both, and especially puts the knowledge of the Lord and obedience to him at the very front.

These are the basal hints on family training in this conspicuous teaching in Ephesians and Colossians, and it is very noticeable that in these companion passages, where so many similar exhortations occur, a strikingly similar injunction precedes: in one case, *be filled with the Spirit*, and in the other, let the *word of Christ dwell in you richly* in all wisdom. No such nurture and admonition of the Lord is possible except where the parents are filled with the Word and the Spirit. All parents should be sustained by the recollection that when God made his representative covenant with Abraham the central and permanent provision was this, "*I will be a God to thee and to thy seed after thee.*" The other provisions concerning the land, a numerous seed, etc., and the special rite of circumcision, belonging to the Hebrew people and were more or less transient; but the central promise was universal and perpetual: "I will be a God to thee and to thy seed after thee."

Godly "nurture and admonition" seem to include such elements as the following: habitual instruction in the Word of God, as the authoritative law of life; constant recognition of God as the supreme father and household head; a prayerful atmosphere pervading home life, and breathed by all who share it; a cherishing and exalting of scriptural ideals of character and conduct; a kind but firm oversight of companionships, occupations and amusements; a study to make home attractive, so that its associations are a delight; but, above all, the centrality of the person and work of the Lord Jesus Christ.

Careful parents will not overlook even the unconscious influence of a child's surroundings. The books, papers and periodicals that find their way into a home; the pictures that hang on the walls; the occasional guests that sit at the table—these and a thousand other quiet and subtle forces give shape to character. A prominent sea captain once declared that the marine paintings in his home sent him to sea, and an Indian missionary said that the life of Harriet Newell sent her abroad.

Family *unity* is of momentous importance. The household force should be centripetal, not centrifugal, if children are not to break loose from its solar system and become wandering stars. The ideas and ideals of the household should be *one*, especially on moral and religious subjects, and as far as may be, on *intellectual*. In a sense, every true family should be exclusive and seclusive. The most abundant hospitality should not turn a home into a hotel. Some elements are often, in a bad sense, "foreign." The Holy Scriptures quaintly record how "outlandish women caused Solomon to sin"—women from *outside the land* who came into his harem bringing notions and customs foreign to the life and habits of Israel, idolatrous, irreligious, un-Jewish. A prudent mother, whose success in household training was unusual, would not allow her children to spend a night among strangers, not knowing what family heresies, wrong notions or practices they might learn. It involves risk to encourage outsiders to make free at all times with the home; visits should be rare, invited and select. God never meant the sacred precincts of home to be a sort of free runway for indiscriminate waifs from the street or from other houses. The intimacies of children may determine their whole future. Parents carelessly let people have free access to their children, who undermine their authority, overturn their ideals, and sow the seeds of frivolity if not iniquity before they are aware. In a sense, every household is to be a little church with "close communion."

So far as the family is one, much depends on *keeping* it one. Children should be taught—while under the parental roof, dependent on the parents and forming part of the family life—not to bring into it discordant elements, to introduce new ideas and practices. The intimacies of children should be guarded, for it is easy for members of another family, brought up in a totally different school or none at all, to bring in what is essentially a foreign speech and notions utterly repugnant to the parent.

It is questionable whether children should be permitted to attend places of worship where they hear doctrines or witness practices which are opposed to parental convictions. When they get old enough to think for themselves, should they come deliberately and conscientiously to a new conviction concerning church matters, wise parents will help them to follow convictions. But ordinarily wanderers to other church folds are moved not by conscientious convictions, but by unreasonable and childish caprices which should be suppressed.

The main elements that together make up an ideal household, according to the scriptural pattern, are law, love, liberty, life, unity, sanctity and ministry; in other words, authority, affection or sympathy, a living example, freedom of action, a common aim, a holy atmosphere, and a training for unselfish service. Without any of these there is a serious if not fatal defect, and the highest results are forfeited.

There must be *authority* in order to any true unity. No family can be properly brought up without household law asserted and enforced. Law implies sanctions, reward and punishment, and these are especially important in early childhood, when as yet moral character is unformed and moral motives not fully understood or appreciated. Rules should be simple, clear, reasonable and inflexible, like the Ten Commandments—a few great moral rules, instead of a multitude of petty restrictions. One way of needlessly provoking children to wrath is to hamper them with a thousand trifling restraints and minute regulations that are capricious and are due to a fastidious temper in the parent. These sometimes constitute a yoke that neither our fathers nor we were able to bear, such as must have constrained a little girl in America, when her teacher asked her full name, to answer, "Mamma always calls me Mary *Don't!*"

As to punishment and reward, a small recognition may be as effective as a much greater one, if associated with the idea of reward, and a slight punishment, if it invariably follows an offence, as effective as a severer penalty that is uncertain and capricious. But punishment should always be administered calmly and deliberately and lovingly, and not passionately, hastily and angrily. The spirit and temper of the parent in chastisement will be likely to awaken a similar spirit in the child—if impatient, or angry, or resentful, or harsh, it kindles its like; if a punishment is inflicted in sorrow and love it is apt to soften and subdue and often draws the child closer to the parent. It should always be plain that the punishment costs more to the parent who inflicts it than to the child who suffers. Here lies the great power of the cross: it shows the love of God. It was a visitation of penalty upon sin that *cost God* everything and cost the sinner nothing. The lawgiver took the punishment on himself!

But authority there must be, and it must be maintained.

"For I know him, that he will command his household after him, and they shall keep the way of the Lord, to do justice and judgment; that the Lord may bring upon Abraham that which he hath spoken of him." Notice, "he will *command*"—there was simple authority, but it concerned the *greatest* matters—the gravest issues—to keep the way of the Lord, etc., fidelity to God and man—and this fidelity on Abraham's part was the necessary condition of the blessing God had promised to his house.

As we have seen, the second table of the law puts submission to parental authority supreme among all human obligations, as in the first table, the worship and service of the one God; because obedience to parents is paramount, not only the basis of all human society and welfare, but the basis of piety towards God; for it is a basal fact and truth that there is a period in child life, when as yet he has no idea of God, when the parent stands to him in the place of God. As, therefore, he is taught and learns to treat his earthly father he will be likely to treat his heavenly Father when old enough to apprehend the fact of his existence and claims.

Great importance attaches also to *household habits*, which may create an atmosphere in which morality and piety thrive and vice and unbelief are stifled.

In Deuteronomy 6:4–9 is pictured a family life, where Jehovah is supremely loved by the parents, where his law is written on the fleshly tablets of the heart, and out of the abundance of the heart the mouth speaketh. God's commands are a habitual subject of conversation and guide to conduct, whether seated in the house or walking by the way, when lying down or rising up; bound for a sign on the hand and worn as frontlets between the eyes; written upon the door posts of the house and the gates. Such figures of speech plainly imply that, whether resting or moving, beginning or ending the day, thinking or working, God's name and Word are to be supreme, and even strangers going in and out are to see and feel this supremacy of God.

Nothing tells on the child like this general *life* of the home. Teaching that reaches no further back than the *lips* will commonly pierce no further in than the *ear*. What teaches most is character—character that stands like a grand oak of Bashan or cedar of Lebanon in the crises of storm—a faith that trusts in promises when human props give way, a courage that dares to follow in face of danger, an unselfishness that both lives and gives to the point of real self-sacrifice, an integrity that can stand firm before seductive temptation. What parents do and are in the *crises* of life—that is what most teaches and impresses children.

Chapter 4

The Church of God

Four texts of Holy Scripture again form our basis:

(1) Upon this rock I will build my church; and the gates of hell shall not prevail against it (Matt. 16:18).

(2) The house of God, which is the church of the living God (1 Tim. 3:15).

(3) Ye are the temple of God, and the Spirit of God dwelleth in you (1 Cor. 3:16).

(4) The church of the firstborn, which are written in heaven (Heb. 12:23).

In the first we have the rock-basis of the church; in the second the divine ownership of the church; in the third the presiding presence of the Holy Ghost in the church; and in the fourth the church register.

The family and the church are intimately associated. The family may be, and ought to be, a smaller church—"the church that is in the house," as in olden times, with the father as a kind of officiating priest, with prophetic powers and kingly authority. And as the family is a smaller church, the church is a larger family. But, while the family originated in Eden, there would have been no church but for the fall. The family pertains to man's sinless state; the church to man's redeemed state.

It is always necessary to return to biblical ideas and ideals, because of a remarkable tendency to deviate from divine conceptions. Man is always swinging like a pendulum, from sin on the one side to sorrow for sin on the other; but, unfortunately, prone never to hold the golden mean of fidelity and loyalty to God; and we shall need some intrepidity, some courageous candor, to discuss this question of the church so as to have the approval of our master, for in nothing, perhaps, have we more departed from divine ideas and ideals than in our church life. Let us therefore seek to ascertain from the Word of God what is God's thought concerning his church. If we examine the Bible carefully, we shall find seven things that enter into the scriptural conception of the church of God:

(1) Separation;

(2) Society, or association;

(3) Service, or mutual helpfulness;

(4) Worship;

(5) Work in the evangelization of the world;

(6) Witness to the truth of God in his Word and especially as represented in the person and work of Jesus Christ our Lord;

(7)—greatest of all, and giving emphasis to all the rest—the presiding presence of the invisible God, the Holy Spirit, making the church his habitation.

Taking these divine ideas from the Word of God, we might construct a definition, for practical and ethical purposes, somewhat thus: "the church is an organized body of Christian believers, indwelt by the Holy Spirit, called out into separation from the world, for mutual service and spiritual worship, for the great work of a world's evangelization and permanent witness to the Word of God and the Christ of God." I ask attention to a few elements that enter into this definition, dwelling specially upon some of them.

First, the idea of *separation*. That word is written, as in letters of flame, on the whole of the Bible, Old and New Testaments. In Lev. 20:25–26, we are taught what was the great ulterior purpose of the Levitical dispensation, and its distinctions between clean and unclean persons and animals and things. It was designed typically to teach the people of God that he had severed them from all other peoples that they should be his. And in the New Testament we have the doctrinal unfolding of the typical truth indicated in the ceremonial law. In 2 Cor. 6:17 to 7:1—that most memorable passage—we read: "wherefore come out from among them, and be ye separate, saith the Lord, and touch not the unclean, and I will receive you, and will be a Father unto you, and ye shall be my sons and daughters, saith the Lord Almighty. Having, therefore, these promises, dearly beloved, let us cleanse ourselves from all filthiness of the flesh and spirit, perfecting holiness in the fear of God."

Thus we have the law of separation, in the Old Testament, typically enunciated and exhibited; and the spiritual explanation and application of the law of separation in the doctrinal portion of the epistles. This idea of separation is absolutely fundamental in the conception of the church of God.

2. Next, look at the feature of *association*. The church of God is an organic body with a social bond. It is the body of Christ, and all are members one of another. It is in the highest sense a celestial democracy, established upon the earth, in which there are to be no divisions—barbarian, Scythian, bond, free, male, female; but "all one in Christ Jesus." It need not be said how far the church of God has departed from this divine ideal.

This is one of the most melancholy things in human history. For three centuries the church preserved much of its original equality; the poor and the rich were on a common plane, with very little distinction between them. There were *no invidious* distinctions in apostolic days. When Constantine was converted, in the beginning of the fourth century, he introduced into the church an ecclesiastical hierarchy, with a score of grades and ranks, based not upon spiritual attainments, but in the interests of political preferment; and the *via crucis*, the way of the cross, became the *via lucis*, the way of worldly light and glory. The period of formation of the church was past, and the period of deformation began, and waited a thousand years for the period of reformation. During that period of deformation there were two melancholy characteristics of the so-called church—putrefaction and petrifaction—the loss of godly savor and the loss of godly sensibility. The church has never recovered herself from her inoculation with the virus of the caste spirit, and we are bold to utter a protest against all these invidious class distinctions in the church of Jesus Christ. God never meant that there should be these sharp lines between high and low, rich and poor, learned and ignorant, inside this celestial society. And it is a suicidal policy for the church to encourage it. John Wesley said: "God has chosen the poor of this world, rich in faith, and heirs of the promises. The rich may make good scaffolding, but they make very poor building material." The best building materials of the church are God's poor. And not only is this a suicidal policy in breaking up the unity which God meant should characterize the Body of Christ, but it is utterly fatal to the work of winning souls. Chalmers said: "The neglecters of the church are the people that have first been neglected by the church." John Hall said that while in Britain the distinction is between churchmen and dissenters, there is getting to be, all over the world, a difference between churchgoers and absenters.

We have all seen painful illustrations of this caste spirit. In India is a caste system—a cellular structure of society so rigid that the cells never interpenetrate; but we have a caste system in the very church itself, and the cells have little or no communication. Dr. Josiah Strong tells of a New England city where, in a great conflagration, a poor workingman, unknown to those present, rushed into a burning house and rescued a poor sick woman and her helpless children, and then as quietly retired to his own home. A minister of the gospel, moved by his heroism, sought him out and asked him, "Where do you go to church?" "Nowhere." "Why not?" "I cannot pay pew rent, and it is more than I can do to get enough money respectably to clothe my family. We have not fit clothes to go into a house of worship in." "Well, I will see that you have clothes, and that you do not have to pay any pew rent." The minister sent him clothing for himself and his whole family, and then brought the family to church next Sunday, and seated them in his own pew. In the midweek service he went into his church meeting with a glowing heart, and told his people what he had done. One of the members, and principal financial supporters, rose and said: "I think the pastor has made a mistake. We do not want such men in this church. They would not be at home here, nor should we be at home with them. The man and his family would better go to some mission!" The pastor rejoined, "If this is the sentiment of my people, I resign my charge, for God forbid that I should be the pastor of any church that will not open its doors wide to any soul that wants to hear the gospel."

I had some similar personal experience in this matter when in 1876 my church building was burned and we held services in the opera house, free to all, where I preached the gospel to the people for sixteen months, with remarkable results. A new church was built, and, like the old one, the pews were both sold and rented, and visitors found a barrier of exclusiveness that they could not easily pass. I besought my people that the pews might be free in the evenings, and this was agreed to. We sent out a band of young men, who scattered invitations at the street corners, hotels, saloons and elsewhere, until we had to furnish extra sitting accommodations, yet some people of that church went to the ushers and said: "If we are not here at night, do not turn any visitors into our pews." So, when the house was otherwise crowded, there were still vacant pews. I went to the ushers, and they told me the instructions they had received. I said: "Obey my instructions; fill these pews, and I will take the responsibility." For a church of God to encourage caste like that, and put barriers in the way of winning souls, is a burning shame wherever found.

3. The question of *service* will be more fully discussed later on. But what words are those in Rom. 12 and 1 Cor. 12 about the body of Christ, and the Holy Spirit distributing spheres and gifts of service according to his own will—room enough for all, so that no one may feel shut out; work given to all, so that none may feel useless; every one necessary, so that all may be helpful; every one receiving the power of God, so that no one may despair; every one dependent on God, so that none may presume. What a wonderful organism is the body of Christ, and what a distribution of service there is in connection with it!

There are three great forms of service: one is the giving of substance statedly, self-denyingly and systematically unto the Lord; another is the witness, both of lip and life, to the truth as it is in Jesus; again there is prayer—supplication and intercession for ourselves and for all men. How simple those three forms of service are! And to them every one may contribute.

4. A great feature of church life is *worship*—that is, "worth-ship"— ascribing worth to Almighty God, describing his worth in fit terms, inscribing his worth upon the whole house of God and every service conducted within it. Worship is nowhere so magnificently expressed as in the Apocalypse. "Thou art worthy, O Lord, to receive glory, and honor, and power." The whole book echoes with these ideal tributes of worship to the only worthy object of worship.

Two things specially enter into worship: the thought of the exaltation of God above all else, and the privilege of spiritual communion with him. Therefore, there are two things that interfere with worship; and they are, more or less, a blight upon the whole church of Jesus Christ. One is externalism and the other is aestheticism.

Externalism is the disposition to substitute forms for spirit; it is what we call ritualism, a word that many use without stopping to think what it means. There is a certain amount of form necessary to the preservation of the substance of worship, just as the skin of the banana, which is not edible, is necessary for the formation and preservation of the heart of the banana, which is edible. But what if some people chew the skin and throw the heart away! That is a Baganda preacher's quaint satire on ritualism.

We must not expect to preserve the heart of worship without some measure of form. That runs to irreverence and fanaticism. We need form, but no more than what is necessary for the preservation and conservation

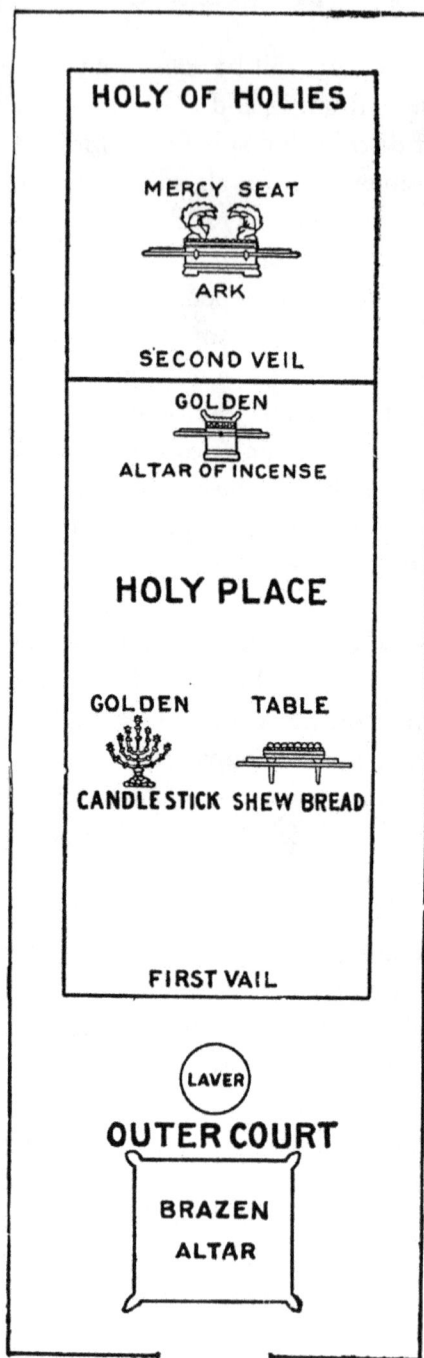

6. Structure of the tabernacle

of spiritual religion. Just so far as the church declines in spirituality she multiplies her forms and sinks into formality. It was so with the Jews. When spirituality declined among them, they took refuge in their rites and ceremonies. Their forms became mechanical, oppressive and arbitrary to the last degree. And in the church of God, whenever spiritual religion declines, formalism prevails; and whenever the spiritual revives, forms are burst asunder, just as the cords about Samson were when he woke up and shook himself. Let the church become spiritual, and she throws away whatever forms are superfluous, what are really fetters on the soaring wings of supplication.

Then, too, aestheticism involves great danger. We justify art; we say: "Nothing can be too good, no building too beautiful, no choir too artistic, no preacher too eloquent."

This is often a great mistake. Whatever attracts attention to itself and away from God is hostile to worship. If we build a beautiful building, and everybody that goes into it is gazing at its architecture, and stained windows, its garniture and furniture, and forgetting God, it is a hindrance to worship. As for eloquent oratory, as such, it has no place in the church. The pulpit is not the place for any eloquence, except it be the eloquence of the Holy Ghost. Wisdom of words makes the cross of Christ of none effect, for the essays of the rhetorician and the arts of the declaimer only tend to obscure the great purpose for which preaching is established in the world. Beware of aestheticism! The punctilious, fastidious taste, the unsanctified art that exalts the aesthetic, lowers the spiritual!

Look for a few moments at the tabernacle (represented on chart 8), erected in the desert. There was scarce a feature of it that was beautiful; in fact, some of it violated all aesthetic laws. Those cherubic figures represented a complex being, with one head of an ox, one of a man, one of a lion, and one of an eagle. Can you put these together and make real beauty? An animal with these four heads would be thought a monster. Then look at the colors. Blue and purple and scarlet and white put together on the same curtain—some would call it tawdry.

But God, in all this, had a spiritual purpose—not an artistic one. He was teaching some great spiritual truths. He directed the cherubic figure, with those four different faces, to be wrought there, because he was not calling his people's attention to an artistic display, but to spiritual types. Truths lay behind the device. And he had those strongly contrasted colors because scarlet is the color of blood, blue represents the fidelity of

God, purple is the color of royalty, white the color of purity, and again he was teaching great lessons about spiritual things.

A distinct command follows immediately upon the giving of the Decalogue, as though there were some particular significance and intention about it. "And if thou wilt make me an altar, thou shalt not build it of hewn stone; for if thou lift up thy tool upon it, thou hast polluted it." Why is this? If he had allowed them to erect an altar of hewn stone, the aestheticism of the altar might have caused the spiritual purpose of it to be forgotten. He wanted their eyes fixed upon that bleeding victim, not on the beauty of the altar that held it. Afterward, Ahaz, like modern aesthetic people, went over to Damascus and saw an altar there which had some sculptured images upon it, and so he displaced the true altar of God and put another altar, like the Damascus altar, in place of it. That is what the church of God does when simplicity is crowded out to make room for elaborate art. A congregation sent a committee to look for a minister. The committee came back and reported in favor of a man who was eloquent as an orator and a fine platform speaker. One who had listened to the report of the committee said: "I should like to know whether he preaches the gospel." "Well, we did not really inquire as to that."

In many a church and chapel there is a godless man presiding at the organ and a choir of worldly people leading the service of sacred song. Has anybody a right to preside at such an instrument, or lead the service of song, in the house of God, who is not appointed and anointed of the Spirit for the work? These are not palatable truths, but they are truths. Whatever does not exalt God drags him down from his high exaltation in the church and is a desecration and a disgrace; and we must be very careful not to corrupt our worship, on the one hand, by externalism, and, on the other, by aestheticism.

5. The church's function in the world is, largely, *witness*. Like the word separation, this is written large over the Old Testament and the New. "Ye are my witnesses, saith the Lord." How often that occurs, especially in the evangelical prophecy of Isaiah. And what does our Lord say? "Ye shall receive the power of the Holy Ghost coming upon you (margin); and ye shall be witnesses unto me unto the uttermost part of the earth." What do the apostles say? "We are his witnesses of these things."

"Witness" is derived from an old Saxon root (witan, to know), from which comes the word wit, which in its original sense is knowledge. Witnessing is therefore telling what one knows—that is all. You cannot tell what you do not know, though you may attempt to; you may know what you do not tell, which, unhappily, many also do. But a witness for God is one that knows God, and simply tells what he knows. It requires no elaborate statement, no high degree of education, no eloquent presentation. Anybody who knows the Word, and knows Christ, and knows the Spirit, and, out of a full heart, even with a stammering tongue, speaks of what he knows, is a witness for God. And here is the universal privilege into which every child of God is welcomed.

It is very important for us to know *to what* we should bear witness, and here we shall not differ. There are two or three great subjects and objects of witness.

One is the inspired *Word of God*. Unto us, as unto the Jews, are committed the oracles of God; only that the Jew had not the complete oracles. He had the Old Testament, and considered it his highest privilege to be the conservator and curator of the Old Testament Scriptures. We have also the New Testament, which he did not. The church of God is like the ark that went in the midst of the children of Israel in their journeyings, which they regarded as a sacred treasure entrusted to their keeping. And what did the ark contain? Look in Hebrews 9: The tables, written by the hand of God—the tables of an unbroken law, typical of Jesus Christ, the perfectly obedient one; Aaron's rod that budded and bore at once buds and blossoms and almonds—a very peculiar fact, remarkable in its typical teaching; and then the pot of manna. We shall not be pressing typology to an extreme if we say that the ark thus represented the treasures of God's Word, Christ as the bread of life, the true manna of God from heaven, the great high priest and teacher, who, like Aaron's rod, swallows all others, and is the only one among them all that buds and blossoms and bears fruit. The church of God is the custodian of the Holy Scriptures, God's living oracles, of the doctrine of Christ as the bread of life for a perishing world, and as high priest and intercessor before God, and man's infallible teacher.

Observe this: God's seal of verity and reality is upon the church of Christ as such just so far as this witness is maintained; only so far has the church assurance of stability—as built upon the rock; and assurance of victory, that even the gates of hell shall not prevail against it; and assurance of conquest of an unbelieving world, which is to be accomplished through the power of the Spirit working through the truth of her testimony. With charity to all, and with malice toward none, we express the deep conviction that any church that denies the infallibility of the Holy Scriptures, and the deity and atoning work of Jesus Christ, has, in God's eyes, no claim to be a church. It may be a religious club, it may be a philanthropic society, but it is not a church of Christ. There are some solemn warnings in Revelation 2 and 3—that a church that denies the infallibility of the Scriptures, and the deity and atoning work of Christ, may become even a "synagogue" and "seat of Satan."

The tabernacle was God's first permanent object-lesson about all the great truths of redemptive history and redemptive plan, representing Christ as the altar of burnt offering, the source of regeneration, the bread of life, the light of the world, the medium of all supplication and intercession, the ground of all acceptance, and the intimate personal fellow-deity with God.

This same tabernacle illustrates the whole life and career of the disciple. Whether designedly typical of it or not, everything we have found characteristic of the church of Jesus Christ finds expression in this remarkable structure.

For instance, the church of Christ is, first of all, indwelt by the Holy Ghost. That is one great cardinal fact. In the tabernacle, in the holiest, the Shekinah fire, the presence of God, dwelt in power.

It was this presence that made the *naos*, or inmost temple, the holiest of all.

Then the church of God is based on the idea of separation. In connection with the tabernacle was a people, separate from all the nations round about them, and drawn into immediate fellowship with God; separated from the world, separated unto God.

The church is a society. All the tribes systematically, by divine arrangement, encamped round about the tabernacle, and in the march moved with it in the midst of them, all the tribes with their standards arranged about the ark of God.

The church is ordained for service. In the holy place we have exactly the three forms of service typified. There was the table of shewbread, representing the offering of substance systematically and statedly to the Lord. "Upon the first day of the week let every one of you lay by him, in store, as God hath prospered him, that there be no gatherings when I come"—that there may be meat in God's house. There was the golden candlestick, representing the witness of the church. "Ye are the light of the world"—shedding light in the midst of darkness, and dispersing the darkness. In the golden altar of incense we have a typical representation of prayer—"Supplications and intercessions for all men," in the name of our Lord Jesus Christ. There are no other forms of service, even as there were none other articles of furniture in the holy place. Is it not at least very suggestive that in the tabernacle these three forms of service should be thus typified and illustrated by the table of shewbread, the golden candlestick, and the golden altar of incense?

The church is organized for spiritual worship. Was ever anything erected among men that suggested the idea of worship better than the tabernacle? Any approach with irreverence was profanation. Any intrusion, except by God's order, was liable to the death penalty. Worship bathed the whole tabernacle and all its services in its divine light, and made it fragrant with a holy, celestial aroma.

Witness is one great purpose for which the church is in the world. In the front court were two articles of furniture: the brazen altar, representing atonement, and the laver, representing regeneration by the Spirit and by the Word—the "washing of regeneration and renewing of the Holy Ghost," "the washing of water by the Word." What is the witness of the church but, first of all, to the atoning blood, to the person of the Lord Jesus Christ and his great work; and, second, to the work of the inspired Word in the cleansing of the life, and to the work of the Holy Spirit in the regeneration of character?

It is thus remarkable that everything vital to the church is expressed in this typical structure—witness to the blood, the Word, and the Spirit; service in the offering of substance, in the witness of experience, in the offering up of prayer and supplications; the presiding presence of the Holy Ghost, typified by the Shekinah fire in the holiest place of all; separation from the world unto God, and a society of believers.

With two passages of Scripture we close: "thou art Peter, and upon this rock will I build my church, and the gates of hell shall not prevail against it" (Matt. 16:18).

"The house of God, which is the church of the living God, the pillar and ground of the truth. And without controversy great is the mystery of godliness. God was manifest in the flesh, justified in the spirit, seen of angels, preached unto the Gentiles, believed on in the world, received up into glory" (1 Tim. 3:15–16).

Of these two passages, the first is one of the most important; and the second is one of the least understood in the Word of God.

"Thou art Peter, and upon this rock will I build my church."

Did Christ build his church on Peter? He had a very unstable foundation if he did. No, he did not build his church on Peter's *personality*, but on Peter's *confession*. He had declared, "Thou art the Christ, the Son of the living God," and our Lord said to him, "flesh and blood hath not revealed it unto thee, but my Father which is in heaven." And then he added: "thou art *Petros*—a fragment of rock—and upon this *petra*—the bed-rock—will I build my church." Peter himself was built on this rock, he was like a fragment of it. But the great bed-rock underneath Peter was the confession of Jesus Christ as the Son of God. Our Lord therefore said: "upon this confession I will build my church, and the gates of hell shall not prevail against it." Historically this was true, for when the Eunuch asked, "why cannot I be baptized?" Philip said: "if thou believest with all thine heart, thou mayest;" and he said: "I believe that Jesus Christ is the Son of God." "No man speaking by the Spirit of God calleth Jesus accursed; and no man can say that Jesus is the Lord but by the Holy Ghost" (1 Cor. 12:3). There is the Spirit-awakened and Spirit-inspired confession. Paul gives the substance of this same confession of faith in Rom. 10:9, where he says: "if thou shalt confess with thy mouth the Lord Jesus, and shalt believe in thine heart that God hath raised him from the dead, thou shalt be saved" (compare 1 John 4:15). Here, then, is the doctrinal basis—the rock-confession on which the church of Christ is built. That has been the great creedal-confession of the ages, the substance of all true creeds.

Against the church, thus founded, "the gates of hell shall not prevail."

What are the gates of hell? The metaphor suggests a city of God, a great fortress, built on the eternal rock, on the one hand; and another city, a Babel of Hades, built on the other side over against it. From these gates of hell throng the myriad hosts of the devil to assault the church. But it stands firm, because built upon the rock of this confession: "Jesus is the Christ, the Son of God." But if the church forsakes that rock, it has no right to live and no power to prevail. It has the promise of stability and victory only while it stands on the basis of this confession of Jesus as Christ—Messiah, and Jehovah—Lord, or Sovereign. The moment that the church abandons that doctrine it ceases to be a true body of Christ, and has no right to expect stability, permanency or victory.

The other passage may be punctuated a little differently, as it doubtless ought to be: "that thou mayest know how thou oughtest to behave thyself in the house of God, which is the church of the living God, the pillar and pedestal of the truth; and, beyond controversy, great is the mystery of godliness"—the incarnation—"God was manifest in the flesh, justified—proven to be God—by the Spirit, seen of angels"—angels had never seen God in any outward form until incarnate; he was revealed to them, as well as to man—"preached among the Gentiles, believed on in the world, received up into glory."

Here is the house of the living God, that is, the church. But, in that house stands one great central pillar, which is the doctrine of the incarnation; as the central pillar reaches down to earth, Christ's humanity touches earth; and as the pillar reaches upward to the roof, his divinity reaches toward and touches heaven. The incarnate Son of God and Son of Man is the pillar about which the whole church is built—to remove that pillar is to bring the church down, like Dagon's temple, when Samson lifted the pillars from their base.

Once more, the only hope of the conquest of a sinning and suffering world for Christ is by standing by the doctrine of the incarnation and of vicarious atonement. May our tongue cleave to the roof of the mouth, and the right hand forget her cunning, before tongue or pen utters or writes a word against the incarnation, deity, and blood atonement of the Lord Jesus Christ!

How little do we know what the power of the gospel is! The Rev. Edward Payson Scott, a missionary in India—fired with passion for souls—resolved to carry the gospel among a fierce and savage tribe living in the mountains—the Nagas. He had learned a little of their language, and yearned to talk about the things of God to those wild people. He was warned by the British resident officer that he must not go unattended by a military escort. "But," he said, "that would misinterpret the object with which I am going as a messenger of peace. If they saw soldiers coming with me, they would say, 'This means a warlike British assault.' No, I will go only with a native." They came to the bottom of a mountain, on the top of which stood this tribal village. As the people saw them coming they hastened down the mountainside and formed in battle line with their weapons. The chief shouted out, "Back! back! We know who you are. You are the spies of the British, and have come to take us captive and sell our children into slavery!" Mr. Scott took out his violin and began singing in the Naga language:

Alas! and did my Savior bleed?
And did my Sovereign die?
Would he devote the sacred head
For such a worm as I?"

Down went the spears in the dust, and that wild tribe drew nearer and nearer, their chief at their head. Mr. Scott went on singing:

Was it for crimes that I had done
He groaned upon the tree?
Amazing pity, grace unknown,
And love beyond degree!

Before he finished that hymn they were crouched around him, their weapons thrown aside, and the chief said: "Where did you learn that song? We never heard the like of that before. Won't you come and stay among us, and sing that song for us again?" Within half an hour the savage tribe was melted and subdued, and Mr. Scott was enjoying their richest hospitality in their best homes, and making preparation to send a permanent teacher to evangelize them.

Chapter 5

The Problem of the Individual Man

To ascertain what Scripture teaches upon the nature of man, we must resort to a careful comparison of passages, of which the following are but a few:

> The LORD God formed man of the dust of the ground, and breathed into his nostrils the breath of life; and man became a living soul (Gen. 2:7).

> The natural man receiveth not the things of the Spirit of God; for they are foolishness unto him: neither can he know them, because they are spiritually discerned. But he that is spiritual judgeth all things (1 Cor. 2:14–15).

> There is a natural body and there is a spiritual body (1 Cor. 15:44).

> Piercing even to the dividing asunder of soul and spirit (Heb. 4:12).

> The very God of peace sanctify you wholly; and I pray God your whole spirit and soul and body be preserved blameless unto the coming of our Lord Jesus Christ" (1 Thess. 5:23).

The biblical teaching upon this theme is not, to the cursory reader, so obvious and unmistakable as upon many others. It belongs rather among the *mysteries*—those hidden truths, unveiled only by more careful search, collating and comparing scattered hints, and so constructing as out of fragments one comprehensive, consistent whole.

The Scripture "classic" upon the constitution of man is the last text, quoted above, where a threefold nature is represented as being combined in him—spirit, soul and body. It is true that the epistles, in which these distinctions appear so distinctly drawn, were not written, or meant to be read, as psychological essays or treatises on the complex constitution of man; and even inspired language may be unduly analyzed and emphasized, reading into it a scientific or philosophic meaning not legitimately contained therein. It still remains true, however, that many devout students, holding to the plenary inspiration of the Word of God, and believing that nothing in its utterances is accidental, have been wont to find, in the distinction thus drawn, and in all Paul's writings maintained, a key to many perplexities.

The words, quoted from this first letter to the Thessalonians, are very clear and explicit. "I pray God your whole spirit and soul and body be preserved blameless."

In the other texts, quoted from the epistles, the distinction between soul and spirit, and between the "natural" or psychical, and the "spiritual," is not only preserved, but assumed as based upon settled facts.

The Lord Bishop of Derry, in commenting on this passage in Thessalonians, says,

> *Body*, material organization; *soul*, sensitive faculty (Luke 12:20, Matt. 10:39; 16:25–26; 1 Thess. 2:8), would seem to stand for the "animal, sentient life," conceived of as indissolubly connected with breath (Jer. 15:9). *Spirit* is the superior faculty, capable of divine communications, which man lost at the fall, but recovers again in his regeneration. The apostle would thus speak of the sensitive mortal soul; of the immortal spirit of new life and higher reason; and of the body, the seat of both…. The one key to his meaning is the principle that, besides body and soul—which make up man's natural being—regenerated man possesses spirit, the principle of supernatural life. It was a long ascent from the conception of body and soul to that of body, soul and spirit.[16]

Canon Fausset likewise regards this prayer of Paul as directed toward an entire sanctification, specifying all the integral parts of man's triune being.

> All three—spirit, soul and body—each in its place constitute man "entire." The spirit links man with higher intelligence, and is that highest part, receptive to the quickening Holy Spirit (1 Cor. 15:47). The soul is intermediate between body and spirit; it is the sphere of the will and affections. In the unspiritual man, the spirit is so sunk under the animal soul, which it ought to keep under, and bring into subjection, that such men are "animal," "sensual," having not spirit (Jude 19), retaining merely the body of organized matter, and the soul, the immaterial animating essence.

Compare 1 Cor. 2:14; 15:44–48, John 3:6. If so, the unbeliever will be raised from the dead, with an animal soul, an animated body, but not like the believer with a spiritual, spirit-endowed and endued body—like unto Christ's (Rom. 8:11).

16 See Bible Commentary, in locis.

With this conception of man's three-fold nature, many other passages of Scripture acquire new significance. In the earliest account of man's creation, we get a hint of this complexity. Moses uses three Hebrew words, which seem to correspond to body, division (*gahphar, nehphesh, n'shahmah*).

"The dust of the ground" clearly represents the soul and spirit, or at least suggest a three-fold body, and that mysterious Hebrew expression, "breathed into his nostrils *the breath of lives,*" may well consist with the impartation to man of a double endowment—a soul life, in common with other living creatures, and a spirit life shared by none of the lower creation. Spirit is evidently that crowning part of man's nature, which fits him for both a higher revelation of God and communication with Him—a faculty either practically lost, or so darkened and degraded by the fall as to be like a blinded eye. If this be a true distinction, there are at once a hundred doors of mystery, both in the structure of the Word of God and in the temple of humanity, that are both unlocked and thrown wide open. So important and far reaching do these teachings of Scripture appear that they afford a complete guide in the study of man as an individual, revealing at once his perils and his needs.

One of the confirmatory *indirect* proofs of this biblical psychology is found, for instance, in the frequent addresses of the Psalmist to his "soul."

"Why art thou cast down, O my soul" (42:5, 11; 43:5).

"My soul, wait thou only upon God" (62:5).

"Bless the Lord, O my soul" (103:1–2, 22; 104:1–35).

"Return unto thy rest, O my soul" (116:7).

"Praise the Lord, O my soul" (146:1).

Here the higher self addresses the lower self, rebuking, or exhorting and commanding it. This is the most natural construction and is often suggested elsewhere.

In Romans 7 Paul plainly represents the fact that, not only in his body but in his mind, is found a law, or tendency, to which his higher self or spiritual *ego* is opposed.

"The things that I would I do not and the evil that I would not that I do. Wherefore, it is no more I that do it," etc.

Here more plainly, perhaps, than in any other one place in Scripture, do we see the somewhat contrary and inharmonious working of the three different natures—the enlightened, regenerate spirit opposed to the soul and body in their lower tendencies. Similarly in 1 Cor. 4:1–4, when Paul

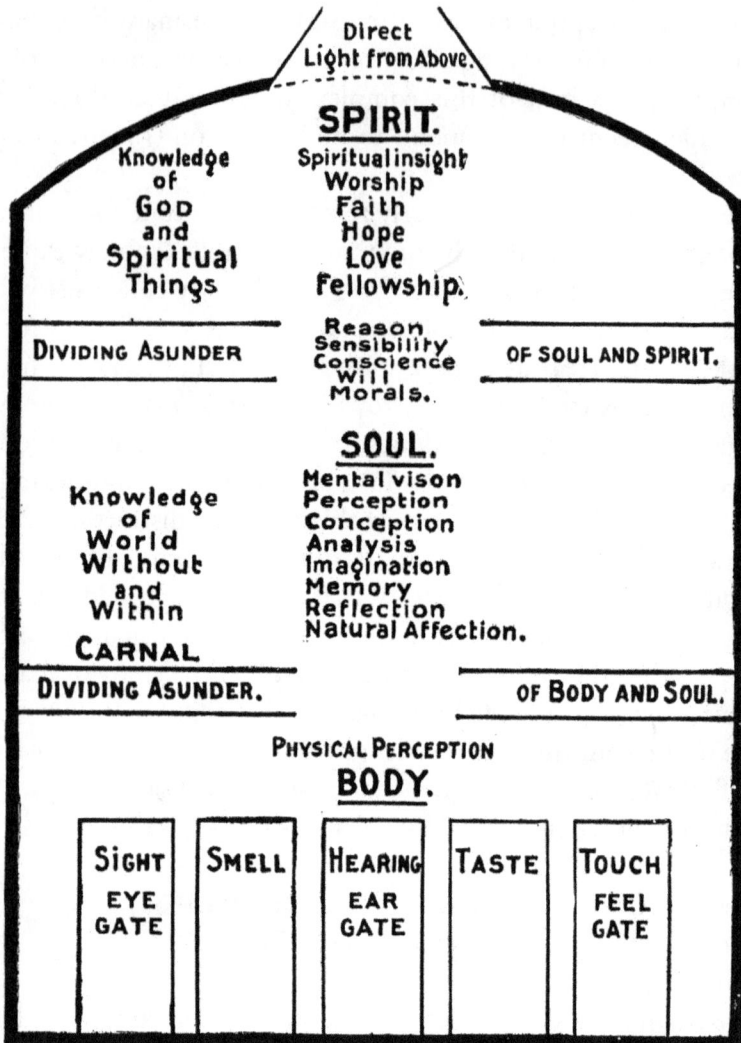

Direct
Light from Above.

SPIRIT.

Knowledge
of
GOD
and
Spiritual
Things

Spiritual insight
Worship
Faith
Hope
Love
Fellowship.

DIVIDING ASUNDER

Reason
Sensibility
Conscience
Will
Morals.

OF SOUL AND SPIRIT.

SOUL.

Knowledge
of
World
Without
and
Within

CARNAL

Mental vison
Perception
Conception
Analysis
Imagination
Memory
Reflection
Natural Affection.

DIVIDING ASUNDER.

OF BODY AND SOUL.

PHYSICAL PERCEPTION

BODY.

SIGHT	SMELL	HEARING	TASTE	TOUCH
EYE GATE		EAR GATE		FEEL GATE

7. Tripartite nature of man

represents himself as sitting in judgment on himself—the higher nature arraigning the lower as before a supreme tribunal.

This conception of the three-fold constitution of man gives new meaning to Paul's three prominent adjectives, "earthy," "natural," "spiritual"— the first suggests man's material part, his body; the second, psychical, or soulish, his soul; the last, his spirit, or *pneuma*. Our Lord, in departing, said: "Father, into thy hands I commend my *spirit*," and Stephen, "Lord Jesus receive my *spirit*"—in both cases, this word being discriminatingly used.

The other three words in 1 Cor. 2, "carnal," "natural," "spiritual," suggest the same *three-fold nature*—the carnal refers to the flesh, the natural to the psychical, and the spiritual to the highest elements of man's being as divinely illumined. Paul was constantly meeting even disciples who were too much controlled by the flesh and its lusts, as when one is gluttonous or greedy, envious or boastful; others who were unduly controlled by the mere intellect, proud of learning, wise in their own conceit; and others who were as plainly ruled by the Spirit of God and responsive in spirit to his leading and teaching. Upon the basis of this three-fold nature of man many of his rebukes and exhortations are founded.

This is by no means, therefore, a merely speculative, metaphysical and trifling matter. It concerns a proper understanding not only of man's being but of his relation to God and his need of the regenerating Spirit.

In Diagram 7, this tripartite being of man is represented as a structure, in which the body is lowermost, the spirit is uppermost, and the soul intermediate. The body rests upon the earth of which it is composed; the soul is next above the body, as its animating principle and intelligence, using the bodily *senses* as its agents in the exploration of the phenomena of matter, and the bodily organs and faculties for its self-expression and communion with the outside world. The spirit receives impressions of outward and material things, through the soul and body, but it belongs itself to a higher level and realm, and is capable of a direct knowledge of God by revelation to its own higher senses and faculties. In an unfallen state, it was like a lofty observatory, with an outlook upon a celestial firmament. Sin closed all the windows and darkened all the chambers of the spirit, and it became as a death chamber, until the Lord once more breathed into this chamber of death his own life-giving Spirit, and once more flooded it with divine illumination and pervaded it with vitality.

The second chapter of 1 Corinthians is beyond understanding or explanation unless this threefold nature of man supplies the key; for here are represented two wholly distinct modes of knowing and apprehending truth. There is the whole vast sphere of intellectual truth, possible of exploration when the mind can use the bodily eyes and ears, and then combine and rearrange sense impressions by the memory, imagination and reason; but we are plainly told that even "the *princes* of this world"—the highest scholars and philosophers—did not and could not know these things which demand a higher capacity, a verifying faculty of a higher order. Eye hath not seen nor ear heard nor heart conceived what is only revealed by the Spirit of God, and even he can successfully address spiritual truths only to spiritual faculties.

The complex constitution of man presents then three separate yet connected realms of being: body, soul and spirit—or the physical, psychical and pneumatical or spiritual.

The body has its senses, or means of communication with the external, material world. These are usually reckoned as five—sight, hearing, taste, touch and smell, or as Bunyan represents them, as the five gates to the city of Mansoul. Later research seems to demand two other senses, the "muscular" sense, whereby we perceive dimension and distance and weight; and the "magnetic" sense, whereby we both impart and receive impressions in a subtle way, defying analysis, yet perceptible and even measurable by delicate instruments, and which seems to find its special field of manifestation within a radius of about ten feet from each individual.

Above this physical department is the psychical, the soul-nature, where mental processes are carried on, with the will and the affections. The soul is shut in a dark chamber. It cannot explore external nature except through the bodily organs and senses. We may think of it as coming down to the lower level, to go out through these sense gates for purposes of exploration and observation; then, as returning to its secret chambers for the elaboration of sense impressions. There is first a *mental perception*, corresponding to the sense-perception and inseparable from it. Then on the basis of this, a mental *concept*—a notion, image or idea of things as gathered from sense. Then, as imagination forms and memory retains such mental images, the thinking powers are able to carry on the process of *classification*; separating and combining; analysis and synthesis; and *ratiocination* follows—reason, by deductive and inductive methods, reaching conclusions.

It will appear how dependent the psychical nature is upon the physical. Were the soul entirely shut in by the closing of every sense gate, it is impossible to see how any correct impression of the external world would be obtained, or even the knowledge of its existence. It is also clear that what we call new conceptions, original ideas, are only new combinations of impressions got from observation of the universe, as a poet's imagination may combine in new forms images first found in nature.

When we reach that highest realm of *spirit*, however, we touch a part of man's being which was meant to explore the unseen world and the realm of immaterial and spiritual realities. It had capacities, at man's original creation, that are as far beyond the bodily senses as the microscopic and telescopic vision surpass the unaided power of the eye. Had man remained innocent of evil and loyal to God, he would have had open doors of access to heavenly chambers of mystery. But sin closed all these gates and windows of the spirit and darkened and blinded the spirit's faculties; so that all conceptions of higher verities became dependent upon physical observation through the senses, and psychical processes of reasoning. This we take to be the real teaching of such marvelous chapters as 1 Corinthians 2.

It is not too much to say that the soul and spirit have also their "senses," faculties which correspond to the organs of sense, and are adapted to the mental and spiritual nature. Paul refers to these when he writes of disciples "of full age" who by reason of habitual use "have their senses exercised to discern good and evil" (Heb. 5:14). Evidently these senses referred to here, which discern *moral* qualities, belong to a higher order, and some of them we may discover. Imagination is the sense of the unseen; memory, the sense of the past, and hope, of the future; reason, the sense of the true and false, and conscience, of right and wrong; sensibility perceives what is repulsive or attractive; and natural affection is the sense of kinship, etc.

In the realm of spirit, there are activities of a yet higher grade. Worship is the sense of holy awe; adoration, of absorption in God; faith, the sense of trust; love, of complacence in moral beauty and response to moral need; while peace is the sense of repose, and joy, of delight in God. These are like open eyes and ears, and receptive physical senses, keenly alive to impression, and through them God reveals himself and his higher verities to the obedient spirit. Disciples have been conscious of an illumination from him which was like a flood of glory—dazzling the vision.

On the diagram has been indicated the "dividing asunder" of body and soul, and of soul and spirit (Heb. 4:12)—the transitions where the different departments of man's being meet and mingle, which is another of the profound hints of biblical psychology. What a mysterious realm is that where body and soul commune—where impressions made on the physical senses, as sensations, pass into thought and become mental images! And so of that yet higher experience, where the psychical passes into the spiritual! Where, for example, the sight of the heavens, having first awakened thought of the creator's power and wisdom, then kindles adoring wonder and praise! Or thoughts of right and wrong having aroused the conscience and will, develop holy resolves fixed on obedience and service!

The Word of God is perpetually seeking to lead us on from experiences that are at first mere sensations, due to the bodily organs, to impressions and convictions that lay hold of our thinking powers, and finally bring the highest being into accord with God. It teaches also how the soul life may injuriously affect the spirit life—how thoughts of evil, lodged in the mind, become debasing to the spiritual character, how hurry and worry, hustle and bustle, break up its peace and trust; how envious, jealous, impatient, ungenerous thoughts and feelings dull and deaden the spirit to all true sympathy and love to men, and to all visions and voices of God; and how to cherish right habits of thinking and feeling pervades the spirit with consciousness of God's presence, and unselfish yearnings after service to humanity.

The theme is inexhaustible; but when once the biblical philosophy of man's three-fold being is clearly apprehended, hundreds of otherwise difficult questions find answer, and perplexing problems a solution.

We begin to understand, for example, how foolish it is to attempt to satisfy man's higher nature with anything short of its natural, necessary food.

The Word of God teaches, as one of the first laws governing these conditions of man's nature, that he must be satisfied, in each plane of his being, only with the nourishment suited to that plane.

Man has a body—that is to say, is built up of what we call earthly constituents—certain chemical elements, and this constitutes the flesh. And there is breath—the air of the atmosphere—within. Man is, physically, at once solid, liquid, and aerial or atmospheric. As related to the ground from which he springs, if he is to keep the body alive, he needs earthly food—bread from the earth because his body belongs to earth. Every form of life must be nourished with food of its sort.

But when we pass into the sphere of reason and thought, what is the use of attempting to feed, satisfy or nourish the soul powers, mind and reason, with a literal meal? They would scorn it. There is in my reason a necessity for higher food; and hence so many are unhappy in the world because they say, "Let us eat and drink." That is their notion of satisfaction. But, having eaten and drunk, they are not satisfied, because God has given them brain and mind which hunger for food as truly and imperatively as the body does. Demosthenes, in the days of his prime, said to his fellow-countrymen in Athens, "For God's sake, think!" That is to say, "You have brains; use them." The mind needs nourishment and strength just as much as the body. A true man feels dissatisfied with every day that passes in which he has not assimilated something mentally and gained some new idea. A German said, "give me a great thought that I may feed upon it." We cannot feed the body with thoughts, neither can we feed the mind with bread, or with even the most dainty viands. Neither can a man feed the highest part of his nature, spirit, with anything which is unfit for it. We must have something also to satisfy that. Where is the food to be found but in God? Let the unsatisfied heart of universal man answer.

The body has its appropriate nutriment and sustenance—it is found in air and food, and its highest welfare is reached through good physical habits of exercise and cleanliness. The soul has its own sustenance and satisfaction: it feeds on thought, knowledge, learning literature and art, human enterprise and natural affection. But the spirit has both higher wants and capacities; and it yearns after knowledge of God and fellowship with him, verifying that ancient maxim of Augustine: "Thou, O God, hast made us for thee, and our heart is restless till it rests in thee."

This subject serves also to interpret man's normal condition and relations. One obvious lesson in this biblical psychology is that God evidently designed that the human spirit, indwelt and ruled by his Holy Spirit, should keep man in constant touch with himself, and maintain in everything its proper pre-eminence, ruling soul and body. Whenever this divine order is lost, through whatever cause, or upon whatever pretext, the true manhood falls into serious degeneracy if not ruin.

For example, in the *carnal* man, the flesh, the lowest and most earthly part of his being, reigns paramount. In the *natural* man, or psychical, the animal soul asserts itself, subordinating the spirit, sinking it into subserviency to the mere intellectual faculties, which are essentially worldly in nature, aim and method. Men lean to their own understanding, become wise in their own conceit, and often despise and blaspheme God. In the ungodly the soul, neglecting the spirit and leaving it to the living death of sin, persists in glorifying intellect and its achievements.

In redemption, the three come into their true relation. In sanctification the human spirit is wedded to the divine, and in this holy union finds power to control the soul, and, through the soul, the body. Even here, however, there must be a true proportion. If undue attention is given to bringing the body into subjection, and the soul is neglected, the result is ascetic practice with wrong doctrine. If the soul is unduly the object of care, the creed may be kept right, the beliefs and convictions guarded, while the fleshly appetites and passions still hold sway. But when God has his way in us, and first of all the spirit is in harmony with him, and proper and proportionate heed is given to the soul and body, all three are preserved blameless, and man may approach very near to a perfect life in Christ.

A brilliant writer, by a powerful use of metaphor, has pictured man's state when the whole of his threefold nature is in rebellion against God's order. Conscience, the judge, bribed or silenced by clamor; the will, the marshal, leading its forces in revolt; the imagination, the poet and artist, lending its powers to evil; the understanding, the student, resorting to curious arts; desire, the merchant, wasting its store of affection, and gazing out into the future in search of some home bound argosy of happiness, but gathering only unsatisfying good—all these powers, untrue to their allegiance; the ermine, the baton, the song, the books, the merchandise, at the service of a usurper, sin.

When the Spirit renews the mind, these faculties are restored to loyalty and reinstated under God. Then conscience seeks to give verdict, according to the divine statute book, and is habitually obeyed. Then the lordly will assumes again a lowly yet noble vassalage. Then the dream of the imagination is transcended by a heavenly reality. Then the understanding burns the magic books in the market place, and breaks the wand of its curious arts, studying now for eternity as well as time. Desire still amasses, for man will lay up treasure, only the treasure is no longer on earth.

It is the crown of such a divine order that the same laws of our being guide our spiritual and natural life: the same self-control and watchful diligence which built up the worldly habits toward the summits of success may be applied at once to those habits which ripen us for heaven. Regeneration imparting no new faculty, gives only a new direction to the old.[17]

Even this metaphor does imperfect justice to the marvels of transformation which take place in man when God becoming the center of his being, all the elements of his complex personality wheel into the orbit of allegiance in harmony with him and with each other.

The subject leads us still further to an understanding of both the nature and need of *regeneration*.

The fall of man left his spirit hopelessly without God and without hope. It was like a dismantled observatory, which some earthquake has wrecked, with its astronomical apparatus for studying the heavens—nay more, it was like the Holy of Holies in tabernacle or temple, forsaken of the divine presence and with the divine, uncreated Shekinah fire quenched, leaving it in midnight darkness. When such was the case in the temple of old, the only light possible in the inmost shrine would be such as could struggle in through the thick veil from the candlestick burning in the holy place, or from the court without, through both veils.

Indeed the whole structure of the tabernacle (diagram 6) strikingly reminds us of the threefold constitution of man. The outer court, open to the sky and dependent on natural light, corresponding to the body; the inner court, without door or window, lit up only by an artificial light of its own, suggested the soul life, with its lamp of intellect; the inmost court, still more shut in, and without illumination save as God himself shed there his uncreated ray, reminding of the human spirit.

After sin left the spirit in the darkness of death, its only light was the uncertain and fallible ray of man's own thinking powers, so often misguided and wholly perverted. And regeneration is the relighting of that quenched Shekinah flame. It is the introduction of the spirit of life into the death chamber, of the spirit of light into the death shade, of the spirit of love where selfishness and hate had reigned. And hence it is that while from the wise and prudent of the world the Father has withheld and hidden the revelation of his higher truths he has revealed them unto babes—those born again in the image of his Son and endowed with the seeing eye.[18]

---

17 *Hours with the Mystics*, 2: 231.
18 Matthew 11:25–27.

This also reveals to us how it is that when men lean to their own understanding, and depend upon intellectual discernment, they are often judicially blinded to higher truth.

No question is more fundamental than whether this book is to be regarded and treated as the book of *God* or of *Man;* whether in it we are to see and recognize a *supernatural element.* It is often said that this is of little consequence and is a mere matter of interpretation. But interpretation is no small matter when it settles the whole *authority of the contents* of Scripture and *our consequent attitude and obligation.* A naturalistic and rationalistic interpretation of its contents may involve a practical denial of its truth and the binding character of its teachings. Christ's resurrection may be resolved into the survival of a holy influence—spiritualized into a poem on the undying character of all self-oblivious heroism; but what becomes of both the credibility of the gospel narrative and the Christianity that is declared to be actually based upon his literal rising from the dead!

Nothing can be much more frivolous and profane than the way in which so-called modern "criticism" coolly disposes of all miraculous or supernatural intervention. By the most tortuous methods of exegesis a plain narrative is wrenched from its obvious meaning.

Take, for example, the experience of Israel at the Red Sea with its two prodigious marvels, the wall of waters and the pillar of cloud.

We are told that a powerful wind, driving down the arm of the Red Sea all the night before, raised the water to an unusual height on the southwestern side, exposing the shallows at the point of crossing. This sounds plausible enough, but the difficulties of this explanation are greater than the supposed difficulties it removes. For not only did Israel go over as on dry land, but with the waters as a wall *on both sides.* A powerful east wind might have caused an ebb tide and reared the waters in a mass to the *leeward,* but the same natural causes would prevent any such accumulation of waters to the windward. And again, what about the pursuing Egyptians whom the same wall of waters that protected Israel overwhelmed and destroyed! That must have been a lucky coincidence—the waters, held back just long enough for Israel to get across, and then loosed from their bonds just in time to fall back upon the pursuers.

Then as to the pillar of cloud, it is no mystery, we are told, but the signal, given on journeys, by the smoke of the caravan fires, each company or division being marked by its own standard, which at night consisted of long poles, surmounted by small beacons, framed of iron hoops filled with combustible materials for light. Each company had ten or twelve, those of each division having its own definite figure and shape, so that every individual in the caravan could find his place. But this was not only a pillar of *fire* by *night*, but also by *day*, a pillar of *cloud*. It possessed intelligence, going before to search out a resting place, and by its movements determining those of God's people, whereas the caravan's movements rather determine those of the beacon signal! And God's pillar was instinct and even *vocal* with his presence! Its position, appearance and altitude, all changing according as the host was in camp or on the march.

We are simply compelled, as believers, to accept the Bible account as genuine, and concede God's interposition, or, while *eliminating the supernatural*, deny also all *historical accuracy*. We must either put nature and chance behind all these phenomena, or else believe that the God of all power was working, using natural agencies to further his own designs. Moreover in Hebrews 11:29, this passage of the Red Sea is classed among the victories of *faith*.

"By faith, they passed through the Red Sea as on dry ground, which the Egyptians assaying to do were drowned."

Here the whole history is lifted to the level of a sublime experience of *dealing with God!* on Israel's part in faith and obedience; on the part of Pharaoh and his hosts, in unbelief and rebellion. In one case we have mere chance coincidences—winds and waters combining to save some and drown others. In the other the God of nature uses his own created forces to accomplish his own purposes.

If modern "Higher Criticism," so-called, be taken as a guide, a *reductio ad absurdum* results from simply compiling and combining some of its teachings.

The story of Eden becomes a mere picture poem to teach the peril of disobedience. Lot and Sodom, a myth, illustrating the risks of too close an alliance with the wicked. Abram, at best a head of an ancient clan, conspicuous for his unselfishness, purity of life and rectitude, whose devotion to a tribal deity became the foundation of a widespread popular worship. Jonah and the great fish are a fable to illustrate a disobedient, selfish and revengeful spirit in a messenger of mercy and judgment. The story of Daniel and the lion's den, an utterly untrustworthy narrative. Who knows but he may have been some ancient lion tamer and the lion's den a menagerie! Even the resurrection of our Lord becomes at best only a symbolic or figurative expression of the survival of a good man in his influence over other men.

All these and kindred errors can be traced to their unfortunate fountain head, if we once clearly perceive how blindly a man may be groping after divine verities, while seeking knowledge and understanding of them only by the help of intellect. Undertaking to unravel the mysteries of God by the mere methods of man, he assumes that the Bible is to be studied and judged like any ordinary book, as mere literature; and that God is like any other author, and can be interpreted by the laws of authorship and the methods of human writers. It is taken for granted that the Word of God has in it no supernatural, superhuman element. Hence at once prophecy and miracle are read out of it, prediction becoming shrewd, sagacious forecast on the basis of probabilities, miracle becoming at most only an occurrence at the time inexplicable. This is reasoning in a circle, like Hume the deist, and Huxley, the materialist; first assuming that anything opposed to the "uniformity of nature" and the "common experience of men" is impossible and incredible, and then assuming prophecy and miracle to contradict both, and therefore fall into the category of the impossible and incredible.

This is like attempting to light up the Holy of Holies with man's wax-taper, when God's Shekinah fire no more burns there; or denying that there ever was such a divine flame because man cannot make his taper burn as brightly and constantly. Every part of man's being demands its own light. Sunlight will do for the body, but it will not light up the mind's secret chambers; neither will mere intellect, however brilliant, serve the place and office of that uncreated flame which made the burning bush so great a sight, and still makes the heart of a little child, indwelt by the Spirit, a presence chamber of God!

Chapter 6

The World That Now Is

Six or seven texts of Scripture are selected, as outlining the general treatment of the Word of God, as to this great problem of the disciple's relation to this present world.

1. Who gave himself for our sins, that he might deliver us from this present evil world, according to the will of God and our Father (Gal. 1:4).

2. Love not the world, neither the things *that are* in the world. If any man love the world, the love of the Father is not in him. For all that *is* in the world, the lust of the flesh, and the lust of the eyes, and the pride of life, is not of the Father, but is of the world. And the world passeth away, and the lust thereof, but he that doeth the will of God abideth for ever (1 John 2:15–17).

3. Ye adulterers and adulteresses, know ye not that the friendship of the world is enmity with God? Whosoever therefore will be a friend of the world is the enemy of God (James 4:4).

4. And they that use this world, as not abusing it: for the fashion of this world passeth away (1 Cor. 7:31).

5. If the world hate you, ye know that it hated me before it hated you. If ye were of the world, the world would love his own: but because ye are not of the world, but I have chosen you out of the world, therefore the world hateth you (John 15:18–19).

6. I have manifested thy name unto the men which thou gavest me out of the world.... The world hath hated them, because they are not of the world, even as I am not of the world. I pray not that thou shouldst take them out of the world, but that thou shouldst keep them from the evil. They are not of the world, even as I am not of the world.... As thou hast sent me into the world, even so have I also sent them into the world.... That they also may be one in us: that the world may believe that thou hast sent me (John 17:6, 14–16, 18, 21).

7. We have received, not the spirit of the world, but the spirit which is in God; that we might know the things that are freely given to us of God (1 Cor. 2:12).

A lifetime of study would not exhaust the lessons contained in these few sentences. The designation "present evil world" is significant; and so important is deliverance from it that it was one of the main objects of our Lord's advent.

The love of the world is forbidden, and so emphatically that he who wills to be its friend is God's enemy.

It is conceded that there is a legitimate use of this world, but we must beware of abusing it by forgetting that it is transient and fleeting.

The last discourse and intercessory prayer of our Lord contains seven phrases which, with singular completeness, define the disciple's relation to the world—*chosen and given to Christ out of the world, sent back into it; in it, but not of it; hated by it, but kept from its evil;* and constraining the world to *believe.*

The characteristic spirit of the world is the opposite of the spirit of God and hinders full knowledge of divine things.

Such are the broad border lines which bound the great territory of this theme and will determine its present treatment.

The subject presents a peculiar difficulty in the fact that so much contained and embraced in "the world" is not of itself sinful, and therefore indulgence in it cannot be; the wrong lies in excess, misuse and abuse, the perversion of what might be harmless or even beneficial, if kept in a right relation to other and higher interests. This fact demands corresponding discrimination in treatment.

Let us inquire what the world *is, has,* and *does.*

1. What *is* the world?

Worldliness and wickedness are by no means synonymous or equivalent terms. Nine words are translated "world"—five in the Old Testament and four in the New. The latter four have various shades of meaning, but all may be comprised in these: two regarding the earth as a material sphere and habitable globe; another, as an exhibition of divine order, symmetry, arrangement and beauty—a cosmos—the remaining word expresses the idea of time; either indefinite, in contrast to eternity, or one's own lifetime, the brief span of human existence. These distinctions might be maintained in the English version by using four simple phrases: material world, created world, habited world, and time world. Combining these meanings, the general idea suggested by "the world" is: the earth as the habitation of man, with everything that pertains to its material beauty, order and symmetrical arrangement; but, in connection with this, the notion of that which is fleeting, passing away, perishing.

A worldly life is wrong, not because it is profane or blasphemous or openly violates the commands of the Decalogue—offending against virtue, chastity, truth, purity; but because it is *taken up with things material and temporal.* The grandest thing about a man is not material at all, but spiritual; not mortal and temporal, but eternal, immortal; and a worldly life, at best, is unworthy of him.

It has already been said that one word translated as world is "cosmos," which expresses the notion of order and beauty. Can it be wrong to be attracted by the cosmic beauty and symmetry of God's universe? To dwell on the wonderful system that prevails in the solar and stellar worlds? To be absorbed in the study of the wonders of nature? Of course not, except so far as, our attention being attracted to these things and engrossed by them, we forget that higher, spiritual glory and beauty of which at best these are only outward types. Suppose a man to have stood in the ancient tabernacle before that veil that hid the Holy of Holies from view; to have looked on the blue, the purple, the scarlet, and the embroidery of the cherubim; and, having attention so taken up with that material curtain, as to have forgotten the Shekinah, the divine presence, within! Not the attention to the material and visible in itself, but the neglect of the spiritual and eternal constitutes the wrong.

We have already seen on the charts representing the constitution of man and the universe (6, 7) how the two correspond. There is in man what is material, and what is spiritual, and a territory intermediate, uniting both—a dividing asunder of body and soul, and again of soul and spirit (Heb. 4:12)—where the physical and the psychical, and, higher up, the psychical and the spiritual meet and mingle.

Exactly correspondent is the structure of the universe. It has a material and a spiritual realm, and another that lies between, where the visible and invisible come into contact, and matter touches spirit. The "Ladder of Life" (7) shows, step by step, the ascent from the grossest forms of matter which can be tested by all our senses, to those which appeal to only four, three, two, one—like light which can be detected only by vision; still

	Good Spirits.		Evil Spirits.

GOD

Good Spirits.		Evil Spirits.
Archangel. Principalities. Powers. Thrones. Dominions. Authorities.	Spiritual Realm Higher order of Senses	Archangels. (?) Principalities Powers World Rulers. Wicked Spirits.

		Supersensuous
	Mystery of Being Mind Psychic Realm. Intellectual Senses	Phenomena.
Transition	Mystery of Matter Invisible Forces of Nature.	
Number 1	Realm	
of Senses 2	of	Sensible
Available. 3	Physical	
4	Senses	Phenomena.
5	The Ladder of Life.	

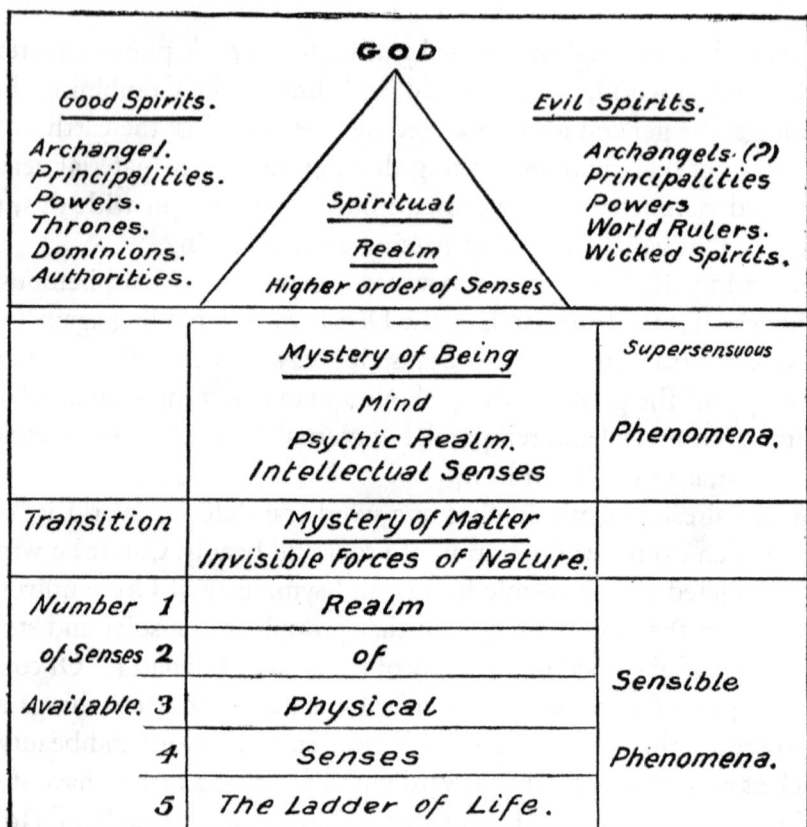

8. Constitution of the universe

further up is the realm of invisible forces, like gravitation and cohesion, which pertain to matter and yet are not themselves material.

Still above is the psychic realm—the realm of supersensuous phenomena, like the life principle itself, the greatest reality of the created universe. It manifests itself through material forms and physical organs, yet is itself essentially invisible and intangible; it uses the senses and yet cannot be detected by any of them, being too subtle and evasive, yet universal and pervasive.

The Word of God reveals, yet above this psychical realm, one purely *spiritual*. God himself presides over it—the uncreated SPIRIT; and under him a whole hierarchy of spirits, both good and bad, in apparently seven ranks or orders, from archangel down to the lowest grade.

In this exact correspondence, itself, between the constitution of man and of the universe, lies the great lesson God would teach. Each is the exact counterpart of the other and hints mutual adaptation. The bodily senses are, as Bunyan called them, the five gates of Mansoul, both for ingress and egress. They are channels of communication between man and the material universe. Between the psychic department of man's being and the like realm of creation there is also a connection: the invisible forces of his nature correspond to the sphere of life and subtle intangible agencies outside of him, while his highest spiritual entity has its counterpart in that lofty realm of spiritual being where God dwells sovereign over vast hosts of spirits.

Not only so, but man was meant to commune with these higher realms of the universe and has faculties and powers which are to soul and spirit what senses are to the body. And because both in man and in the universe these invisible realms are higher and grander than the lower, it is plain that they should have his supreme thought and attention. This is a *natural* inference from the very nature of things; but it is enforced tremendously by the *spiritual* motives which the Word of God inspires. Here the true character and importance of the spiritual world is unveiled for the first time. Man is taught that he was originally an offshoot from the central life of the universe—not simply an animal, however exalted in rank, but made in the image of God, and that he was made and meant to know God, and commune with him; that this upper chamber of his being, darkened by sin, is capable of becoming a holy of holies, where the uncreated life of God burns and shines, and of receiving light from him who is Light.

To engross himself in that which is *material* is therefore to neglect the higher realm of the universe and starve his own higher nature. It is to make the visible and temporal order an idol and substitute it for the worship of Deity. It is to give all heed to the life that perishes and none to the undying life beyond. To state this course is to expose its unspeakable folly, wrong and crime. It is the disaster which this brings about, of which our Lord says that the fool's house "fell—and great was the fall of it."

The "world," then, is, in the Bible sense, material, visible, temporal. While man belongs to a temporal order, he also belongs to the spiritual and eternal, his better part being immaterial and invisible. While the world passeth away, he abides forever. We have only to put these two great classes of facts in opposition to see why this existing order is called "the present evil world."

2. What *has* the world?

It is briefly summed up in that message of John—"all that is in the world, the lust of the flesh, the lust of the eyes, and the pride of life."

These "lusts," or carnal cravings, characterize and often control man: appetite, avarice and ambition. And here all three are referred to: "the lust of the flesh"—appetite; "the lust of the eyes"—avarice, gloating over externalities—the splendor and glitter of wealth, luxury; "the pride of life"—ambition—selfishness, seeking prominence and pre-eminence, the display of worldly honor, power, glory. All these attractions the world has, and these are *all* it has; but they are great snares. They all appeal to *self*—that root of all sin and pride and rebellion. With pleasures, gains, crowns, which are but for a season, it ensnares and enslaves the man.

3. What *does* the world?

We are now prepared to understand what the world DOES with man when it has him under control. We have seen what it *is* and *has* and has *not;* and it is not difficult to see that its practical power over its mistaken devotees must be harmful and ruinous.

1. The god of this world uses these things to *take up the attention* of men. We are creatures of habit; and there is nothing in which the power of habit is more evident than in the life of thought that we lead. We think of some things for no assignable reason except that we are accustomed to think of them. Our minds run in the channels which have been scooped

out by our customs and habits of thought, and our thoughts determine our character; they give shape and mold to our conduct, our conversation and our destiny. If Satan can take up attention with things that have no influence in developing and enlarging the spiritual life, one great end of his snares is accomplished; and hence we are told of the wicked man, that "God is not in all his thoughts." The first charge that God brings against him is that he leaves God out of his plans, out of his daily life; not that all his thoughts are bent against God, that he meditates dethroning God, if it were possible, but simply that he has not God in all his thoughts. Satan takes up his attention with the things of the world and he has no thoughts of God's kingdom. Things material and temporal crowd out things immaterial and immortal.

2. In the second place, Satan uses the things of this world to *blur and blind the vision* to the power of spiritual things. He deals in illusions and delusions, and makes men interested in the magnificence and glory of the things of the world, and so indifferent to the powers of the world to come. Words often express in themselves great ethical conceptions. Look at three words in our English language, quite similar, and peculiar: The words "blare," "glare" and "flare." Blare expresses a sound as of a trumpet, and the effect of such a sound is to render the ear temporarily deaf to any other; it paralyzes for the moment the organs and faculties of hearing. Glare represents a brilliant light, by which for the time the vision is blinded and dazzled, so as to be insensible to other objects of sight. The word flare expresses the effect of bold, strongly contrasted and brilliant colors. You look, for instance, from a deep red, and cannot discern the exact hue of something else which is over against it. Your vision has been confused by the brilliance of these strongly contrasted colors. Satan uses worldly things to produce a similar effect on the mind. He deafens the spiritual ear by the blare of his trumpets; he confuses, dazzles, blinds, bewilders the spiritual vision by the glare and flare, the brilliance, the grandeur, the high colored magnificence of worldly display. Lot saw the plain of the Jordan well watered, fertile, a capital place for his flocks and his herds. True, Sodom was there, and the men of Sodom were sinners against the Lord exceedingly; but Lot's vision was dazzled and confused by the external splendor and beauty of the land that was before him, and he chose that plain as his inheritance, notwithstanding the wickedness of the associations that cursed it. Ahab looked over on the beauty of Naboth's vineyard, its fertility, its southern exposure and

enviable position, and his eyes were dazzled by its external attractions, until his judgment and conscience ceased to give a true report of his duty to God and man. That is Satan's method—the method of *spiritual eclipse!* Just as this world at times may come between the inhabitants of other worlds and the sun and eclipse the sun; so this world comes between the vision of its inhabitants and the sun of righteousness, and eclipses the glory and the splendor of spiritual things. Some render 2 Cor. 4:3-4: "if our gospel be hid, it is hid *by those things which are perishable; by which* the god of this world hath blinded the minds of them that believe not," etc.

Boys catch birds with paper funnels, which they stick in the soil, dropping into them seed. The birds thrust in their beaks to get at the seed, but cannot withdraw them, and so can neither see nor take wing and are easily made captive. The master fowler uses similar snares to blind men's eyes and keep them from taking wing to loftier heights. Robert Hall rebuked an avaricious brother by writing the word God on a card and covering it with a gold piece. "Do you see that word now?" "No." "I thought a sovereign, put between, would make it hard for you to see God!" The sun, though eighty times as large as the earth, and with it the whole arch of the heavens, may be hidden from view by the intrusion of a very small object, however trifling, before the eye. True advance in anything depends on seeing where one is going and what are the relations of things.

3. Again, Satan uses the world not only to absorb attention but *affection.* A merchant in Britain grew so to love gold that he would spend hours in gloating over the sight of his hoarded treasure. Beau Brummel, the arbiter of fashion and dictator of dress, who boasted of his intimacy with lords and ladies and even royalty itself, so worshiped clothes that he spent a thousand pounds a year on his tailor's bill, and studied for hours the tying of a cravat. He wasted fine powers in follies and frivolities, and his character was worn on his back and made at so much a yard.

Thus Satan leads by subtle steps from that which is not sinful in itself to that which *is.* He begins with innocent self-indulgence. There is no inherent wrong, for instance, in enjoying what ministers to the pleasure of the senses; but by the power of self-indulgence we become selfish, and the love of pleasure becomes prominent and pre-eminent; and so, that which we think of, which we plan for, to which we are devoted, is nothing but the advancement of self, the indulgence of selfish propensities and pleasures! A man may come to be a monster of wickedness through the simple power of selfishness—to put his own interest habitually before him; to think of and care but little for the advancement of his fellow men; and when the question is, "Shall I give up self-advantage in order to promote the welfare of the greater number, or push self-advantage to the detriment of my fellow men?" he chooses his own gratification, letting the rest of mankind go. If the question comes up, "Shall I enjoy myself and forget the interests of God and his kingdom; or deny myself, that I may promote them?" the selfish man, by and by, sets up self in the place of God; nay, he may even become so titanic in wickedness that, if the question arose whether God or himself should rule in the heavens, and he had it in his power to put God out of the way, he would have no hesitation in dethroning him in order to occupy his throne. Such is the ultimate tendency of selfishness!

Satan leads on from what is sensuous to what is sensual. Those words are similar in sound, and the things they represent lie so close together that they are oftentimes confused, but in reality they are different. The word sensuous relates to the impressions derived through the senses. To smell the perfume of flowers, hear the melodies and harmonies of music, perceive the symmetry of form and the beauty of color are sensuous delights. Now what are sensual pleasures? Those which, through the senses, arouse and inflame the passions. Satan uses the things which are sensuous to awaken passions which are sensual. For instance, Absalom saw the splendor and grandeur of the kingdom of his father David, and Satan used these sensuous attractions to inflame his carnal ambition; and he said, "I will be king, too, even if, in order to sit on the throne, I put my foot on the neck of my own father." And so he plotted his father's ruin. Achan saw the Babylonish garment with its embroidery, and the wedge of gold—sensuous attractions; but avarice was awakened, and he said, "I will have the garment and the wedge of gold, although God has devoted them to utter destruction." So he stole them and hid them in his tent and destruction overtook him. Ahab looked on the external beauty of Naboth's vineyard, sensuous attractions, and covetousness was awakened. He said, "I will have the vineyard, though I have to destroy the owner of it in order to have it." David looked on the charms of Uriah's wife, and the lust of appetite was awakened, and the great king fell into the foul sins of adultery and murder. And so you may find illustrations all through sacred and secular history, and it is still true that Satan leads on man by things which are simply sensuous to those which are sensual.

And hence the expression "the lusts of the eyes and the pride of life" has so intimate connection with "the lusts of the flesh" because the latter are excited through the lust of the eyes.

4. The world is used by its "god" to *sway the judgment*. What was meant to be an arbiter, occupying the seat of authority, weighing evidence and deciding in favor of what is true, right, and best, yields to the bribes of this world. All safe and sound decisions become comparatively impossible.

The things of this world thus cheat the worldly man of all that is permanent, substantial, satisfying, enduring. Some things come unsought; as for example when a man possesses great wealth because his father was wealthy before him. Without knowing any of the labor, the toil, the economy, the frugality and industry by which fortunes are commonly acquired, he comes to his majority to find himself the owner of an immense estate; perhaps he is the scion of some noble house and inherits the title of a baron or even a kingly throne and scepter. Many things come unsought, but one peculiarity of spiritual things is that *they never come to us unsought* or without our striving—agonizing—to enter in at the strait gate. "Let us labor therefore to enter into that rest, lest any man fall after the same example of unbelief;" and we are further bidden to take heed lest we let these things slip. The highest good never comes to us unsought; and if we do not earnestly, persistently, and importunately seek after these things, we shall find them slipping from our grasp, even when we seem to have a hold upon them. Satan, by taking up the attention and affection of men with the things of this world; by blinding their eyes to spiritual things; leading them from that which is sensuous to that which is sensual; is preventing them from seeking after the high and spiritual forms of good, which cannot be attained without earnest striving, laborious effort, prayerful, careful and persistent search.

Thus the world cramps and cripples man's better self. The magic skin was fabled to empower the wearer to realize every wish, but it shrank with every new gratification, until at last it stifled him. Selfishness is the magic skin, and our very indulgences shrink and shrivel us up until there is a sort of mental and moral atrophy, and we become incapable of what is noble and heroic.

Worldly indulgence ends in a strange *recklessness*, as may be seen pathetically in the drunkard, the debauchee, the gambler. A follower of Pizarro in Peru got as his share of booty a priceless golden image of the sun, which in one night he staked and lost at the gaming table. A woman at Monte Carlo, in ten days lost $250,000—$25,000 in one cast of the dice—and then blew out her brains.

That picture, "*Le Chasse de Bonheur*," portrays a young man of kingly mien madly pursuing a golden bauble in the hand of a fair woman who floats in the air before him, while his steed is trampling with his hoofs his wife and child; and just ahead a break in the bridge reveals a frightful chasm into which he is unconsciously about to leap. It startlingly hints how men in mad haste to get money, pleasure, fame, tread down all that is most precious and crush out all higher aspirations and plunge into ruin.

5. Satan uses the things of this world to leave a man at the last moment utterly poor, miserable, wretched, blind, naked and destitute. When we come to the dying hour, how does everything in this world appear? Suppose we have gathered to ourselves all possible material possessions. They slip out of our grasp. We go out of this world without one of all those material forms of treasure that we may have spent a lifetime in accumulating. Everything temporal, passing away, seems insignificant, and at the threshold of life that, like God's own existence, has no end, we have nothing left. Satan has taken up our attention, blinded our vision, led us on to sensual joys, prevented our seeking after the things of God, and now, how does he pay us? By ushering us through the portals of death into the great hereafter utterly stripped and desolate. The things we most of all cherished, for which we lived and labored—not a solitary fragment to be carried through that gateway into the awful forevermore! I do not wonder that the Bible warns us against this evil world more emphatically even than against terrible and flagrant forms of wickedness; for this world has caused the great bulk of the human race to start upon eternity without any hope, any faith, any joy, any preparation, any capacity for holy pleasure, or any accumulation of heavenly treasure.

The verse quoted from 1 Corinthians, is especially interesting as the only one in which the phrase occurs: "*the spirit of the world.*" It is important to understand just what this spirit of the world is, especially as we are told that "we have received not the spirit of the world, but the Spirit which is of God." The Spirit which is of God is put in contrast to the spirit of the world, as peculiar to disciples, and it is intimated that the reception of the Spirit of God enables them to know and understand certain things that are freely or graciously given of God; but that, so far as we receive and possess the spirit of the world, we can not understand or know those things which are only revealed by the Holy Spirit. The drift of this entire chapter and the preceding one is that he who has received the Spirit of God has his eyes opened to understand things hidden from the natural or worldly-spirited.

What, then, is "the spirit of the world?" It is a disposition which gives undue value to the things that are material and temporal, neglecting the things that are spiritual and eternal. The god of this world has very subtle snares for the feet even of disciples. He dazzles our vision with splendid and beautiful things; dazzles our senses with sensuous attractions; dazzles and bewilders our judgment by the intoxicating influences of things that appeal, through the senses, to the imagination; and so he shuts out of our lives the consideration of the infinite things of God. When we come to understand the methods by which Satan leads sinners astray through the power of this world, and the spirit that works in the children of disobedience, we shall be able to understand why, in the Bible, we are so warned against worldliness! Paul says, concerning the carnal mind, in the eighth chapter of Romans: "the carnal mind is enmity against God." James, the apostle of action, and John, the apostle of contemplation, utter the same emphatic admonition against the world. James says, "the friendship of the world is enmity against God; whosoever, therefore, will be a friend of the world, is the enemy of God." John is no less emphatic (1 John 2:15-17): "Love not the world, neither the things that are in the world. If any man love the world, the love of the Father is not in him." And in the book of the Revelation, although terrible curses are pronounced against various forms of wickedness, the church is warned as with trumpet tones against the encroachments of the power of the world, the fashion of the world, the love of the world, and the disposition that rules in worldly bosoms!

Those phrases in our Lord's intercessory prayer briefly answer all honest questions about the disciple's relation to the world. He is chosen out of the world, but sent back into it as a witness; he is, therefore, in it, but is not to be of it; he will be hated by it, but kept from the evil that is in it; and is so to live as that the world may know and believe.

Whatever relation is necessarily sustained must be a consecrated one. We are to spiritualize the secular, not secularize the spiritual. Whatever our worldly "calling," we are to account it our divine vocation and therein abide with God (1 Cor. 7:20–24). Thus the very tools and implements of daily work become sacred by a partnership with God. Like Baruch the son of Zabbai, a man may build or repair a piece of wall "earnestly" as part of his high calling (Neh. 3:20), putting his conscience into brick and mortar.

When the Queen of Sheba visited Solomon, she was most impressed by the "ascent by which he went up to the House of the Lord." Dr. Robinson identified this as a viaduct, 350 feet in length, and 150 in height at the central arch, whereby the king connected his own house with the Lord's. That ascent may well typify the life that, in going from the sanctuary on the Sabbath to one's own house and work, maintains, throughout, the same sacred level; it is not necessary to go down to a lower plane to business and then struggle up to a higher when we go to worship!

The Christian disciple should know that the spirit of the world makes impossible the *growth*, even if not the *existence*, of spiritual life. It is a question never settled yet how far the possession of a worldly spirit is compatible with the existence of spiritual life; but one thing is sure, that growth is utterly impossible so long and so far as a worldly spirit has possession and control. For the spiritual life has its own form of sustenance: it grows by familiarity with spiritual things and can not grow otherwise. If, therefore, it be possible for a spiritual man to have a worldly spirit, it is impossible for him to grow in resemblance to Christ. He is starving his spiritual nature, at best. By familiarity with spiritual things the soul grows mighty in the graces and in the virtues of Christian life. And in proportion as you let these things alone and cultivate the spirit of the world by familiarity with worldly things, in such proportion you grow thin and weak spiritually, even if you do not lose all hope that you are a child of God.

So far as the worldly spirit possesses a disciple it makes him ignorant, even if he loses not perception altogether, of the things of God. "We have received not the spirit of the world, but the Spirit which is of God, *that we might know the things that are freely given to us of God*." God has made no more glorious revelation of himself, except in the Holy Scriptures and in the person of Jesus Christ, than in the personal lives of true disciples. It is necessary, in order that the teachings of the Word of God and the power of the example of Christ, and the illuminating influences of the Holy Ghost, should be received by the disciple, that he should have first of all a spiritual mind. These things are not seen by the eye of sense or reason or imagination, but by the spiritual eye of faith, which depends, for quickness of discernment, upon the indwelling power and presence of the Holy Ghost. The worldly man may be a very good man in the ordinary sense, companionable and lovable, and yet not understand the things of God. A worldly man ought to have no position of influence in the church of God whatever, from the highest to the lowest, though some such men are oftentimes men that we love, even as Jesus Christ loved the young man in the Gospel. But the worldly man, or the professor of religion with a worldly spirit, cannot understand the things of God. If I were to practice medicine without a practical knowledge of medicine, I might be a very respectable and estimable man, but I would not make a good doctor. If I should attempt to practice law without a knowledge of law, I might be a very respectable man, but people would not want me as a counselor at law. Just so a man of the world, or a Christian with a worldly spirit, may be very lovable and yet, not having the capacity to understand and perceive the things which are of God, he is not a fit man to preach the gospel in the pulpit, to hold any official position, or exercise any controlling influence in the church: because the church of God is regulated by spiritual measures, and the worldly man cannot perceive the wisdom of those methods.

In proportion as the disciple is a worldly man he loses the power to discern spiritual things. When he is taken up with the things of the world and gives them undue value, by his undue dependence upon them, he is, for the time being at least, blind to the things of God's kingdom; whereas another man who may have no learning, culture, social position, or influence in a worldly sense, may have deep spiritual perception, penetration, and wisdom. He may have that profound insight in reference to the things that pertain to God's kingdom, which gives him an infinite superiority over the most learned, cultivated and influential persons according to the world's judgment of capacity and power.

The disciple who is worldly-minded, possessed and controlled by the spirit of the world, can not be a useful man with respect to the kingdom of God. God's work is best performed by men who are impressed with the power of an unseen life, and manifest the beauty of God's character; and the influence of those who live in communion and fellowship with the unseen God can not be calculated: in proportion as the disciple gives prominence to the things that are material, in such proportion does he make it impossible to get that strength and effectiveness in Christian work that is found in an unworldly life.

There are some professors of the religion of Christ, good citizens, fathers, husbands, sons, and brothers, admired for intellectual faculties, for culture; respected and honored, and not undeservedly so, by the world, for capacity, and influence among men; who, when they come by divine grace into the kingdom, if so be that they are scarcely saved, will find that their spiritual influence in leading men to Jesus Christ has been paralyzed, simply because of a worldly spirit; simply because others saw no difference between them and themselves, because they have seen them pursuing the phantoms of this world, occupied by the things that blinded and dazzled their own vision, and having no spiritual discrimination and discernment with regard to the things of God. It is an awful fact that there are some that will be "scarcely saved"—saved because of faith in Jesus Christ, but whose whole life will have been practically thrown away, because what they have labored for has been what perishes. Suppose I have spread a network of railroads, or built canals, that have spanned a continent; suppose I have erected great structures having to do with human arts and industries, and have accelerated the progress of the race in civilization; and yet have done nothing to provide men with bags which wax not old, treasure in the heavens which faileth not, where no thief approacheth, nor moth corrupteth; what will be my feelings in the eternal state, when this world with all its triumphs of art, and industry, and commercial enterprise shall be burned up, when all its magnificence of worldly splendor shall be no more; when I behold millions upon millions of the human race standing before the bar of God to receive the sentence of final destiny, and remember that *not one soul in all the millions of the saved I have brought to a knowledge of Christ, and not one soul in all the millions of the lost, I have turned away from the absorbing devotion to the things that perish!* These are tremendous thoughts! All past years are gone forever, with their opportunities. Shall we continue pursuing the same course that we have been? Shall we live for this world or the world to come? Shall we live as witnesses to men of the power of the unseen God and the life of faith or shall we devote ourselves to things that perish, to the accumulation of material wealth and the extension of material enterprise? Shall we seek to promote commercial interests and yet not turn the thoughts of men to the life that has no end?

Orcagna, the Italian, in his painting of the last judgment, represents Solomon as rising from the dead in regal robes, with crown and scepter, and looking round in bewilderment, not knowing whether he belongs on the right or left hand of the Judge. What a satire on worldly disciples, who have been so controlled by the carnal that they know not whether they will be acknowledged at all as the Lord's! How different Pannecker, the German sculptor, who, asked to make a statue of Venus, replied with tearful eyes, "For eight years I have been studying to chisel the face of Christ; can this same hand now sculpture a heathen goddess?"

We are bidden to "use this world as not abusing it; for the fashion of this world passeth away"—literally, its *stage scenery*. Satan uses this world as a stage, and its framework of superficial scenery, tinted in glowing colors, to fascinate the eye for a little; and when it ceases to charm, he substitutes another bit of the same stage scenery to keep up the illusion. Oftentimes we recognize the hollow and shallow character of worldly things and do not expect them to last nor our relish for them. But meanwhile, like the wooden framework on which the stone arch is formed, these trifles are giving shape to character, and what we by and by renounce will already have molded us for eternity. We may discard the pleasures as we burn the wooden framework, but the shape given to character lasts.

A few winters ago, in the rapids of Niagara, an eagle was seen upon a block of ice, feasting on the carcass of a lamb. Just on the brink of the falls the great bird spread its wings for flight, but the feet were frozen fast to the ice, and all plunged together into the abyss. Many a slave of this world counts on escaping from its bonds at last, but finds it too late at the dying hour, and often before that, when the fetters become galling. Beau Brummel, already referred to as an example of a wasted life, after reckless vices and gambling had made him both a financial and moral bankrupt, fled to France to escape his creditors, and there died in poverty and exile. His last earthly pastime revealed the mockery of his worldly idolatry. He amused himself with a phantom feast, alike his brilliant company of guests, his dainty viands and costly wines, his servants and surroundings being the creatures of his own fancy.

At the Milan Cathedral, three significant inscriptions surmount the respective doorways. Over the right hand portal, a sculptured wreath of flowers, with the motto: "all that pleases is but for a moment." Over the left hand entrance a cross and crown of thorns, and under it, "all that troubles is but for a moment." But over the central door, a simple sentence: "nothing is important save that which is eternal."

Chapter 7

The Unseen World of Spirits

This theme is scarcely outranked in importance, solemnity and gravity, by any other in the whole range of spiritual truth, and hence the need of again carefully following Scripture leading. We select six suggestive texts:

God is a Spirit (John 4:24).

The number of them (the angels) was ten thousand times ten thousand and thousands of thousands (Rev. 5:11).

The angel of the Lord encampeth round about them that fear him, and delivereth them (Ps. 34:7).

Put on the whole armor of God, that ye may be able to stand against the wiles of the devil. For we wrestle not against flesh and blood, but against principalities, against powers, against the rulers of the darkness of this world, against spiritual wickedness in high places (Eph. 6:11–12).

We look not at the things which are seen, but at the things which are not seen: for the things which are seen are temporal; but the things which are not seen are eternal (2 Cor. 4:18).

The LORD opened the eyes of the young man; and he saw: and behold, the mountain was full of horses and chariots of fire round about Elisha (2 Kings 6:17).

From these Scriptures we learn:

1. That there is a spiritual realm over which God, himself a spirit, reigns.

2. That countless hosts of spirits inhabit this realm.

3. That good angels specially minister to saints.

4. That evil angels continually seek to deceive and destroy.

5. That we should live for the unseen and eternal.

6. That only a lack of vision prevents us from seeing the encompassing hosts of spirits.

Some grave hindrances beset the treatment of this subject, foremost among which is the *mysterious and occult nature* of this whole realm. It evades our senses and defies adequate exploration and investigation. We have seen that, in studying the complex constitution of man, the moment we pass beyond sensible phenomena, we find mysteries which need subtler faculties to examine them. Our thoughts themselves belong to the invisible realm, and even their connection with audible speech and visible action we cannot comprehend. We know that, when we will to raise the arm, the will influences the nerves of motion, the nerves, the muscles, and the muscles, the bone. But the explanation needs explaining, for how an invisible purpose links itself on to a visible action no one can tell.

Another hindrance to investigation lies in the fact that this realm of mystery is also one of *doubt and uncertainty;* indeed, not a few deny its existence, and hold that man is nothing but matter, highly organized, and at death goes to dust and ceases to be. The Sadducees refuse to believe in the existence of spirit, and hence, in any survival after death, or resurrection from the dead.

There is but one real source of knowledge of this spiritual universe: it is the Word of God. Though there have been endless conjectures and countless speculations about it, even philosophers and sages have never agreed, and the only clear light ever thrown into the darkness of this unseen world has been what shines from God's own book, where what eye hath not seen, ear heard, or heart conceived, is plainly revealed—things which no mere intellectual search or psychic investigation ever unveiled. One of the grand proofs that the Scriptures are God-inspired is found in the air of absolute positiveness and infallible certainty with which these occult mysteries are treated. There is no timid feeling after truth or hesitating utterance concerning it, but a consistent body of teaching concerning the unseen realm, that has at least this to recommend it, that, for the first and only time, it gives man a simple and satisfactory solution of perhaps his greatest problem. Here is teaching which has about it *finality;* it is the utterance of one who speaks as confidently as about the most common facts or phenomena, and treats what is hidden from the senses as a familiar commonplace. He who, after vain attempts to find in man's hypotheses and philosophies any solid ground to rest upon, comes with open mind and heart to inquire at God's living oracles, gets an answer to all his inquiries and a sure basis for faith and hope.

The realm of the unseen is, therefore, to a believer in the Word of God, an undisputable reality, whose existence and importance are never *argued* but *assumed*. Skepticism attacks the whole position merely on the ground that, in the researches of natural science, there are no traces of the supernatural, and that the very idea of disembodied spirits is inconceivable. Dr. Alfred Barry well remarks "that while both facts are true, the inference is false."

Natural Science deals mainly with things material and visible; if it touches the unseen at all, it is only because invisible energy works as force in the realm of matter. In all its research, science reaches a limit, a region of darkness beyond which it cannot penetrate. Yet this very darkness in which science ends, when it approaches *soul* and *spirit* and their relation to matter, so far from contradicting, rather implies the existence of an unseen world and of supernatural influence. In fact *scientific inference itself points in that direction*, so that it is difficult to understand how a scientist can escape the conclusion that there is an unseen realm.

Again we cite 2 Cor. 4:16–5:4, the leading Scripture passage which contrasts the two worlds.

> Though our outward man perish, yet the inward *man* is renewed day by day.
>
> For our light affliction, which is but for a moment, worketh for us a far more exceeding and eternal weight of glory;
>
> While we look not at the things which are seen, but at the things which are not seen: for the things which are seen are temporal; but the things which are not seen are eternal.
>
> For we know that if our earthly house of this tabernacle were dissolved, we have a building of God, an house not made with hands, eternal in the heavens.
>
> For in this we groan, earnestly desiring to be clothed upon with our house which is from heaven:
>
> If so be that being clothed we shall not be found naked.
>
> For we that are in this tabernacle do groan, being burdened: not for that we would be unclothed, but clothed upon, that mortality might be swallowed up of life.

Note the phrases used here: "outward man," "inward man;" "for a moment," "temporal," "eternal," "things which are seen," "things which are not seen," "earthly house," "house not made with hands," "mortality," "life," etc.

Here the realms are plainly contrasted: the material, temporal, visible; the immaterial, eternal, invisible; both treated as equally real and indisputable.

We have seen that life is a ladder, resting on earth and reaching up to heaven, and like any ladder, lifts us, rung by rung, from what is below to that which is above. Where the ladder touches earth we find matter so gross that it can be tested by all five senses; but as we ascend, material forms become more and more ethereal and evasive, until we reach what no sense can detect, yet which we are sure *is*. No sense can perceive gravitation, cohesion, centrifugal and centripetal forces, but we trace their *effects*. Life itself defies all analysis, yet we find it everywhere, in earth and sea. A dead body—a corpse—and a living body—a corpus—are alike in structure, appearance, features, yet in one is *something* not in the other, which cannot be confined within walls or bounds; and which where air and water and light cannot pass, passes unhindered. It is independent even of conductors, and cannot be insulated, like electricity, nor isolated. Thought is the most important thing about us, none of us ever saw, heard, felt it, or subjected it to any physical and sensible tests. Speaking *scientifically*, research shows that, as we go up life's ladder, we come successively to material forms and forces which appeal to all the senses, then to four, three, two, one, and finally to *none*. Is it not a natural inference that if we could climb up higher we should find a realm of pure spirit where life is not limited by physical and material conditions; and, at the summit and crown of all, one supreme being, who is a *spirit* infinite, invisible, eternal, without form or similitude, whom no man hath seen or can see?

Just this is what the Word of God teaches: at the point where science finds its limit—where the *Mare Tenebrum* stretches away toward a limitless horizon, Holy Scripture offers to guide man's barque safely. There is no doubt about the wonderful handling of this inscrutable mystery in the Bible. What all the study of thousands of years could not illumine, one ray of God lights up.

God is the all-presiding, all-pervading, uncreated spirit. Between him and man there lies an intermediate realm, inhabited by a higher order of intelligences, neither pure spirit like God, nor so physically constituted as man. They are called angels because they appear in Scripture as messengers of God to man. They appear to exist in a hierarchy or organized body with orders or ranks, and of these we find even the *names* given. This is what we could expect, for, as among men, there must be different degrees of capacity, sagacity and ability, and consequently, authority.

The late Prof. William G. T. Shedd was wont to condemn the common notion that by the natural is meant the material and visible, and by the supernatural the immaterial and invisible. He pointed out with rare acumen that nature may be as invisible and immaterial as spirit. Back of this world of nature which we apprehend by the five senses there is an invisible world which is nature still, which is not supernatural, because there is no moral element in it.

Confessedly, then, no realm of being throughout the whole universe is so mysterious, baffling our utmost research; so that, after five thousand years we have not arrived at any scientific certainty, and even the foremost scientists themselves are divided; some of them considering that they have found some of the facts of the psychic realm; others remaining absolute agnostics and regarding all so-called "discovery" as an illusion.

The only clear and consistent unfolding of these mysteries is that contained in the Word of God and, if we accept this solution, however incomprehensible this realm, it is at least apprehensible: all is *clear*. And as in this series of studies we professedly base everything upon the Bible, we propose, without suggesting a doubt of its truth, to present the Scripture teaching as to *this unseen world and its relation to man*. We make no apologies for boldly accepting as a platform the whole biblical revelation on this subject; and if the scriptural teaching is scouted even by some who profess to be believers; if many would refine away all *literal* statements by giving them a mystical or mythical meaning; one comfort will be ours, that the further afield we wander from the simple Biblical position, the more difficulties we have to confront and the more mysteries to leave unsolved.

The teaching of the Word of God upon this subject may be comprehended in the following dozen statements:

1. There is an unseen world, not only invisible, but insensible—neither its forces nor its phenomena capable of being tested by the physical senses.

2. This unseen realm is infinitely more *important*, and potential for good or evil, than the realm of the material and visible.

3. This unseen world belongs not to the temporal but the eternal order. It is the realm where *life* is found and from which all *life* proceeds, and which we have *no* proof that literal *death* ever invades.

4. This unseen world is a world of intelligent and conscious being—independent life, peopled with spirits which, if not disembodied, are independent of a material organism.

5. In this unseen world the one ruling all pervasive *spirit* is *God*—source of all *being*, who only hath inherent and uncreated life.

6. In this unseen world are countless forms of inferior and created spirits, differing in intelligence, dignity and power.

7. These spirits are called in the Bible *angels* and exist in a vast hierarchy with several ranks, to which six or seven distinct names are applied in Scripture: such as archangels, principalities, authorities or powers, thrones, rulers, dominions, cherubim, seraphim, spirits, etc.

8. Among these spirits, or angels, a mysterious revolt once took place, headed by Satan, who drew after him in his fall multitudes, now known as "fallen angels," demons, etc.—and among them exist similar ranks, at least four names being applied to them—principalities, powers, world rulers, wicked spirits.

9. All spirits, good or bad, have access to man's *spiritual* being and actually do influence him for good or evil. And more than one spirit may operate upon or even occupy his spirit.

10. Man's only hope of deliverance from the power of evil spirits, or even of *discerning* whether or not the spirits are good or evil, is to be indwelt by the Holy Spirit of God.

11. A disciple may be influenced at one moment by God's good spirit and the next by the spirit of evil and even Satan himself, so that there is occasion for perpetual watchfulness and prayer.

12. Evil spirits acquire their greatest power from their subtlety. They are masters of the art of deception, and aim to *counterfeit* that which is good rather than suggest what is obviously and wholly evil.

Satan, who led this defection of angels, appears to have been an archangel, endowed with great wisdom and power, whose very excellence inspired the pride which led to his downfall, and led him to aspire to the throne of the universe, to be as *God*.

This body of fallen angels, commonly referred to as "*devils*," should be known as *demons*, for there is but *one* Devil, and the Word of God refers to them as in league, as powers of darkness, against God, holy angels and all obedient human beings. There are two opposing hierarchies, eternally at war! Good angels in alliance with God and all saints, to promote all that is good; evil demons, confederate with each other and all evil men, to work disaster and ruin and, if it were possible, supplant even the Almighty. These demons are represented as the authors and abettors of all evil to man's body and soul, having power to afflict with disease; and, as the frequent epithet "unclean" implies, impart spiritual pollution also. They are the agents of Satan in his work of evil, subject to the kingdom of darkness and doomed to its condemnation.

There can be no doubt to the believing student of God's Word that they are real beings. All modern attempts to make out that the Bible merely accommodates its language to current traditional beliefs among the Jews are incompatible with the plain and uniform attribution of *personality*, with all its attributes to both angels and demons, just as much as to men or to God; and, if carried out in principle, such methods of interpretation must destroy the truth and honesty of Holy Scripture itself (*Smith's Bible Dictionary*, vol. 1, 425).

Satan is represented as the head of all fallen angels (Matt. 12:24–30; Mark 3:22–30; Luke 11:14–26; Rev. 16:14); and they are angels of the Devil (Matt. 25:41; Rev. 12:7–9).

These demons "believe and shudder" in terror of coming judgment; they recognize and confess the deity of Christ as the son of God, and they were exorcised or cast out of those possessed by them by the power of his name. They had a strange passion for such possession. Why, we can only conjecture; possibly because they craved the control of bodily organs to work greater harm.

Beyond the limits of all matter, and even those invisible operations of the human mind that manifest themselves through matter, there is a realm of *spirits*, so far as we know independent of material forms and manifestations. Over this realm God is supreme—the eternal, uncreated SPIRIT. Under him are inferior spirits. There is a vast host of these spirits—"innumerable angels in festal assembly" (Heb. 12:22–23). Many are the hints of their countless number. When Peter sought to defend his master with the sword, he said, "Thinkest thou that I cannot now pray to my Father, and he shall presently give me more than twelve legions of angels?" If a legion was six thousand, twelve legions would be seventy-two thousand; and one angel of the Lord slew in one night 185,000 Syrians! Surely the suffering Son of Man needed no human weapons to be unsheathed in his defense. Even his self-emptying was only a voluntary suspension of his omnipotence. He chose to be helpless, and had only to assert his authority and claim his rights to summon an army of angels to his side!

In Revelation 5:11 the number of them is "ten thousand times ten thousand"—a hundred million—and "thousands of thousands"—that is apparently another multiple—the hundred million multiplied by millions more—literally "myriads upon myriads, and chiliads upon chiliads"—a vain attempt to express in human language a countless host of unfallen angels, standing about the throne of God, waiting his will.

To this spiritual realm man is closely allied by the endowment of a spiritual nature. As his soul-life, or psychic nature, allies him to all intelligence, his higher spirit-life makes him akin to all spiritual being, and even to God, who is a Spirit. This latter was probably the image and likeness of God in which he was created.

Man is therefore especially open to all influences of the spirit realm, whether good or bad. Just as his bodily organism makes him susceptible to impressions from physical nature, and his animal life and intelligence to contact with all forms of conscious life; so his spiritual being responds to the unseen approach of other spirits, who are as distinctly personal as himself, but not limited to sense channels for contact.

Some who seek to improve on the Bible deny the personality of the Devil and make "Satan" simply a name for a *bad influence*, whether proceeding from one's self or others. But such views must find support outside of Scripture. In at least six places in the New Testament the "world" and the "flesh" are distinguished from the "Devil"[19]; and everywhere in Scripture personal attributes and activities are ascribed to Satan as truly as to any other being, human or divine. To identify the Devil with the world, with evil men, or with the fleshly nature in man is to introduce hopeless chaos and confusion.

Man is, moreover, represented as actually more or less under the sway of the good Spirit of God and other good spirits, or of evil spirits, and without exception (Eph. 2:2–3). "The spirit that now worketh in the children of disobedience" is "the prince of the power of the air"—one of the names of the Devil—and "among these children of disobedience we all once had our life-course." Such is the plain language of the Word. There are, in God's eyes, only two great classes of men: sons of obedience, under the control of the Spirit of God, and sons of disobedience, under the control of Satan and the spirits of evil. This is a humiliating classification, but it is God's own.

Again, the Word of God teaches that a man may be swayed by *more than one* evil spirit at the same time. Out of Mary Magdalene our Lord "cast out seven demons"; the man out of whom the evil spirit departed

---

19 Compare Ephes. 2:2, 3; 6:11, 12; 1 John 2:14, 15, 16, etc.

was re-inhabited by the same demon, who brought back with him seven others more wicked than himself (Matt. 12:43–45). When the two demoniacs of Gadara gave a name to the spirits possessing them it was "Legion, for we are many"—and they may have been permitted to go out into the herd of swine—two thousand—to show both their multitude and their malignity.

In matter, the law of impenetrability forbids two particles to occupy the same space at once, so that a nail driven into a board must crowd other particles into closer contact. But as spirits occupy no space, no such law obtains in the spirit realm, but more evasive and subtle than the perfumes of thousands of flowers, mingling in one atmosphere, yet leaving room for thousands of new odors, spirits may occupy the same body without interference with each other.

Every *unregenerate man* is a territory of Satan, the only difference being in the *extent* of Satanic working. In some unsaved souls it is a partial and hindered working. Conscience—a godly training—social respectability—motives of worldly policy—may keep one from entire and reckless surrender to Satanic power; but he works in *all*. In some it is *operation*; in others, *occupation*. Few facts are taught with more tremendous significance than this, that every human being's spiritual nature is the haunt and home of spiritual influences, holy or unholy, benevolent or malignant.

Evil spirits are continually on the alert to harm both body and spirit—to inflict physical evils and to corrupt intellectual convictions and pervert the heart's affection and weaken the will—in every way to lead away from truth and God. Their one business is to provoke and promote sinful revolt against the creator.

No greater mystery invests the spiritual realm than that of demon possession. A Jewish theory is that when the angels "kept not their first estate" part of their penalty was to wander henceforth through space *disembodied*. This, of course, would lessen greatly their capacity to do harm, as they could only work through mental suggestion but could control no bodily organs; and hence their craving to possess and control the bodies of their victims, making use of their bodily powers for mischief. If so, this partly explains the desire of the legion to enter into the herd of swine, thinking to infuriate these beasts and by them work destruction, but not foreseeing that they would drive them into the lake.

The Bible traces idolatry to demoniac influence, and makes the worshipers of false gods, worshipers of "devils" (1 Cor. 10:20–21). And yet Christian writers and speakers can flatter the Hindus for their sublime "oriental consciousness of God" and salute them as "brethren" while they worship over three hundred millions of deities! Behind all systems of false religion and idolatry lies the influence of the Devil and evil demons.

"What say I then? that the idol is any thing, or that which is offered in sacrifice to idols is any thing? But I say, that the things which the Gentiles sacrifice, they sacrifice to devils and not to God; and I would not that ye should have fellowship with devils. Ye cannot drink the cup of the Lord and the cup of devils; ye cannot be partakers of the Lord's table and of the table of devils" (1 Cor. 10:19–21).

"Now the Spirit speaketh expressly, that in the latter times some shall depart from the faith, giving heed to seducing spirits and doctrines of devils" (1 Timothy 4:1).

"And the rest of the men which were not killed by these plagues yet repented not of the works of their hands, that they should not worship devils, and idols of gold, and silver, and brass, and stone, and of wood; which neither can see, nor hear, nor walk" (Rev. 9:20).

Thus the word "devils" (*daimonia*) is used of objects of worship. Even while admitting that an idol is nothing in the world, and there is no other God but one, Paul says that all that is offered in sacrifice to idols is offered to demons. In idolatry we are therefore to recognize the influence of demons at work—agents of Satan, who is their chief (Rev. 16:14).

They are both subjects of and agents of the kingdom of darkness, and doomed to its condemnation, and they are sometimes called "the Devil's angels" (Matt. 25:41; Rev. 12:7–9).

Satan's *methods* with men are marked by extreme subtlety and awful power.

1. He deceives the understanding. Like a master optician, he uses his various magnifying and minifying glasses. He makes things near by appear to be great and great things to appear small. Paul compares him to a magician who by sleight of hand and cunning craftiness makes the eyes the fools of the other senses, so that he makes you believe that he does what he cannot do.

2. He allures the heart. He spreads his dainty bait of worldly pleasure and makes it the trap for his snares to entangle the feet. The powers

and capacities of loving which God meant for the noblest objects are degraded to what is unworthy and unsatisfying.

3. He hardens even the conscience. He bribes the moral sense to uphold wrong because it ministers to self-indulgence and temporary pleasure; and finally, as the Word of God expresses it, men have their conscience seared as with a hot iron. There is Satanic *hypnotism*. The prince of this world so attracts the fixed gaze of his victims as to lull them to sleep by his soft sayings and dazzling visions, until they become unconscious of any other world beyond, hear no voice calling from on high, and are made captives of him at his will.

Satan *hardens the heart* by leading one to continuance in sin, cherishing unbelief, neglecting what are called means of grace because through them as channels the grace of God commonly works, and habitually postponing performance of duty. Even in the absence of flagrant forms of wickedness, a human heart may become so hard as to resist all convictions of truth, all claims of duty, and become fatally insensible to all the approaches and appeals even of the love of God (Heb. 3:7–4:11).

The Devil himself is said only on one occasion to have entered into a man—Judas Iscariot. The most damnable deed of all history was to be done, and he would trust no one else to see to its accomplishment (John 13:27). But evildoers are often judicially abandoned to demon influence, as when Jehovah sent an evil spirit to possess Saul (1 Sam. 16:14), whose paroxysms of murderous rage and hate toward David are traced to this malign possession.

On the other hand, good spirits and unfallen angels are entrusted with a special ministry and mission to saints. "The angel of the Lord encampeth round about them that fear him, and delivereth them." May it not be that, going through crowded thoroughfares, and exposed to countless risks, many escapes and deliverances are due to angelic guards? They came to comfort and minister to the "Son of Man" in the crises of temptation and agony and, could we but see clearly, we might find them still active in errands of consolation and instruction to his followers. Particularly do they appear to minister to dying saints (Heb. 1:14), and we are told that Lazarus was "carried by the angels to Abraham's bosom." What a funeral procession that was! "The rich man died and *was buried*"—nothing is said about any stately human burial for the beggar—

> Rattle his bones over the stones!
> He's only a pauper whom nobody owns!

But, beyond the limits of human vision was a convoy of angels to bear him to his celestial abode—a funeral cortège indeed!

That last verse of the opening chapter of Hebrews asks, "Are they not all ministering spirits, sent forth to be of service to them who are just *about to be heirs of salvation?*" May this not hint that, just as the exchange of worlds is about to be made, their ministry is specially in exercise? And may not some of those visions of glorified beings, which have so often cheered departing saints as the veil parted between earth and heaven, have been glimpses of this angelic convoy?

This same Word of God encourages us by the promise that, at the final advent of our Lord, Satan himself is to be crippled of his power and with all his hosts overwhelmed with eternal defeat. This last victory is reserved for the crowning glory of his second coming, and in it every redeemed saint shall share.

This brief résumé of Scripture teaching vindicates the statement at the beginning of this chapter that the Word of God sets forth this theme in a clear, consistent body of doctrine, the like of which can nowhere else be found nor any approach to it.

A few practical inferences may still claim our attention.

1. We must properly *measure our great adversary*. It is both foolish and fatal to safety to belittle the subtlety and malignity of our awful foe. We believe him to outrank all other created beings; and there is one description which, it has long been thought, can be applied only to him.

> Thus saith the Lord God: thou sealest up the sum, full of wisdom, and perfect in beauty. Thou hast been in Eden, the garden of God; every precious stone was thy covering, the sardius, topaz, and the diamond, the beryl, the onyx, and the jasper, the sapphire, the emerald, and the carbuncle, and gold; the workmanship of thy tabrets and of thy pipes was prepared in thee in the day that thou wast created. Thou art the anointed cherub that covereth; and I have set thee so; thou wast upon the holy mountain of God; thou hast walked up and down in the midst of the stones of fire. Thou wast perfect in thy ways from the day that thou wast created, till iniquity was found in thee. By the multitude of thy merchandise they have filled the midst of thee with violence, and thou hast sinned; therefore, I will cast thee as profane out of the mountain of God: and I will destroy thee, O covering cherub, from the midst of the stones of fire. Thine heart was lifted up because of thy beauty, thou hast corrupted thy wisdom by reason of thy brightness: I will cast thee to the ground, I will lay thee before kings, that they may behold thee. Thou hast

defiled thy sanctuaries by the multitude of thy iniquities, by the iniquity of thy traffic; therefore will I bring forth a fire from the midst of thee, it shall devour thee, and I will bring thee to ashes upon the earth in the sight of all them that behold thee. All they that know thee among the people shall be astonished at thee: thou shalt be a terror, and never shalt thou be any more (Ezek. 28:12–19).

These words are addressed to the "King of Tyrus"—which probably should read *"tutelary god* of Tyrus." But, however applied, many phrases contained in this marvelous apostrophe could apply to *no human being*— such as "full of wisdom, perfect in beauty"; "thou hast been in Eden"; "thou art the anointed cherub that covereth"—an apparent reference to the cherub's wings as covering the altar of God, etc.

Taken as a description of the original and unfallen dignity, beauty and glory of Satan, this is one of the great glimpses given in divine revelation of the inconceivable majesty and greatness of the great adversary. How utterly false and misleading all those travesties and caricatures of the truth that represent the Devil as half man and half beast—a mongrel and monster, with horns and hoofs and forked tail! How little his slaves and victims understand his capacity to transform himself into an angel of light! And how little do even saints appreciate the fact that nothing short of a complete panoply of God, and the Spirit of God to enable us to wear and wield it, can make us strong enough to stand before such a foe!

We are to think of Satan as a magnificent being—great in knowledge, power and wisdom—next to the Son of God, whom for that very reason he sought to rival and even corrupt and destroy—as doing things evil on a grand scale, and as a master in the art of dissembling. He imitates everything—*prayer* by forms without the spirit; *alms giving* by selfish donations which promote personal glory—humility by hypocrisy; even defense of the faith by a zeal without knowledge. He has his theological schools where, under the cloak of scholasticism, rationalism is taught, and his churches, which are in God's eyes synagogues of Satan.

The Devil has been dealing in shams ever since he began the business in Eden. His method is *"wiles"* and *"lies,"* and part of his wiles consists in disguising lies. He approaches man with half-truths, plausible apologies for disobedience, and so skillful are his devices that he can make vice appear as virtue and wrong as right, veiling formalism with the show of devotion, and heartless externalism with the show of piety. He imposes on men by a form of godliness which utterly denies its power, and so imitates truth and goodness and counterfeits the gospel of grace as to deceive, if possible, the very elect. Probably even Antichrist will not be the open foe of God and Christ, so much as a deceptive counterpart, imitating the person and work of the Son of God, even to the point of "prophecies," and "miracles of falsehood," assuming the form and disguise of an angel of light.

We must not be surprised, therefore, if his ministers cloak abominable heresies and denials of the Lord that bought them in attractive rhetoric, false liberalism and winning manners. Satan is too wise and subtle to pose as a blasphemer and profligate. He showed in the desert temptation what a master he was even in quoting Scripture and making disobedience seem lawful, counterfeiting dependence on God by independence of him, faith by presumption, and loyalty by compromise. We must expect the heresies and iniquities of the last days to parade in the white robes of charity and piety. But, however respectable the guise, he is our enemy and God's who denies the Lord Jesus Christ.

2. It is, therefore, of immense importance to learn how to detect and discern the *sources* of all suggestion and discriminate as to their true character. Even a Christian disciple must not be heedless and self-confident.

"Beloved, believe not every spirit, but try the spirits whether they are of God; because many false prophets are gone out into the world. Hereby know ye the Spirit of God: Every spirit that confesseth that Jesus Christ is come in the flesh is of God. And every spirit that confesseth not that Jesus Christ is come in the flesh is not of God: and this is that *spirit* of antichrist, whereof ye have heard that it should come; and even now already is it in the world" (1 John 4:1–3).

In Matthew 16:21–23 we have a startling example:

> From that time forth began Jesus to shew unto his disciples how that he must go unto Jerusalem, and suffer many things of the elders and chief priests and scribes, and be killed, and be raised again the third day. Then Peter took him, and began to rebuke him, saying, be it far from thee, Lord: this shall not be unto thee. But he turned and said unto Peter, get thee behind me, Satan; *thou art an offence unto me;* for thou savorest not the things that be of God, but those that be of men.

At one moment Simon Peter, marvelously moved by the spirit of God, gave utterance to those words of confession: "We believe and are sure that thou art that Christ, the Son of the living God, that should come into the world." That became the rock basis of all Christian creeds; but, straightway after, he was so moved by Satan as to suggest to Christ to spare himself by avoiding the cross, and thus, for the moment, became the mouthpiece of *Satan*. And not least significant is it that in neither case was he *conscious* of being controlled by either the spirit of God or the spirit of the Devil—showing how subtly both the spirit of God and the spirit of evil work, possessing and controlling the human so that there is no consciousness of any foreign influence.

3. We must beware how we intrude unlawfully into the spirit realm. To lift the veil and penetrate the unseen is one of the greatest of human temptations, and against it God's people are warned—prohibited from all intercourse with spirits.

"There shall not be found among you any one that maketh his son or his daughter to pass through the fire, or that useth divination, or an observer of times, or an enchanter, or a witch, or a charmer, or a consulter with familiar spirits, or a wizard, or a necromancer. For all that do these things are an abomination unto the Lord: and because of these abominations the Lord thy God doth drive them out from before thee. Thou shalt be perfect with the Lord thy God. For these nations, which thou shalt possess, hearkened unto observers of times, and unto diviners: but as for thee, the Lord thy God hath not suffered thee so to do" (Deut. 18:10–14).

The command is most comprehensive. Observers of times, who pretend to foretell by the clouds and plants—enchanters: diviners by means of serpents, flight of birds, entrails of beasts; witches, who used magical incantations, fumigations, etc.; charmers, with spells, tying knots, peculiar conjunction of words, and all consulters with familiar spirits—the pythoness, the necromancer, who seeks inquiries of the dead. This is an expansion of briefer commands in Ex. 22:18; Lev. 19:26–31; 20:26–27; Num. 23:23; 2 Chron. 33:6, and many other places. So long ago as when the Hebrews encamped at Sinai, all these modern practices were in vogue, and upon them all God set the stamp and brand of his positive prohibition.

This same Word of God, therefore, which thus unveils this mysterious realm, discourages and *forbids all curious investigation into its secrets* through divination, familiar spirits, etc. Its prohibitions are both explicit and repeated with emphasis. Yet how many who claim to be disciples dabble with these mysteries!

These prohibitions include the "curious arts" used by the magi of Ephesus (Acts 19). Prognostication by observing clouds, birds, entrails, currents of wind and water; those who hissed like serpents, practiced ventriloquism, fascinated by the glance, hypnotized and mesmerized, practiced magical incantations and hallucinations in the interests of superstition, bound others by magic spells and mystic knots, consulted with the dead and evil spirits, dealt in prodigies and false prophecies, astrology, palmistry—this first full prohibition covers at least ten forms of occult practices. Will any one show us one substantial benefit accruing to the race from any attempts to invade this forbidden realm, even scientifically, which begins to overbalance the sad wrecks of body and spirit, that lie all along the shores of this *Mare Tenebrum*!

For such prohibitions in Scripture human history furnishes manifold reason. All attempts to enter this forbidden realm save in one way, by communion with God, have proved dangerous, if not fatal, to spiritual life, and sometimes even to sanity.

Among the reasons for this prohibition are the following:

1. The difficulty of discerning the character of spirits;
2. The danger of being misled by half truths into grave errors;
3. The supernatural power with which demons are invested (Acts 19);
4. The danger of a visionary and unpractical curiosity; "curious arts."
5. The weird and mysterious nature of the whole realm;
6. The impossibility of any thorough investigation;
7. The historical argument in the actual results of such practices;
8. The actual influence, especially in promoting and developing insanity.

This realm of spirits is, by its very nature, the most subtle, deceptive, elusive and dangerous of all spheres of the universe, and wields an influence whose power and malignity cannot be fittingly described. Evil spirits, being disembodied and unseen, can intrude, unconsciously to us, into the very arcana of our being, and there work as fertile sources of evil suggestion, kindling passions, desires and resolves inimical both to God and man.

When human beings begin to depart from Christian truth as revealed in the Word of God and dabble in the mysteries of the unseen on their own account, there is no extreme of absurdity to which they will not go.

Someone has well asked, as to "Christian Science," "how can there be any value in an atonement which is not an atonement, connected with suffering which is not suffering, in a body which is not a body, offered in expiation for sin which is not sin?"—a question worthy the attention of adherents of that strange system of paradoxes and platitudes.

Professor Austin Phelps in his volume on *Men and Books* says:

> In a certain parish in Massachusetts, spiritualism had stolen a march. Starting with a fortune teller, it crept into a group of respectable families. An educated physician gave it prestige. Seances were held every fortnight. Soon Dr. Channing and Benjamin Franklin began to dance on the tipping tables. The intermediate state and eternal retribution were revised. Several church members dropped their ancient faith at the bidding of the ghosts of their grandmothers. Their pastor, when inquired of about the still revolution which was going on in his parish, scouted it because of its origin. He was preaching that winter upon the parables of our Lord. He could not descend from so lofty a height to contend with the twaddle of the seances. But his people could. Ought he not to have followed them? Ought he not to have known what they were thinking of and talking of, and whither they were drifting under the lead of the skeptical physician? Christianity never stands on its dignity.

To meddle with this awful realm of spirits may bring us under the sway of malignant supernatural agents and forces. Not only God, but wicked spirits wield weapons which, to us, are superhuman and supernatural, because alike beyond our knowledge and control. Hence (in Rev. 16:14) the "spirits of demons" are represented as "working miracles." The Devil, belonging to created intelligences of the highest order, can sway man by powers that belong to a higher realm; and to dare to invade those forbidden precincts is to venture into an unknown territory and run corresponding risks, risks that are proportionate to the success of our experiments!

While admitting demonic power to work wonders, the Word of God implies no proper parallel with the wonder working of the Lord Jesus Christ. We may not be able always to distinguish by appearances, but it is because of our ignorance and incompetency to deal with such mysteries. Investigation into such a realm is perilous on account of our blindness to our danger and the subtlety of the foes and forces to which we expose ourselves.

Moreover, such researches never reach certainty of result. Outside of God's Word, we can only conjecture; certainties evade us, even a safe conclusion lacks confirmation. Our so-called discoveries never become certainties. We are exploring a realm of phantoms and shadows.

These perils are *historical*. "Psychic research," however it may assume a scientific guise, has never led to any beneficial goal—it has promoted vague and visionary notions, and a dreamy life, and sometimes landed men in insanity. It is also a significant fact that for some reason those who become familiar with spirit phenomena often wander into immorality and sensuality. It is well known that spiritualism has helped stock asylums with insane patients and broken up pure family life by new "spiritual affinities." All unbiblical practices somehow entail disaster. A notable convert from spiritualistic ranks has described it as "one-half fraud and the other half devil."

How far demoniacal possession is a *present* fact, we may not say.[20]

In conversation with a man who had been converted from the depths of drunkenness, he made the startling statement that it was his conviction that delirium tremens is a possession by demons; and his argument was that, in almost if not quite all cases, the victim's visions take certain shapes—he is surrounded by frightful or loathsome animals, has terrible and ghastly visions of serpents and vipers that coil about him and sting him, is burned by livid flames, is pursued by murderers; the patient is generally filled with fear and terror, and cannot be persuaded he is not the prey of demons, and even harmless animals that may happen to be about him are transformed into demoniac shapes.

The Word of God refers to certain offenders as being "delivered over to Satan that they may learn not to blaspheme" (1 Tim. 1:20).

What this means we may not, at this distance of time, confidently say. But a few authentic modern cases of a very remarkable nature may perhaps serve to give some hint of the awful danger of being given over by God to Satanic control.

For the first, Dr. Horatius Bonar is responsible. It took place at Warsaw, in Russian Poland. A bold young scoffer scouted the idea that there is any such thing as sin. Whereupon an old Polish Jew offered the blasphemer twenty-five rubles if he would make a contract to take upon himself the whole burden of his sins. The reckless scoffer made the bargain and the price was paid. But soon after he became strangely ill and no remedy could reach him. At last he confessed that it was his blasphemous bargain that was the load upon him. The old Jew was offered 1,000 rubles to cancel or undo the bargain, but stubbornly refused, and the scoffer sank under his self-assumed load.

---

20 Dr. Nevis, *Demon Possession and Allied Themes*; Mrs. Howard Taylor, *Pastor Hsi*.

Another startling incident belongs to American history. A western village was founded by German infidels upon the very cornerstone of denial of God, and every effort made to keep out everything Christian. A mock procession was conducted in the streets to hold up Christ to ridicule and a mock Lord's Supper celebrated around a stuffed effigy of the blessed Redeemer. That village has been destroyed at least three times—once by fire, once by tornado, and once by the Indians; and in the last case the principal sufferers—the first that died by the tomahawk were the very men that led that blasphemous procession—mimicked the apostolic company.

Within ten miles of a house where I lived, some young men met on a certain night in a hall. They said, "Here we are, thirteen, let us celebrate the Lord's Supper." After an hour's revelry over wine and viands, they made a travesty of the Lord's Supper. Before six o'clock in the morning the leader was dead and every other man in that company was down with a disease that threatened his life. It is a dangerous thing either to meddle with the malignant spirits of the unseen world or to treat with ridicule the glories and verities of the gospel of Jesus Christ. Beware! for God is not dead!

Chapter 8

The Problem of Salvation

A gain we lay a biblical basis for what follows:

Thou shalt call his name Jesus; for he shall save his people from their sins (Matt. 1:21).

Unto you is born this day, in the city of David, a Savior, which is Christ the Lord. (Luke 2:10–14).

Let all the house of Israel know assuredly, that God hath made that same Jesus whom ye have crucified, both Lord and Christ (Acts 2:36).

The word of faith, which we preach: That if thou shalt confess with thy mouth the Lord Jesus, and shalt believe in thine heart that God hath raised him from the dead, thou shalt be saved (Rom. 10:9).

We preach not ourselves, but Christ Jesus the Lord; and ourselves your servants for Jesus' sake (2 Cor. 4:5).

And that every tongue should confess that Jesus Christ is Lord, to the glory of God the Father (Phil. 2:11).

In these six texts the common peculiarity is that they all contain one or more of three significant names applied in the New Testament to the person and work of the Messiah: "JESUS," "CHRIST," "LORD."

These three names are so exhaustive that to master their meaning is to understand the whole scope of his great work of redemption. In the text quoted from Luke, these names follow the *historic order*, outlining the actual progress of redemptive experience. Their significance and order are in every case important, for they unlock the mystery of salvation, and singularly illustrate the divine skill with which, in so narrow a compass, the author of the Scriptures comprehends truths that, like many of his creative marvels, demand microscopic examination to reveal their real beauty.

Two announcements of the birth of our Lord are recorded—one to Joseph, before the event, the other to the shepherds immediately after it; and both are made by that august personage "the angel of the Lord." The two announcements, taken together, are scarcely paralleled even in Scripture as thus supplying, in the fewest possible words, the clue to the whole problem of salvation.

The pre-announcement gives a general, comprehensive statement of the main, central purpose of the advent of *"Jesus." He shall save his people from their sins*—not their *penalties* or judicial *consequences* only, but their *sins* themselves—their pollution, power and even presence. In the post-announcement, the *threefold name*, "Savior," "Christ," "Lord," reveals the threefold aspect of the character and work of the God-Man, and the successive stages in its progressive development.

"Jesus," "Savior"—the *human* name—points to his work as a vicarious substitute for sinners—an atoning Savior. It reminds of the *cross;* that, as Peter says, "he bare our sins in his own body on the tree;" or, as Paul expresses it, "when we were enemies we were reconciled to God by the death of his Son."

"Christ"—the Anointed One—the Messianic name, points to his reception, possession and transmission of the Holy Spirit without measure; and hence to that part of his saving work accomplished in the believer by the impartation of the spirit of grace as an indwelling presence and power—a truth briefly expressed in Romans 8:2: "The law of the spirit of life in Christ Jesus hath made me free from the law of sin and death."

"Lord"—or sovereign—the Jehovah name—carries the idea of *personal rule*. It points to his second advent, when he establishes the throne of his kingdom and identifies his people with his final conquest; when he shall put all enemies under his feet and God shall be all in all.

Thus these three names represent as many grand stages in salvation. As *Jesus*, by his death and resurrection he saves his people from their sins, as to their guilt, penalty and condemnation. As *Christ*, he imparts to them the Holy Spirit—the very life of God— to work in them mightily both to will and to do, thus supplying a power within, as the antidote and counteractive to the power of the world, the flesh, and the Devil. As *Lord* and *King*, he finally destroys all remaining foes, even the Devil and death, raising his people from the dead and clothing them with final and glorious perfection. It can be no accident that thus, the very first authoritative announcement by the angel of the Lord, of the birth of God's appointed Savior, outlines in these few, short, simple words, applied to him as names, the whole plan and progressive history of salvation, and in the exact order in which he accomplishes and develops it. (Compare Peter's sermon, Acts 2:36.)

To get this more fully in mind and appreciate the gravity and importance of this threefold announcement it is needful first to understand the enormous *threefold barrier which stood in the way of man's salvation.*

To begin with, the race was sunk in a double ruin: first, by nature, in a state of alienation from God, under control of a lawless disposition; and, second, under condemnation for sin and actual guilt.

Again, there was a host of evil spirits, with Satan at their head, possessing and controlling fallen men, by inward suggestion and outward temptation, using the world and the flesh as their allies.

And finally, what Paul calls "the bondage of corruption," which holds the body as well as the spirit under its sway, putting restraint and limitation upon the attainments and achievements even of the most self-surrendered servant of God, and in some way involving the whole material creation (Rom. 8).

1. The first of these conditions needs and demands some way of *reconciliation with God;* the second, *regeneration of spirit*, or a new and divine life dwelling and working within; the third, *reconstruction of character*, nothing less than a re-creation, making all things new. In this divine scheme of salvation all these demands are fully met: the first, at Calvary; the second, at Pentecost; the last, at the second coming.

At the *cross*, the believing sinner becomes by faith so one with Jesus as his vicarious substitute and Savior that, in him, the penalty of his sin is judicially paid and he is reconciled to God. At Pentecost, the Holy Spirit given, thus makes the saved sinner to become a partaker of the divine nature. Here is a second substitution—the spirit of God entering within and displacing the spirit of evil and disobedience as the controlling power over the inward life. Then, at the second coming there will be a third substitution—Christ as perfect Lord of lords and King of kings, displacing all other rulers of this world and bringing in a state of perfection instead of an imperfect and partial condition in the spiritual, and even the material, realm.

The wonder of all this only grows as it is studied the more. When a sinner is first brought to consciousness of guilt and condemnation, he feels that between him and God there is a "great gulf fixed" which no human works can bridge, and over which chasm of moral separation neither God can pass to him in mercy nor he to God in reconciliation. But in the gospel he learns that a living mediator—the God-Man—in his own person, bridges that gulf, somewhat as at the fire in the Iroquois Theatre in Chicago, a human hero actually stretched his own body from the burning building to another near by, over which living bridge scores of people passed in safety though it cost him his own life!

But even the forgiven and reconciled believer finds, in his inner self, tendencies to evil, lusts and passions too strong for absolute control, and yearns for full deliverance from the *power* of sin as well as its *penalty*. He finds a divine provision made for this also. The Holy Spirit of God actually descends and dwells in him, makes his body his temple, and prompts to all that is good. A *new order of "lusts"* or overmastering desires henceforth sway him, contrary to the lusts of the flesh (Gal. 5:17). These "lusts of the spirit" are spiritual and heavenly, not carnal and earthly; divine, not devilish; and as the lower lusts come up from beneath to overcome his higher nature and drag him down, so these, coming from above, subdue his lower nature and lift up his whole being to a loftier level.

Then at last comes the resurrection of the dead, the new creation, when there is a final and complete sundering of all connection between the carnal and the spiritual. The life-long conflict is henceforth and forever at an end. "The body of our humiliation" is now exchanged for "the body of his glory." Sin is finally cast out and eliminated, and death, the last enemy, is destroyed, and the Devil no longer permitted to harass and annoy. Even the material creation is reconstructed, a new heavens and a new earth taking the place of the present order, upon which are everywhere found the signs of the curse. Every thorn and thistle that grow on the soil, every storm cloud and lightning flash in the sky, every microbe and germ of disease in air and water; every earthquake, tempest and tornado—all these represent the virus and venom of the serpent, pervading even creation. But in the new creation, wherein dwelleth righteousness, all these will disappear; moral order will be so restored as to correct even the material disorder, and God will, in a peculiar sense, be all and in all and through all.

The Bible, therefore, is first of all the book of *salvation*. Cecil Rhodes' famous saying was, "Let us paint Africa red." This whole Book is, in another sense, "painted red"—dyed scarlet with the blood of atonement. And the attentive student is often amazed to discover a hidden meaning where at first no such sacrificial hue was seen. Years ago a Jewish convert called attention to the fact that the names of the first ten patriarchal heads of the race, as given in Genesis 5, in their historic order, literally translated, supply material for a sort of redemptive sentence, thus: Adam—Seth—Enos—Cainan—Mahalaleel—Jared—Enoch—Methusaleh—Lamech—Noah. The respective meanings are: man—placed—fallen—ransomer—light of God—the descending—teaching—his death brings—stricken—rest. More recently, from another source, a Jewish Rabbi has suggested a similar construction: "The red earth—hath appointed—mortal man—wailing—for the dead; why praise God? There shall descend, a mortal man, dismissing death, (bringing to) the weary—rest." The two are so essentially alike as to intimate a possible divine design that this list of historic names should spell out a mystical sentence giving a succinct history of redemption.

These two redemptive sentences might thus be rendered:

Man, placed on earth, and fallen, the ransomer, light of heaven, descending, teaches stricken men, by his death, rest is given.

Red earth appoints to mortals to wail, for dead, distressed; praise God! Another man descends, to bring the weary, rest.

There can be no reasonable doubt that in the Word of God, the basis of all human salvation is laid in substitutionary sacrifice—the death of Jesus, Savior, upon the cross.

All through the Word of God there was the scarlet thread, as in the heart of the cordage of the British Navy, so that cut it where you will you find that red cord at the heart.

The Bible presents three sides to the *crucifixion* of our Lord Jesus Christ: the side of man's hate, cruelty, malevolence; and the side of God's love, mercy and benevolence; and the side of Christ's voluntary self-offering. From one point, it is the most awful *Tragedy of Crime* ever perpetrated, and nothing could be added to the terrors and horrors of the whole scene. But, from another point, it is the most awe-inspiring *strategy of grace* ever imagined; and nothing could be added to the beauty and glory of the wisdom and love that shone amid that darkness. So long and so far as infidelity prevails and skepticism beclouds even the intellectual atmosphere, men see no higher or farther than the human tragedy, and Christ becomes no more than the leader in a procession of martyrs who have laid down their lives for the truth. But, when faith revives, and prayer opens the doors of God's audience chamber and place of vision, men begin to see that this human display of man's sinful will and habits of evil is also a divine display of infinite love and compassion, and that God made the wrath of man and the plot of demons to work out the ends of his grace, so that life came out of death, victory out of defeat, gain out of loss—and he who seemed the victim was in reality the victor. The cross will always be a stumbling block until behind it is seen the overruling purpose of the infinite and eternal God and the voluntary assumption of the sinner's place before the law by him who bore our sins in his own body on the tree.[21]

The work of Jesus as Savior only *begins at the cross*. The life he there laid down he took again; and the riven tomb witnessed that, out of this new virgin womb of death he was born anew—as "first born from the dead," the Lord of life to all who believe.

Hence those wondrous words of the intercessory prayer: "And this is life eternal, that they might know thee, the only true God, and Jesus Christ whom thou hast sent." The word here translated "that" is commonly construed as having the force of 'namely' and expressing an equivalent. But such usage does not consist with the almost uniform usage of the same word elsewhere. It conveys a higher meaning, if understood to teach that this gift of life eternal is *in order to* the knowledge of God—the indispensable means to that result.[22]

Here is deep, divine philosophy. Only life can understand or appreciate life. God is essentially life eternal—the mysterious I AM; without beginning of days or end of time, he abideth continually. He represents the sum of all being—the same yesterday and today and forever. He is eternally and essentially the unknown—a Spirit whom no man hath seen or can see. Invisible, unsearchable, he evades alike our senses and our ideas—our investigations and our imaginations. After our researches into nature have been aided by microscopic and telescopic lenses, we know indeed a little of his created works, but we know not the *creator* himself any more than we know Edison when we have seen and studied the phonograph.

---

21 *The Message and Meaning of the Cross*, H. C. Mabie.

22 The Greek word is final, as marking the end or purpose for, or on account of which, anything is done: to the end that, or in order that, it might be so and so; but it is also efficient, as marking the event, result, upshot of an action, that in which it terminates; so that it was, is, will be so and so.

To have eternal life in Christ is to have the very nature of God. The Spirit of God who knows the things of God, now dwelling in us, makes us to know him by partaking of his life (1 Cor. 2).

2. Hence the significance of this second name, "CHRIST"—one who has received the *Chrism*, or anointing, and, having the Holy Spirit without measure, imparts that Spirit to the penitent and believing sinner.

God can *reveal himself* to man only by *imparting himself.* Regeneration prepares for illumination. Faith makes possible such revelation: it is the verifying faculty to which the verity appeals, the receptive faculty that responds to the impartive grace. In wireless telegraphy, results are obtained only so far as the receiver is in tune with the transmitter, otherwise the vibrations of the ether cannot be detected and reported. From the eternal generator of life, pulsations vibrate through the universe, but only he who is indwelt by the spirit of life can become a receiver, or ever knows, or feels the power of, the message that God would transmit to man.

It is this truth, especially, that makes the whole Gospel according to *John* alive with divine and quickening energy. The narrative scarcely opens before the inspired writer reminds us that he is writing of him in whom is life and light for men. But immediately he tells us that death cannot receive life nor darkness comprehend light. But he adds—"To as many as *received him*—even to them that believe on his name—gave he authority to become the sons of God." Vain, even the divine transmitter, without the believing receiver.

This grand truth fills and thrills the whole Gospel like an omnipresent electric current. It reappears in various forms of statement, as in the teaching of the third chapter concerning the new birth from above, without which none can *enter* or even *see* the kingdom of God; and there is not a chapter that follows without some new hint of this fundamental fact, that God can be truly known only through Christ, and even Christ known only through the indwelling and in-working of his Spirit. Consequently the world cannot see, know, or receive him (John 14:17), because it lacks the faculties of perception, conception, reception. Only as we are made partakers of the divine nature, which is to have eternal life, can we know him.

Here, then, is the *second stage* of salvation. The first was deliverance from judgment, because that judgment was vicariously borne. But to escape penalty in itself works no change in *character;* and without that, such deliverance might only encourage more presumptuous sin. It would have been a fatal defect in the redemptive scheme had there been no provision for a new nature—a transformed character. Justification could not itself be justified if it did not assure regeneration, and God would not have been just in becoming a justifier (Rom. 3:26).

Behold the wisdom and righteousness of a pardoning God! He who was delivered for our offenses and raised again for our justification, ascends up on high and receives of the Father the promise of the Holy Spirit, that he may, in turn, become his crowning gift to man—his renewer and transformer. And now holiness of heart and life are provided for, a character and a conduct, such as become salvation and imply a higher deliverance from the *power* of sin, providing for a radical change of disposition—that inmost stronghold of sin—until anger, wrath, malice, covetousness are displaced by mercy, kindness, humbleness, meekness, longsuffering—the meek and quiet spirit, the ornament which burns and glows in the heart like the jewels of the breast plate, and is in the sight of God of great price.

3. Even this is not enough. Jesus Christ is also LORD.

The fall of man was the awful wreck of a throne, and the loss of a crown and a scepter. Man was made to have dominion; but instead, he has lost mastery even over himself, and God's anointed sovereign has sunk to Satan's abject slave. For six thousand years man has been seeking for a master and found none that could break his chains and set him free. Even the believer feels his bonds but half broken. In his body, soul and spirit, the remains of his moral wreck and ruin wait for full repair and reconstruction. As in a healed body, where muscular and nervous power has never been restored, but the traces of past injury remain, even saints find themselves hampered and hindered in sanctity and service by the relics of the old life and the "old man," and sigh for full deliverance from the "body of this death."

To the Lord's second coming, we are taught to look for the final revelation of Jesus Christ as Lord and the final manifestation of the sons of God. Then the body of our humiliation will be exchanged for the body of his glory; then the last traces of sin and even infirmity will instantly disappear, and all the limitations of our present spiritual life be removed. Sin will become doubly a thing of the past, and Satanic wiles and lies cease forever to perplex and annoy. For the first time man will know what it is to have a perfect *sovereign*, whose will is law and whose law is love; and a new heaven and a new earth wherein dwelleth righteousness shall displace the present disorder—cosmos out of chaos—no more death, sighing nor crying, pain nor tears—a city of God, with bridal beauty and divine purity—into which entereth nothing that defileth, worketh abomination or maketh a lie.

This is all a *present* salvation, for in a sense, even the final consummation casts its glory backward upon our present experience.

While the Lord Jesus Christ was in the flesh in the form of a servant, it behooved his believing people to be as their master. How could they realize or even recognize their high privilege and standing in him as *sons!* Like him, they were in a state of servitude and humiliation; but now "our citizenship is in heaven"—a present fact—though its full realization and enjoyment waits for his coming to lift his people to the full inheritance of their privileges. To deny the present "heavenlies," taught in Ephesians, is to deny the present "citizenship," taught in Philippians. In the heavenlies we are to find the present *sphere* of our identification with Christ. There are our citizenship and our treasures (Matt. 6:20-21), our hope (Col. 1:5; Titus 2:13); our aims and affections (Col. 3:1-2); our inheritance (1 Pet. 1:4). It is one of the greatest redemptive facts, that our Lord has by his own resurrection and ascension actually, in himself, raised all believers to the heights of heavenly privilege from which sin had shut us out, and into which, until his ascension and the Spirit's descension, it was impossible for us *experimentally* to enter.

If anyone objects that such a view is inconsistent with the believer's present experience of actual conflict with the world, the flesh and the Devil, let him remember that there is more than one phase or aspect of our relation to our Lord. There is the aspect of suffering and conflict, for as yet all enemies are not made the footstool of his feet; and there is the aspect of sovereignty and even of conquest, for he is on the throne. More than this, even in our experience of earthly conflict there is also an aspect of heavenly conquest. For it is written of him that he is "set down at the right hand of God, from henceforth *expecting*"—an emphatic word conveying the idea of receiving in expectation—as though there were such certainty as made future victory a present reality (Heb. 10:12-13). Therefore, so far as our position is realized, we shall from henceforth be *expecting*, and our experience in him will be far less one of *fighting* than of *subduing*. We shall in him dare to count or reckon ourselves as already victors. It is our present privilege to clothe ourselves in the panoply of God and become proof against even the powers of darkness. After his session at God's right hand, victory over our foes is uniformly represented as assured in him, and dependent, not on our effort, but on our standing in him. The greatest of our foes, the representative adversary, is the Devil, and yet we are told simply to "*resist* him"—steadfast in the faith, and he will flee from us (1 Peter 5:8–9; James 4:7). Astonishingly easy victory—simply by taking the attitude of resistance! And so (Eph. 6:10–20) we have only to put on the Lord's panoply and then *stand*—as an anvil stands under the hammer, not to be broken, but to break the hammer. If our position in him and possession of him is once fully seen and felt, we also shall *sit down* in conscious sovereignty, and from henceforth confidently *expect* our enemies to be made our footstool.

A singular phrase occurs in Ephesians five times and nowhere else: "in the heavenlies"—not accompanied by any definitive noun. As yet we are not in the heavenly *places*, but in the earthly; yet it is ours to recognize and realize our heavenly *states* and privileges and potential victories even in the earthly places.

To refer this phrase to heavenly *places* and to the *future* exaltation of saints is a serious if not fundamental error in exposition, for it overlooks a fact of vital importance to the understanding of our Lord's work and its effect on believers, namely, that we, unlike Old Testament believers, are blessed *in* Christ Jesus, with *all* spiritual blessings—the word *all* being emphatic.

Judaism had its blessings (Rom. 9:4–5), but how little did even Abraham, Moses, David and Daniel know of the believer's blessings as a whole, and as now revealed and realized in Christ by the Spirit! This brief phrase—in the heavenlies—expresses a fact not fully presented until we reach Ephesians and Colossians, that the believer, who in Romans is seen as one with Christ in death, burial and resurrection; in Corinthians, as one with him by the indwelling of the Spirit; and in Galatians by the walk in the Spirit, is further identified with him in his ascension to the heavenlies. It is true we are as yet actually in the earthly sphere; but the church is the body of Christ. It reaches from earth to heaven. The feet stand on the earth, but the head is among the stars; and though the feet are on earth, the lower members thrill with the life and vitality of the head.

It is only in the light of such truths as these that we can understand the *true value* of the Scriptures of truth.

Out of all the marks of the divine adaptation of the Bible to man, two stand conspicuous: first, *its revelation of God and spiritual truth;* and second, *its clear exposition of the way of salvation.*

Much knowledge—in fact, a vast area of knowledge—is open to man, naturally, and without help from the inspired Word. From other books in God's library, much may be learned—from the material universe—the book of nature; from the annals of the race—the book of history; from the experience of man—the book of human nature. For the study of these, the natural man has his bodily senses and his mental powers of observation and recollection, reason and reflection. But another vast area of knowledge lies outside of all these—an entire universe, wholly beyond the reach of the senses or natural faculties, in which are contained the deepest truths about God and man. As man looks at nature or himself, he finds a limit beyond which he cannot pierce or penetrate—mysteries that even telescope and microscope can not explore, depths and heights that defy all search and pass all knowledge.

For example, as we have seen in another connection, the heavens and earth may suggest a creator and evidence his wisdom and power and even goodness. But of his *moral* nature, nature can only hint vaguely and uncertainly. It is guesswork. Man is not sure that the creator is even *good;* for there are so many evidences of destructive forces at work, producing disaster that, left to unaided reason, he can at best conclude with the followers of Zoroaster that there are two rival powers, Ormuzd and Ahriman, one working good and the other evil. The full knowledge of God he cannot thus attain.

Again, when he discovers, in himself, a nature prone to evil, and sees himself a transgressor of law, absolutely nothing in the natural world or his own little world within answers such questions as, how can a sinner be reconciled to God? Is there forgiveness with him, or any way to be saved from sin? To such moral questions in vain he seeks an answer. The depth of the sea saith it is not in me, and in the profounder depth of the sky, as he looks upward for a voice, the silence is awful. All the history of heathenism is one pathetic groping in the dark. Conscious of having offended against God—in despair of self help—holocausts and hecatombs of victims—the first born of the body for the sin of the soul. In India today see the fakirs on their beds of spikes, sitting in summer heats between roasting fires, starving themselves into a passionless state, sleepless, homeless, self tortured—all in hope to attain the favor of the gods and find deliverance from sin and suffering in extinction—*nirvana*.

It is here that the *Bible* especially interposes. It is the revelation of those truths about God which can be known *in no other way*. His *attitude toward men*—his grace in forgiveness; the stupendous fact that he actually *seeks* the lost instead of leaving the lost to seek him.

Here is the reason why the Word of God so unmistakably teaches and supplies the need of a spiritual revelation. The spirit of man is a dark chamber. The body has its senses for contact with the material world. The soul through these senses goes out to gather a knowledge of physical facts and then from these by mental processes evolve what are called science and philosophy. But as to those more exalted facts and truths of the unseen world, pertaining to God and the higher needs of man, the spirit needs other avenues of knowledge.

This is the grand office of the Bible—to let light into the chambers of man's spirit. It brings direct ray from God and pours it into the spirit of man. Everything we need to know about him and his attitude to us is here revealed, and this knowledge comes *only from the Word*.

That Word pierces to that dividing asunder of soul and spirit which, even to man himself, is a dark chamber of mystery, and discerns the thoughts and intents of the heart. But if it pierces like an arrow or a dart, it carries on its sharp point not a poison but a balm—it wounds to heal; it reveals to relieve; it cuts to cure.

Nothing is risked in the broad statement that, from man's creation and fall unto this day, not one problem of spiritual life has perplexed humanity that does not find in this book an adequate solution, and more than this, its *only* perfect solution. Not one great question as to man's origin, nature, need, peril, duty, highest interest or final destiny, which does not meet here—and here only—its satisfactory answer.

If this be true, it is obvious that here is the supreme *evidence* of the superhuman, supernatural origin of the Bible—the highest form of *apologetic*. No greater or more conclusive proof that this is God's book can be found than the fact that it thus corresponds to man's deepest wants as only God could meet them—that, after the wisest and best of the human race have worked and worried during all the ages over the problems of spiritual life, like boys struggling over a mathematical problem, one sentence of the Word of God often solves the difficulty as a key unlocks a door. This has been the satisfaction of the simple minded and the surprise of the great minded, that the Word of God proves a lamp unto the feet and a light unto the path—the wisdom of God in a mystery, flooding with sunshine the obscurest realm of inquiry, and pronouncing a final and ultimate verdict where even the most sagacious of human counselors and judges have failed to reach a decision; or where, even when a judgment was formed, there was still a hopeless conflict of opinion.

Two wonderful marks of the Bible's adaptedness to man are most conspicuous and important: Its revelation of truth unknown and undiscoverable by any other means; and particularly this: its exhibition of the complete way of salvation.

In what are known as the Burne-Jones Mosaics, in the American Church at Rome, art has sought to pay its tribute to the work of Christ on the cross.

Outside the great arch of the chancel, and immediately beneath the roof, is seen the annunciation; and beyond, the crucified Christ, boldly conceived as fixed, not upon a mere instrument of shame and torture—the cross; but on a Tree of Life, whose branches cover the whole heaven. Adam, with sheaves of garnered wheat, is seen on the one side of the crucified; on the other, Eve with her children and lilies. Beyond this arch, in the semi-dome of the apse, is pictured a glory of angels, and, below, the enthroned Christ surrounded by seraphic figures, holding in his hand the terrestrial globe. Fountains of life spring from beneath the throne, but so separated from it by a strongly defined arch as to divide the spiritual realm above from the earth below. On each side are two attendant figures representing the four archangels. Above the outer arch are inscribed, in Latin words, the angelic salutation; above the inner arch, also in Latin words: "In the world ye shall have tribulation; but be of good cheer, I have overcome the world."

Our subject also makes clearer the value of a true *preaching of the gospel*.

The reason is apparent why the New Testament so emphasizes the preaching of Christ.

The method whereby it has pleased God to save men needs far clearer apprehension, and especially the mutual relation of the *preaching of Christ* and the working of the *Holy Spirit*. Attention may be so fixed upon the work of the Holy Spirit as to risk a possible obscuration of that other equally important factor, the faithful preaching of Christ, or conversely. But the bearing of each on the other is vital. The Holy Spirit is first of all the spirit of *truth*—he uses truth, and most of all the truth about the Lord Jesus Christ, as the basis for all his regenerating and sanctifying work; so that in exactly that proportion in which men are taught this great essential truth of Christ crucified, risen, ascended and coming again, is the foundation laid for the Spirit to work his wonders in salvation. It is therefore possible to offer prayer in a mistaken and misguided way for the Spirit's outpouring and manifestation when we are not giving heed to the preparation for his regenerating work in the full, clear and constant presentation of the Lord Jesus Christ.

One of the most emphatic of our Lord's sayings is that double "verily" in John 5:24–26:

> Verily, verily, I say unto you, he that heareth my word, and believeth on him that sent me, hath everlasting life, and shall not come into condemnation; but is passed from death unto life.
>
> Verily, verily, I say unto you, the hour is coming, and now is, when the dead shall hear the voice of the Son of God; and they that hear shall live.
>
> For as the Father hath life in himself; so hath he given to the Son to have life in himself;
>
> And hath given him authority to execute judgment also, because he is the Son of Man.

This is the declaration of a *spiritual resurrection from among the dead*, as that which follows is the prophecy of a future and *physical* resurrection; and it is made in both cases to depend upon the voice of the Son of God, an equivalent phrase for his word (24). Three things are the conditions of this spiritual resurrection—Christ's voice, the hearing of it and the quickening by it. The last is the work of the Spirit which we cannot command or control, except by fulfilling the conditions: there must be the *word of Christ spoken and heard*. Of this teaching in Chapter 5, the incident in Chapter 11—the raising of Lazarus—is designed to be both type and illustration. Lazarus had been four days dead—there was therefore no doubt of his death and already offensive decay and dissolution. Yet our Lord had only to speak the three words, "Lazarus, come forth!" and, behold the result! The dead man lived, and corruption not only was arrested, but the process of decay was actually reversed and undone!

The word or voice of Christ has never lost power. We make a fundamental mistake in attaching even a secondary importance to the power of his own utterances in raising dead souls and quickening them. This is the one miracle, sign, wonder that never fails. And let us think and speak of it reverently! The true preaching of the gospel is the utterance of the *Word*—the echo of his voice. It is given to everyone who faithfully proclaims the gospel to speak in his name, that is, in his *person* and with his authority. We can even command dead souls to arise and come forth! That is magnifying the Spirit's work out of the due proportion of faith which overlooks or belittles the power which supernaturally inheres in the true preaching of Christ crucified. It is not too much to say that men and women who know very little intelligently and consciously of the Holy Spirit have wrought great marvels by the power of his name, so that it is safer to preach the full gospel of salvation through Christ without conscious dependence on the Spirit than to plead for the Spirit's presence and power without providing that grand preparation for his working, found in the Scriptural and incessant proclamation of the gospel message.

I know no more august conception of the whole work of preaching than this—that it is, as ambassadors for Christ, acting in his stead and speaking by his authority, becoming mere echoes of his voice and word—and in the name of Jesus Christ of Nazareth bidding the lame rise up and walk and the dead "come forth!"

Whenever this is faithfully done, results will always follow. Whether or not we formally feel and recognize our dependence on the Holy Spirit, he will not fail to do his work, for he recognizes the voice, word, name of the Lord Jesus.

This explains two great crises in the acts of the Apostles—one on the day of Pentecost; the other that Roman Pentecost in the house of Cornelius. In both cases it is most noticeable that the point at which the great manifestation of the Spirit was realized was when Peter had given his *full* testimony about Christ. Note the clear indication in both cases.

This Jesus hath God raised up, whereof we all are witnesses.

Therefore, being by the right hand of God exalted, and having received of the Father the promise of the Holy Ghost, he hath shed forth this, which ye now see and hear.

For David is not ascended into the heavens: but he saith himself, the LORD said unto my Lord, sit thou on my right hand, until I make thy foes thy footstool.

Therefore let all the house of Israel know assuredly, that God hath made that same Jesus, whom ye have crucified, both Lord and Christ.

Now, when they heard *this*, they were pricked in their heart, and said unto Peter and to the rest of the apostles, men *and* brethren, what shall we do? (Acts 2:32–37).

So also at the house of Cornelius:

That word, *I say*, ye know, which was published throughout Judaea, and began from Galilee, after the baptism which John preached;

How God anointed Jesus of Nazareth with the Holy Ghost and with power: who went about doing good, and healing all that were oppressed of the devil; for God was with him.

And we are witnesses of all things which he did both in the land of the Jews, and in Jerusalem; whom they slew and hanged on a tree: him God raised up the third day, and shewed him openly; not to all the people, but unto witnesses chosen before of God, even to us, who did eat and drink with him after he rose from the dead.

And he commanded us to preach unto the people, and to testify that it is he which was ordained of God *to be* the judge of quick and dead.

To him give all the prophets witness, that through his name whosoever believeth in him shall receive remission of sins.

While Peter yet spake these words, the Holy Ghost fell on all them which heard the word (Acts 10:37–44).

In both these cases it is of first importance to observe that each of these brief discourses embraced *all* the fundamental facts of Christ's vicarious death, resurrection, ascension and all sufficiency. Had our Lord himself been present and speaking, we can scarcely imagine a more *explicit* and comprehensive announcement of his complete work as Savior, Christ and Lord. In one case the whole of the testimony as to Christ's work is contained in less than four hundred words, and in the latter in less than two hundred; but so soon as there was enough spoken to become the basis of a saving work, the Holy Spirit began to act wondrously. In the former case they were pricked in their heart and compelled to ask, "What shall we do?" In the latter, "While Peter yet spake these words, the Holy Spirit fell on all them which heard the word," as though the Spirit were divinely impatient to bless men and waited only for a sufficient declaration of saving truth to begin at once to manifest his power.

The discourse of Peter at Pentecost has great interest and importance as the *first Christian sermon*—first utterance of the Holy Spirit as the Spirit of *truth*, guiding into all truth, and "taking of mine and showing unto you;" and Spirit of *power* in witness for Christ—already breathed into them as Spirit of *life* on the evening of resurrection (John 20).

Here Peter, overflowing with Holy Spirit knowledge and power, in few words, recites and explains the career of Jesus of Nazareth—his work on the cross, his resurrection as Prince of Life, ascension and Pentecostal effusion, and present session on the throne of God as King and Conqueror. The past, present and future of Christ as redeemer is thus set forth clearly, briefly, comprehensively and powerfully, and they were pricked in their heart and three thousand added to the Lord that day.

Within the compass of that one discourse the whole plan of salvation is found, and nothing new remains to be said except to expand what is here stated germinally.

It is at least hinted in our Lord's talk on the way to Emmaus that his image is to be traced throughout the whole Old Testament. It is not too much to say that, in some form, his impress may be found, however faintly, on every page of Scripture, so that an inspired teacher might begin anywhere and, like Philip, preach Jesus. We need only the illumined insight to recognize the often invisible tracing which like the waterline in paper is seen only when held up to the light.

A visitor at the home of an English clergyman of devout habits was amazed to find written on every page from Genesis to Revelation—"CHRIST," and resolved to ask him the meaning of all this. He stared as in astonishment, and after a pause replied, "I always thought you knew your Bible well, but you seem not to know an all-important Scripture that quite warrants me in putting 'Christ' where it is; for except I see *him* from beginning to end of Scripture, I am as dark as the Emmaus disciples." "I at once," says the writer, "confessed my ignorance of Luke 24:27; but from that day to this have been led of God to make much of this glorious fact."

Here likewise is to be found the reason why the simple gospel story, surviving all assaults of unbelief and disbelief, still proves to hold sinning souls under its charm.

Bishop Whipple used to tell of a young man whom he knew—a thoughtful and scholarly man—who had searched all literature to find objections to the Christian religion and arm himself with a panoply of weapons against the truth. He was compelled, however, to confess that he was kept back from confirmed infidelity by three things:

First, I am a man; I am going somewhere; tonight I am a day nearer the grave than I was last night. I have read all such books can tell me; they shed not one solitary ray upon the darkness; they take away the only guide and leave one stone-blind.

Secondly, I had a mother; I saw her go down into the dark valley where I am going, and she leaned upon an unseen arm as a child goes to sleep on the breast of its mother. I know that was not a dream.

Thirdly, I have three motherless children. They have no protector but myself. I would rather kill them than leave them in this sinful world if you blot out from it all the teachings of the gospel.

Is there any answer to the arguments that held this man from the abyss of infidelity? Life and death are realities. They are in us, before us and around us. Life has problems and death has terrors, and nothing the world can give can satisfy the soul.

From all this discussion several practical conclusions are clear.

1. This book should be handled with great humility and docility. It should inspire reverence. It is quite possible to approach it with an undue intellectual conceit and mistake the ideas we read into it for the ideas we find in it, reminding again of Parke Godwin's witty remark about "original investigation" where "the originality surpassed the investigation."

2. Its credibility does not hang on the inherent *probability* of the facts narrated. Sometimes the improbability of a prophecy and the strange and unprecedented character of the fulfillment become strongest proofs of actuality; since it would not occur to a prophet to predict what would be most unlikely to happen, nor to a historian to record what was equally without precedent, if they were simply writing from a human point of view and seeking to commend their writings to human confidence.

3. Whenever a clue unlocks a maze we need no other path, especially if any other leads us only to a wall of impenetrable mystery or back to our starting point. This book is confessedly a mystery. There is one and only one possible solution, namely, that it is what it claims: on that basis we find all that is strange and unaccountable reasonably explained; but as Mr. Frank Ballard has shown in his striking book, "the miracles of unbelief" are absolutely greater than those that unbelief sets aside as incredible.

Were I asked what is the most unanswerable argument for the divine origin of Christianity, I would unhesitatingly answer, *Calvary*. Archbishop Whately and Dr. Pusey after him long since framed the axiom that when what is in the highest degree *improbable* is foretold ages in advance and then actually occurs as foretold, it furnishes the highest evidence of a superhuman origin. It is often said that the whole tragedy of the cruci-fixion—the incarnation of God in man for the purpose of such vicarious atonement—and the resurrection of the crucified one in a body no longer mortal—that all this is so improbable and impossible as to be *incredible.* But in the very *impossibility lies the credibility!* For sane men, common men taken from common walks of life—men of all varieties of temper-ament, accustomed only to deal with the commonplace monotony of life, are not likely to dream a dream so transcendent, so extraordinary, so superhuman. Now, notice that while this whole prophecy and history of incarnation, crucifixion, resurrection, ascension and ultimate return is extraordinary and entirely above the whole common level of human experience, it is entirely *self-consistent.* Grant that the Son of the eternal God actually does undertake such a mission in behalf of man, and the rest is in harmony with the supposition. Start with Calvary and you have no explanation, for no crucified and speared man can pour out his life blood, be buried and rise the third day to die no more. But once go back from Calvary and accept the Bible story of his *birth*—once admit that this is no mere *man* upon the cursed tree, but the God-Man, and you are prepared to understand his own mysterious saying: "No man taketh my life from me: I have power to lay it down and I have power to take it again." He who hangs on the cross is not the helpless victim he seems. One word from him even now and twelve legions of angels would sur-round his cross, waiting to do his bidding. All this is voluntary, because he has undertaken to redeem man by dying, the just for the unjust, that he might bring us to God. But in the God-Man there is a *divine* as well as a *human* factor. The human may die, but the divine cannot. He is even in dying still the "Prince of Life" and cannot remain under the power of death. Resurrection to die no more is but the natural finale of this tragedy and so is ascension to God's right hand; for when his errand is completed what is more to be expected than the Son's return to his Father's house and heart!

I expand this thought because it is not appreciated at its true value. The very *objections* of infidels and skeptics to the facts of Christianity are in truth its unanswerable arguments. For thousands of years the whole machinery of the heavens was an inextricable maze of mystery, with its sun and planets and satellites, its fixed stars and comets; it seemed as though there must come some mighty crash of collision, some universal disaster—the paths of moving orbs seemed irregular and uncertain and without definite order or system. But the trouble is stargazers had not got the *right point of view!* They were led by such as Ptolemy to take their stand on the *earth* and it became to them the center around which all else moved. But Copernicus took his stand on the *sun.* He found a new center, a new point of prospect; and lo, all the inexplicable mystery of the solar system became plain. The problem of ages was solved. And since then, astronomers have found a still grander center for the *stellar* universe, for they find that this whole visible body of stars are in motion around one point which Mädler indicated as the brilliant star Alcyone in the constellation of the Pleiades!

Men have studied the story of Calvary, taking their stand on the earth, and making the *human will* their center. From this point of view only one thing is plain: the malice of men might crucify a good man. But how many other acts go unexplained! This crucified man claimed to be the Son of God in so unique a sense as to be equally entitled to worship and endowed with power and eternal life; and if the testimony of hundreds of credible witnesses is to be trusted he both foretold his rising from the dead and actually did as he said, and forty days later, in their sight, rose heavenward and was received into a cloud out of their sight. All this, while *earth* is our point of view, is not only inexplicable, it is absurdly incredible. It belongs to the realm of fable and fancy.

But now take the point of view suggested in the Word. Take your stand at the throne of God—the center of the moral universe. See the whole mystery of the birth, death, rising from the dead as one consistent plan of redemption, devised by God and wrought out by him as he only can plan or perform. And now all comes into order and harmony. There may be mystery still, but it is the mystery of love and wisdom passing human thought.

When Prof. Rendel Harris of Cambridge went to Armenia, after the massacre, on a mission of mercy to the orphans of those modern martyrs, he was permitted to speak in one of the Greek churches in the district desolated by Turkish assassins.[23] Seeing before him forty or fifty of the men who had survived the slaughter, scarred and maimed, he felt impelled to bring them a message suited to their experiences of suffering. But back of them stood a company of soldiers, spies of the government

---

23 A reference to the Hamidian massacres of 1895.

sent to catch him in his talk, and any reference to the massacre might involve him in peculiar peril and even forfeit his own life. Nevertheless, he did not hesitate. Choosing as a text Isaiah 49:16,

He hath graven thee upon the palms of his hands,

he showed that the palms of our Lord's hands were the place of the nail-prints—the stigmata of the crucifixion. How could he look on those marks of his own suffering for their sakes and not remember their sufferings for his sake? Their sorrows as his witnesses identified them with the master himself and would not be forgotten or unrewarded.

It was at immense personal risk that Prof. Harris dared thus to refer to the awful scenes through which they had passed. But he suffered no harm. As he afterward learned, those very soldiers went and reported to the authorities, "Never man spake like this man."

It was a new demonstration and illustration of that great fact that the story of the cross never loses its charm. There is something about it so grand yet so pathetic, so sublime yet so tragic, so unselfish and heroic, so overwhelming and subduing, so indescribable and incredible—that God's only Son should become man, and in some strange sense become *sin* for man that in him man might become the righteousness of God, and all this by simple faith—that in all ages and among all classes it has had a power absolutely *unparalleled*, and after nineteen centuries its power is still undiminished and undecaying.

We are told that when the risen Christ appeared to the disciples on the mount and in Galilee, they worshiped him, but some doubted.

It will always be so; side by side with the most devout worshipers, and even before the indisputable evidences of the risen Christ, there will be some who *doubt*. But let us continue to worship. Quite enough for us if he says, "All power is given to me … and all the days I am with you."

JESUS—CHRIST—LORD

Watching shepherds heard redemption's song,
Bursting from angelic choral throng:
"Unto you, this holy natal morn,
In your city, Bethlehem, is born,
Jesus, who is Savior, Christ and Lord."
He is Jesus, for, upon the tree,
He bore sin, to set the guilty free:
Free from load of penalty for sin,
Free from alien heart that hides within.
Christ and Lord, but *Savior*, first of all.
Christ—anointed of the Holy Ghost,
He hath shed his promised Pentecost:
Breathes God's Spirit into human hearts,
God's own nature graciously imparts.
Jesus, Savior, Lord, is also *Christ*.
Lord—he comes again, to reign as King—
Full Redemption to his saints to bring:
Perfected, in body, spirit, soul,
All creation finally made whole.
Jesus, Savior, Christ, at last is *Lord*.
Then shall end the age-long mystery—
Death itself, last enemy, shall die—
Then shall Satan's throne and kingdom fall,
Every foe beneath his feet! Amen!
That God, henceforth, may be all in all!

Chapter 9

The Problem of Faith

On this question, Scripture lessons are singularly *progressive*, beginning with the simplest and most rudimental, and advancing to the most complex and complete. Some of the leading steps of this teaching may be indicated at the outset:

> Abram believed in the Lord, and he counted it to him for righteousness (Gen. 15:6).

> The just shall live by his faith (Hab. 2:4).

> They that know thy name will put their trust in thee (Ps. 9:10).

> Believe in the Lord your God; so shall ye be established: Believe his prophets; so shall ye prosper (2 Chron. 20:20).

> Have faith in God
> or
> Hold the faith of God (Mark 11:22).

> He that believeth on the Son hath everlasting life (John 3:36).

> Faith is the substance of things hoped for; the evidence of things not seen. By faith the elders obtained a good report (Heb. 11:1–2).

> She judged him faithful who had promised (*ibid.*, 11).

> If we receive the witness of men, the witness of God is greater (1 John 5:9).

It is of first importance to understand the nature and province, powers and possibilities of faith, for upon it depends the existence and development of all true life in the Spirit. Hence on this subject, perhaps more than any other, the divine teacher, in his Word, begins with the alphabet of faith, the simplest rudimentary lesson, and gradually leads on to the most advanced level; but to understand the advance lessons, it is needful to master the primary and fundamental.

The word *believe* is first found in Gen. 15:6, where it is said, literally, that "Abraham *amened Jehovah*, and it was imputed unto him for righteousness." The verb *"amen"* means not *let it be so*, but *it shall be so*. When the Lord promised Abraham a son after Sarah was beyond the age of bearing he simply responded to Jehovah's word, "it shall be as the Lord hath spoken." Hence James adds, "and he was called the friend of God," for it is a sign of friendship that another's word affirmed by him is confirmed by us.

This first lesson on faith is followed by a second, twelve hundred years after (Hab. 2:4): "The just shall live by his faith."

The importance of these two texts will appear in the fact that they are *thrice repeated* in the New Testament epistles, and, where they occur, mark critical points in the argument.

Gen. 15:6 is repeated in Rom. 4:3, Gal. 3:6, James 2:23.

Hab. 2:4 is repeated in Rom. 1:17, Gal. 3:11, Heb. 10:38.

God gave his people twelve hundred years to learn that first lesson before he gave them the other. The word "faith" is found but once before it is found in Habakkuk (Deut. 32:20), "Children in whom is no faith," where it means *faithfulness, i. e.,* they neither have faith in me nor keep faith with me.

The word "believe" also seldom occurs, with relation to God, in all this interval.

Isa. 28:16 is a marked exception: "He that believeth shall not make haste." Dan. 6:23 is another: "No manner of hurt was found on him, because he believed in his God."

If the two main passages already quoted from Genesis and Habakkuk be followed in the New Testament, it will be seen that they occur at critical points, in every case, and that, by emphasizing some one word, the peculiar relation to each particular context will be plain. Thus, in Rom. 4:3, it is the word *counted;* in Gal. 3:6, the word *believed*, and in James 2:23, *righteousness.* Again, in quoting Habakkuk, in Rom. 1:17, the emphatic word is *just*, as though answering the question, who is the just or righteous man? In Galatians, *faith*, as though the question were, how does the just live? And in Heb. 10:38, *live*, as though the question were, what is it that the just does by his faith? He *lives*—is both *made* alive and *kept* alive by faith.

The English word, believe, means primarily to be *willing*, and faith is from *fido*, "I trust," both roots conveying the notion of voluntary and restful confidence in another's word.

The simple, literal meaning of the word "amen"—*it shall be so*—gives much light on the subject. In several conspicuous instances of faith this *very form of words* is used, as also in rebukes of unbelief.

In Luke 1:20, twice we find the *shall be* which is in such contrast to Zacharias's doubting frame, the unbelief which proved an instant paralysis of testimony. And in verses 37 and 45 we have the two statements that "with God nothing shall be impossible," and that she shall be blessed that "believed that there *shall be* a performance of those things which were told her of the Lord."

In Acts 27:25, Paul says to the shipwrecked company, "I believe God, that *it shall be* even as it was told me," as if Gen. 15:6 were in mind (comp. 2 Cor. 1:20). All this is *amening* God.

Between these two lessons in Luke 1 and Acts 27 lie all the sixty years of gospel history, one incident being before the birth of John the Baptist and the other after Christ's ascension and within a short time of the destruction of Jerusalem. Many are the lessons in the interval, emphasizing what the angel taught Zacharias, and the Spirit taught Mary, in the first chapter of Luke. We are to say *"it shall be"* to all *promises of God,* and act as though we believed.

Thus the first great lesson on faith was found in Abram's saying to the promise that, humanly speaking, was impossible of fulfillment, "it shall be so;" and the fundamental principle of the imputation of righteousness on account of faith, likewise taught in that same verse in Genesis, is further confirmed and amplified in Habakkuk.

In the matter of righteousness before God, no one is ever regarded or treated as righteous on the ground of anything beginning and ending in himself, but solely because of his laying hold by faith on the righteousness of God in Christ; and to such union with him is wholly due whatever God thinks of us, counts us to be, or judicially declares to be, as accepted in his sight. This, says Canon Hay-Aitken, is "not a legal fiction but a divine anticipation." Our standing in justification is therefore as much the gift of grace as the body of glory which in resurrection shall displace the body of our abasement; for "God giveth a body as it hath pleased him."

This word, "faith," one of the most prominent in Scripture, is found about three hundred times; and, including its near equivalents, "believe," "trust," etc., the number is much increased. But the number of times of recurrence fails to indicate its importance, for it holds the commanding position, at the vital points of Scripture argument and appeal, and at the critical and pivotal points in holy living. It reminds us of a general-in-chief in an army; however many hundreds of thousands of private soldiers there may be, his authority and influence outweigh them all; his word or signal wheels into line whole regiments and battalions. We constantly meet faith in commanding positions in the Word of God and in every conceivable application to spiritual life.

On the *human* side of salvation and of all man's relations to God, faith is the one thing on which all else depends, and hence most necessary to be understood.

The nearest approach to a definition proper is found in two places, Luke 1:45 (margin): "blessed is she that believed that there shall be a performance of those things which were told her from the Lord;" and in Hebrews 11:11, "Sarah judged him faithful who had promised." In both cases these godly women are commended because they held fast to God's good faith and reckoned on it.

A definition might perhaps be framed, somewhat thus: "Faith is such confidence in the faithfulness of God as leads to a reception of his testimony, to such love and trust as becomes a personal bond of union with him, and to corresponding obedience and testimony." But, like other very simple things, it is difficult to define because of its simplicity, but even a child knows what it is and shows it in action. It begins in a simple act of *reception*, than which no act can be simpler. It grows by the exercise of *confidence*, more and more implicit, of *dependence* more and more absolute, and *obedience* more and more cheerful and unquestioning.

Two conspicuous texts in the Gospel according to John belong among the rudiments.

> As many as received him, to them gave he power to become the sons of God, even to them that believe on his name.
>
> Which were born, not of blood, nor of the will of the flesh, nor of the will of man, but of God.
>
> But these are written, that ye might believe that Jesus is the Christ, the Son of God; and that believing ye might have life through his name (John 1:12–13; 20:31).

The main purpose of John's narrative is to induce faith that Jesus is the Christ, the Son of God, so that life may come through believing. It is important, therefore, to understand what believing is, and at the opening this is made clear—it is *receiving him*. In every case where the word 'believe' is used throughout this Gospel the word *'receive'* may be substituted without impairing the sense.

Here, then, is the starting point for anyone who would exercise saving faith: he must *receive* Jesus as Savior, Christ, Son of God; not simply the witness God gave concerning his Son, but the Son of God *himself*, as a child receives his father's word, "jump and I will catch you," by leaping into his arms, or as a woman receives a husband when she links her life to his in inseparable union. Such reception of faith, such receiving by believing, is the initial act of faith. The penitent, believing sinner simply lets go all other dependence and drops into the everlasting arms.

To as many as thus receive him, even to them that believe on his name, he gives authority to become sons of God by a new birth of the Spirit. Regeneration is necessary, but with that we have nothing to do. It is God's act—a gift to the believer. We cannot command the new creation any more than control our original birth; but we can believe on his name and so become new born sons.

This is one of the primary truths of the whole Word of God:

This *reception of God's witness concerning his Son* is the *one* and *only condition of salvation;* all beyond this has to do with sanctification, service and satisfaction in God.

This cannot be made too emphatic; it is always the "present truth"— the truth needing perpetual emphasis. One of the greatest errors to the preacher, and snares to the seeker, is so to misapply the words of Scripture as to make the terms of salvation obscure; either by interpreting injunctions and directions, addressed to the disciple, as applying to the unsaved; or by confusing dispensational truth so as to apply legal maxims to gracious dealings.

Certain texts lay emphasis on the *works of man*, like Ezekiel 18:27; Matthew 6:14–15; Luke 10:25–26, 18:18; Matt. 19:29; 25:34–35; the gospel lays stress only on the works of the Lord Jesus Christ. The new covenant rests on a wholly different basis from the old (Exodus 19:5–6). The old dispensation was founded upon a *theocracy*. Its basis was the old Sinaitic covenant: its demand was implicit obedience. But men proved themselves wholly unable to live in such covenant relations with God, under the most favorable conditions, and hence the *new* covenant, in which the contracting parties are God the Father and God the *Son*—the latter in his capacity as the new head of a fallen race (Rom. 11:32).

At the close of our Lord's earthly ministry this new covenant came into full force. Jewish worship ceased as such. The veil of the temple was significantly rent asunder; the city and temple destroyed, and the nation scattered. No man can "save his soul alive" by the best legal obedience of which he is capable.

This simplicity of *receiving*, however, brings the *having*. Hence the lesson taught in John 1:12 is emphasized peculiarly in chapter 3:16, and, in verse 36, the Holy Spirit gives it conspicuousness by an unusual mode of expression. In the original we have the one and only case of a perfect Iambic couplet with not only rhythmic feet but rhyme, a sentence which may be put into a corresponding English couplet thus:

> Whoso on the Son believeth
> Everlasting life receiveth.

Did not God mean thus to isolate this verse from its surroundings like some elevated mountain peak amid a landscape, or the grand central figure on the canvas of an artist? It is one of the great lessons on faith that life comes through believing.

The apostle John, in one other passage in his writings, again shows how faith works unto salvation in enabling us to *receive* God's testimony concerning his Son.

> If we receive the witness of men, the witness of God is greater; for this is the witness of God, which he hath testified of his Son.
>
> He that believeth on the Son of God hath the witness in himself: he that believeth not God hath made him a liar; because he believeth not the witness that God witnessed of his Son.
>
> And this is the witness, that God hath given to us eternal life, and this life is in his Son.
>
> He that hath the Son hath life; *and* he that hath not the Son of God hath not life.
>
> These things have I written unto you that believe on the name of the Son of God; that ye may know that ye have eternal life, even ye who believe on the name of the Son of God (1 John 5:9–12).

There is no more important scripture than this as containing a sort of résumé of all the fundamental truths of salvation. Even much so-called evangelical preaching is tainted with the spirit of *legalism* which evoked this epistle as well as that of Paul to the Galatians.

Note some truths herein contained:

1. One great fact: the substance of all God's witness—that God hath given to us eternal life, and that life is in his Son.

2. Hence another great fact: He that hath the Son of God hath the life; and he that hath not the Son of God hath not the life.

3. The witness of God is greater than the witness of men, and hence is to be implicitly received.

4. Not to receive it is not only to forfeit blessing, but to impugn God's own veracity; to make him a liar.

5. To receive it is to have life, and having life to have *him;* and to have the witness in *one's self!*

Here is no character described—no inward experience outlined, simply one act called for: To BELIEVE A RECORD—that God so loved that he gave, and that he that hath the Son hath life.

A half idiot, hearing these words, made them the major premise of a simple syllogism; but it brought salvation:

> CHRIST came to save sinners:
> I AM A SINNER,
> Therefore he came to save me.

How plain it is that faith is not to be confounded with, nor measured by, *feeling.* No mistake is more common than to gauge faith by conscious emotion. Faith is confidence in facts and their statement in words. Feeling is a natural *consequence* of faith, but to get our eyes on feelings rather than keep them on the facts is a fatal mistake; for the more we turn attention from facts to feelings the less feeling we have. Steam is of main importance, not for sounding the whistle but for moving the wheels; and if there is a lack of steam we shall not remedy it by attempting by our own effort to move the piston or blow the whistle, but by more water in the boiler and more fire under it. The remedy for little joy in God and his salvation is a clearer knowledge and a firmer grasp of *facts*, to turn attention away from our own frames to God's grace—not to ponder over our little joy, but over the great work of Christ which is the reason for joy.

Rev. Evan Hopkins quaintly says that fact, faith and feeling are to march in the procession in a regular order—fact leads, faith with the eye on fact, following, and feeling, with the eye on faith, bringing up the rear.

All goes well as long as this order is observed. But the moment faith turns his back on fact and looks at feeling, the procession wobbles.

Matthew Henry said that "when he wanted a faith of assurance, he lived by a faith of adherence." Yet these are not two faiths, but different degrees of faith—the faith which begins, and always begins, in adherence to Christ, and then grows into assurance. We first lay hold of Christ in his Word, and then the hold gives us an assurance that we have grasped one who is able to save to the uttermost; properly speaking, faith is only adherence, and assurance the effect of adhering.

Two other lessons in the Old Testament cluster about the word *trust* which is close of kin to the word believe.

Psalm 9:10 "They that know thy name will put their *trust* in thee." To the question, so often asked, "how can faith be increased?" it gives the only answer: *by knowing God better*. His name is his nature—his character; and those that *know* God *will* put their trust in him—not will feel that they *ought* to, for trust is not born of mere duty. Parents sometimes complain that their children do not trust them, without honestly asking whether they have shown themselves trustworthy. How many promises are made to a child that it is not meant to fulfill, and how many threats that it is not intended to carry out—both mere expedients to induce good behavior; and no one detects a lie or insincerity so instinctively as a child. The only way for a parent to insure trust is to inspire it, and then it is involuntarily exercised. So, there is but one way to learn to trust God more, and that is to learn to know him more. We must not look at our faith if we would have it grow, but look at the object of faith: to know how infinitely worthy he is of trust is to confide in him without even *willing* it. We have need only to cultivate personal, practical, living acquaintance with God, and implicit faith naturally follows such fellowship.

The prophecy of Isaiah is rich in lessons on faith. The prophet says to Ahaz in a crisis of peril, "Fear not, neither be fainthearted!... If ye will not believe surely ye shall not be established." About a hundred and forty years after, Jehoshaphat, at another crisis of battle, repeated the same sentiment, only in the positive form: "Believe in the Lord, your God; so ye shall be established; believe his prophets, so shall ye prosper" (2 Chron. 20:20). When the author of the Scriptures would mark some lesson as though to underscore it, he often uses rhyme and rhythm or a play on words. There is an assonance in the Hebrew between these two clauses which it is not easy to transfer. The effect is, "be firm in faith, or ye will not be confirmed in fact."

The Septuagint translates, *"nisi credideritis, non intelligetis."*
We might approximate the original paronomasia, thus:

> If in God ye do not confide,
> Surely in strength ye shall not abide;

or,

> If to believe ye are not able
> Neither shall ye become stable.

The thought is that in faith lies the sole secret of stability.

Chapter 26:3–4 conveys another lesson, and again in a form that no English rendering can do justice to or adequately represent. This occurs in Judah's "Song of Salvation," in the coming day of restoration, and the utmost resources of language are taxed to express the inspired thought, and particularly is that favorite figure of speech—*repetition*—resorted to, to give emphasis.

> Thou wilt garrison him in peace; peace,
> Whose mind is stayed on thee,
> Because in thee he trusteth.
> In Jehovah trust ye forever!
> For, in Jah Jehovah,
> Is the Rock of Ages.

As though overwhelmed with the vision of the eternal and unchangeable faithfulness of Jehovah, the prophet can only pile up the same words one upon another: "in *peace*, IN PEACE," as though at each repetition there were heavier stress on the word. And when he attempts to express the divine resting place of such trust, he can only think of the Rock of Ages that stands—a petrified shaft of eternity—when, like the clouds that mantle it, all temporal things vanish, and reappear and vanish a thousand times. Here occurs the only *triplicate* use of the sacred name, Jehovah, it being thrice found in this one verse, once in its abbreviated form, "Jah." That this stanza in the Song of Salvation is meant to be an inspiration to faith for all ages is shown by its being practically repeated by Paul in Phillippians 4:7:

> The peace of God, which passeth understanding, shall garrison your hearts and minds through Christ Jesus.

Here the Holy Spirit comments on his own word in Isaiah. "Peace, peace," means "peace which passes all understanding"—too deep to be sounded, too high to be measured. The word "garrison" is likewise peculiar to both passages, proving that the New Testament writer had the Old Testament prophet in mind. God's peace is his angel guard, encamping round about the praying and believing soul and assuring deliverance from anxious care.

Turning now again to the New Testament, we have in Matthew 8:10 and 15:28 the only two cases in which faith is pronounced "great;" and this suggests the question, what constitutes great faith?

Both these were *Gentiles*, and, as such, outside of covenant limits; and in the case of the woman, she was under the ban of the curse resting on the Canaanites. This makes these instances the more instructive. Our Lord could never say to any Jews, "your faith is great," though often he had to rebuke even his own disciples for "little" faith; but twice he paid this high tribute to a Gentile.

And why? Most people in those days expected all healing power to depend on his personal presence and touch, but the Centurion, when Jesus offered to come and heal his servant, answered:

> Lord, I am not worthy that thou shouldst come under my roof: but speak the word only, and my servant shall be healed.
>
> For I am a man under authority, having soldiers under me: and I say to this man, go, and he goeth; and to another, come, and he cometh; and to my servant, do this, and he doeth it.

He believed Christ able to heal by a word spoken at a distance; and that he, as Son of God, had under his control all the occult forces of the unseen realm, and could bid disease and even death "begone!" and they would obey. Our Lord found no such faith in Israel—even in Mary and Martha.

The woman of Canaan was a still more marvelous example of faith. Our Lord went from near the Galilean lake to the borders of the Mediterranean, apparently to bless this woman; for the record of the journey to and fro takes note of nothing else. Yet her repeated appeals for mercy on her afflicted daughter met at first a stubborn silence, then formal refusal, and then apparent reproach bordering on insult. Not only did the compassionate Jesus first "answer her not a word;" and then remind her that his mission was "to the lost sheep of the House of Israel," not to those whom they regarded as accursed and devouring wolves; but he finally met her agonizing prayer, "Lord, help me!" by saying: "it is not meet to take the children's bread and to cast it to dogs!" the only time he ever even appeared to insult a humble suppliant.

It is true the original is a milder term—*"little* dogs"—pups, such as were the children's pets and playmates. But we cannot account for this solitary instance of apparent harshness unless it was to draw out and exhibit her unique faith. She triumphantly turned his argument about and, taking the place he gave her as a little dog, transformed his *objection* into a *reason: "truth, Lord; yet the little dogs under the table eat of the children's crumbs that fall from their master's table!"* It was the logic and wit of importunity! The only case in which he was ever refuted out of his own mouth; and, of course, he had to give her what she sought. Our faith, in comparison to such as hers, is so small that it takes God's microscope of love to discover it!

An example of *restfulness* in such faith (John 4:46–54) is found in the man who believed the word of Jesus and went his way, so assured that he appears not to have gone home until the next day, tarrying somewhere over night.

The Epistle to the Hebrews gives two whole chapters to the triumphs of faith and the defeats which come through unbelief (11–12).

Here we are told that "faith is the substance of things hoped for, the evidence of things not seen: for by it the elders obtained a good report," or, "faith is, of things hoped for, a confidence: of facts unseen, a conviction."

The substance of this is that faith gives substantial reality and verity to what is vague and visionary without it, by reason of its distance in the future, or its indistinctness in the unseen. It brings the future near and makes vivid the invisible.

As to the statement that by it the elders or old-time believers had witness borne to them, the simplest construction is the safest, that, while their faith bore witness to God's faithfulness, his faithfulness *bore answering witness to their faith.* That this is the true interpretation the whole chapter, set to this keynote, gives proof; for every instance of victorious faith here adduced exemplifies both parts of this reciprocal witness. All these worthies testified to God by trusting him, and he testified to them that they had not trusted in vain.

Two passages in the Epistle to the Romans also are significant, and like the two from John, stand at the beginning and close like sentinels at the gates: "for obedience to the faith" (Romans 1:5), "for the obedience of faith" (16:26). This is declared to be the purpose of the worldwide preaching of the gospel, and in both cases it is the same in the original—"the obedience of faith," and it seems to emphasize the fact that faith is the mother of obedience. True believing leads to *doing* the will of God. How could it be otherwise! Believing is receiving Christ; receiving Christ brings the new birth of sonship; sonship impels to obedience. As James insists, *faith* is shown by *works*. The works do not justify the believer, but they justify the faith—they prove it genuine.

Abel bore witness to God when he offered the lamb; God bore witness to him when he had respect unto him and his offering—doubtless sending fire from heaven to consume it.

Noah conspicuously witnessed to God by building the ark and preparing for the flood, steadfastly maintaining his testimony to God's truth, amid the jeers of blaspheming rejecters and scoffers of his warning message. God witnessed to Noah by the judgments he poured out on an unbelieving world, and the mercies he showed to one believing household in their miraculous preservation.

Every man and woman mentioned in this holy succession of believers, in confidence, dependence and obedience toward God testified to him as worthy of trust and surrender; and to every such believer he gave answering testimony in such ways as suited their needs. Thus understood, the otherwise obscure statement in the opening verses of this great chapter on faith and its victories becomes not only plain but luminous: "by faith the elders had witness borne to them." This eleventh of Hebrews becomes a sort of monument built to Old Testament heroes—where each has a niche and an inscription, and over the whole memorial structure we read this double motto:

> Faith bears witness to God:
> God bears witness to faith.

The climax of all testimonies to the *power* of faith is found in our Lord's words:

> Have faith in God! For verily I say unto you, that whosoever shall say unto this mountain, "be thou removed, and be thou cast into the sea!" and shall not doubt in his heart, but shall believe that those things which he saith shall come to pass; he shall have whatsoever he saith (Mark 11:22–23).

The original injunction cannot easily be translated, but certainly means more than "have faith in God." Literally, Christ's injunction is *"hold faith of God."* As "faith" and "faithfulness" are so akin as to be often interchangeable, the thought seems to be "hold fast the faithfulness of God"—that is, *reckon on God's good faith;* and, so regarded, it goes far to unlock the whole mystery of the subject.

The statement, however, which accompanies it, ascribing to faith such unlimited power, demands further examination; and a careful comparison of this with other like utterances of our Lord may serve again to illuminate his meaning. Two other conspicuous passages, at least, contain language so strikingly similar that the three should be put side by side, that both the points of likeness and of unlikeness may be apparent.

And Jesus rebuked the demon, and he departed out of him: and the child was cured from that very hour.
    Then came the disciples to Jesus apart, and said, why could not we cast him out?
    And Jesus said unto them, because of your unbelief; for verily I say unto you, If ye have faith as a grain of mustard seed, ye shall say unto this mountain, remove hence to yonder place; and it shall remove; and nothing shall be impossible unto you.
    Matt 17:18–20
	Master, behold, the fig tree which thou cursedst is withered away.
	    And Jesus answering saith unto them. Have faith in God.
	    For verily I say unto you, that whosoever shall say unto this mountain, be thou removed, and be thou cast into the sea; and shall not doubt in his heart, but shall believe that those things which he saith shall come to pass; he shall have whatsoever he saith.
	    Mark 11:22–23
		Take heed to yourselves: if thy brother … trespass against thee, seven times in a day, and seven times in a day turn again to thee, saying, I repent; thou shalt forgive him.
		    And the apostles said unto the Lord, increase our faith.
		    And the Lord said, if ye had faith as a grain of mustard seed, ye might say unto this sycamine tree, Be thou plucked up by the root, and be thou planted in the sea; and it should obey you.
		    Luke 17:3–6

Here the emphasis is so strong upon the possibilities of faith as a wonder working power that we advance not by steps but by strides in the revelation of its importance; and several features are specially noteworthy:

First, faith is represented as *conferring authority.*

Our Lord does not say, "if ye had faith ye might *pray for* the removal of the mountain obstacle," but ye might "*say, be thou removed!*" This is the language of a *fiat*—"let it be so!" God alone issues a fiat, as when he said "let light be," and light was. It is the obvious intention here to teach that faith so unites the believer to God as that *he wields in some sense divine power and authority.* The reference to the "grain of mustard seed" is not to its *size* so much as to its *sort*—to the fact that *it hides in itself the life principle.* The mountain, however large, is but a mass of dead matter, inert, and cannot move itself an inch. But the mustard seed, however small, has life's vital energy and is capable of *growth*—of that strange motion downward, upward and outward which makes possible for the least of seeds to become greatest of herbs. He who is one by faith with God, one by nature with him, learns to wield supernatural power. Spiritual life has its own omnipotent energy and can uplift and remove obstacles that, however gigantic, are, in comparison, but *dead.*

Secondly, this confidence of faith rises to the height of *expectancy.* "Believe that ye *have* received them" is beyond even "and shall not doubt in his heart, but shall believe that those things which he saith *shall* come to pass." Here is a glimpse of how faith rises from height to height of assurance: first, believing without doubt that God's power *will* be exerted and his promise *will* be fulfilled, and then rising higher and believing that it is *already done.* We have a way of expressing similar confidence in men of truth and integrity; we say of a promise from such, "it is as good as *done.*" Much of our business is carried on, on the basis of such faith in others' word or promissory note. A promise to pay in three months is discounted at the bank as though the money were already on deposit. Infinitely more when we have God's promise may we count it as *already fulfilled* and build on it securely.

We read in 1 John 5:14–15: "This is the confidence which we have in him, that if we ask anything according to his will he heareth us:

"And if we know that he hear us, whatsoever we ask, we know that we have the petitions that we desired of him."

We know that we *have* the petitions that we desired of him. In God's action there is no *time* element necessary. "He speaks and it is done." His promise like himself is the same yesterday and today and forever. Thus faith comes to count with such certainty on his faithfulness that the believer's confidence reckons on what he says as already done and goes forward fearlessly, believes in coming good as present experience, enters into its enjoyment beforehand and praises him for what he is about to do.

Further light is thrown on these amazing possibilities of faith when we compare the *occasions* on which such words were spoken.

In one case, a *fig tree* has been withered by a word; in another a *demon* cast out; and in another an *evil disposition* is referred to as thus uprooted. These suggest three departments for the exercise of power, which curiously cover and comprehend the whole range and scope of its operation. The fig tree represents material nature: the demon, the unseen realm of spirits, and the disposition—the stronghold of the self-life. Our Lord seems to teach thus a threefold lesson: that if in the blind forces of nature we meet obstacles that need removal, or in the malignant and intelligent forces of the demon world, or in the deep rooted resentment of our own unsanctified nature—to any or all of them an undoubting faith is equal; and the reason is because such faith is born of God; his seed remaineth in it, and it has the secret of his life and power; and, like any other seed, needs only right conditions for the exercise of its vital energy to demonstrate its true potency.

We are reminded how minute seeds, dropping between the stones, have heaved them apart in the castle of Banias in Syria; and how, when an infidel countess directed that her dust should be guarded from all "resurrection" by huge blocks of granite, again little seeds, borne by the wind and growing in the interstices, crowded the blocks to one side and exposed her costly sarcophagus.

Faith so unites the believer with God as to make him, in his finite measure, a partaker of his nature, a sharer of his attributes, a wielder of his power. When the seer of old laid hold of God's omniscience, he saw through God's eyes both into the past and future. When holy men laid hold of God's omnipotence, they used his power and wrought miracles. Our Lord tells us that faith carries the potency of the divine vitality and makes the undoubting believer a perpetual miracle worker. He has in him the energy that moves masses of matter and withers fig trees; he has in him the almighty Spirit, who drives out demons; he has in him the great renewer of disposition, that plucks up the deep rooted growths of evil and malicious temper and makes plants of godliness grow in their place. How little do we know of such faith!

The power of faith may be due in part to the fact that it is the foe of all slavish *fear*. It is said of perfect love that it casts out fear which is tormenting or brings punishment (1 John 4:18)—the *fear* that inflicts torture creates unrest and disquietude. This is equally true of perfect faith, which is twin sister to perfect love; and this truth may have a far wider bearing than we imagine.

One of the great scientific discoveries of our day is that every mental emotion leaves its physical traces and produces direct effects in the body. The *breathing* betrays anger, resentment, impatience or even excitement—so does the pulse. The microscope reveals in the *blood* the effect of all moods, especially what are morbid. The psychologist predicates fear, as characteristic of the mind, when he finds certain excited or irregular action of the heart; and a skilled microscopist, by close examination of blood corpuscles, can trace the influence of dominant emotions.

This may in a measure account for some of the cures effected by Christian Science. In the "treatment" which these strange practitioners use, their first aim is to persuade the patient that disease and pain are not *real*, but imaginations of "mortal mind;" *mental* fancies rather than physical facts, and therefore that to *believe* them to be unreal is to banish them. They are treated as ghosts of the mind, illusions of the imagination, torturing their victims because their credulity and superstition invest them with actuality. When such persuasion fully possesses the mind, *fear* gives way to a sort of *faith*. The sick man believes he has really no disease. The shadow of prospective suffering, perhaps of near death, is dissipated, and calmness takes the place of agitation. Possibly this is the explanation of many cures. It has long been known to those accustomed to visit sick beds that if they can inspire *hope*, the sick improve—that to create confidence in recovery is better than any medicine. I have seen an apparently dying woman rise from her bed in a half hour when authoritatively assured that she was only the victim of hysteria; and a man helplessly awaiting an operation recover health with incredible swiftness when told by both physician and surgeon that there was actually no need of the knife. Charles H. Spurgeon used to tell how, in a cholera visitation, when exhausted by visits to the sick and dying, he felt the symptoms of the disease, he caught a glimpse of the promise from the ninety-first psalm: "he that dwelleth in the secret place," etc., in a shop window; and at once taking refuge in that promise, all fear disappeared and with it all symptoms of disease. Faith may have power as a *therapeutic* yet undreamed of, and the Word of God often refers to those who "have faith to be healed" (Acts 3:16).

All great forces have their conductors and nonconductors. One of the greatest problems to be settled before electricity could be harnessed to mechanism, as a motor, messenger and illuminator was to determine what media were and what were not conductors. There is virtue in God for all ills bodily, mental, spiritual, and there are conductors and non-conductors. The multitude thronged and pressed our Lord, coming into the close contact of a crowd, yet no virtue went out of him until faith touched him in that woman's hand. Faith is the great conductor of divine blessing. Fear is a non-conductor, as to God, but the Devil's conductor, conveying all diabolical suggestion and malicious interpretation of God.

Peter's faith made him light and buoyant and he walked on the water to go to Jesus. But when *fear* was aroused it made him heavy and he began to sink. While his eye was on Jesus a supernatural power was his. When the daughter of Jairus was *dead*, even then our Lord said, "be not afraid, only believe!" and Psalm 91, the great psalm of immunity from disease, even epidemics of plague, sounds for its keynote, "*thou shalt not be afraid.*"[24]

For all evils in the life of the believer and of the church God has provided remedies, and one of the foremost of them is faith. There are three distinct spheres for the operation of faith, and in each of them it has a special and definite character of its own which particularly fits it for that particular realm. The three spheres are salvation, sanctification, and service. In the sphere of salvation, faith simply *receives;* in that of sanctification, it goes further, and *reckons;* in the sphere of service, it goes

---

24 The bishop of London tells how the wife of one of his clergy, faced with the prospect of an operation which might cost her her life, was, when he visited her, in a state of moral collapse. The physicians and surgeons recognized that the operation could not be performed while she was in that state. He spent a sacred half hour with her, and two days later she walked from her room to the operating table without a quiver. The surgeons exclaimed, "what has the bishop done to you?" She replied, "something that none of you could have done!" The bishop referred to the incident simply as showing that healing and sustaining forces may be exerted upon the body by high exercises of the soul. He adds that by the use of this one truth the so-called Christian Science propaganda has attained its present proportions. Heresy flourishes by the amount of truth it contains. The crude thinking and the absurd pretensions of this cult would never have had the influence they have if the church on the one hand, and the medical profession on the other, had recognized the immense power, amounting often to what seems the miraculous, of the higher mental states upon physical conditions. It is now for both these departments of service to recover their lost ground.

still further, and *risks*. Three leading texts may be selected to set forth representatively these great truths, each of them unique in its way:

John 1:12: "But as many as received him, even to them that believe on his name, gave he power (authority) to become the sons of God." Here *believing* on his name is made equivalent to *receiving* him, and is the one condition of becoming the sons of God.

Acts 26:18: "... inheritance among them which are sanctified by faith that is in me." Here faith in the Lord Jesus is made as vital to sanctification as it is elsewhere to justification.

Philippians 2:17: "... the sacrifice and service (or ministration) of your faith." Paul represents himself as a libation of blood poured out upon the sacrifice and service of their faith and offered to God.

These three representative passages suffice to present this threefold thought—that faith has a saving, a sanctifying, and a serving aspect; and it is important now to learn how it is that faith operates in these its several spheres.

(1) SALVATION lies at the foundation of all the rest; and here, therefore, faith is seen in its simplest possible form and exercise. Salvation is offered unto all, and hence it must be adapted to the worst and the weakest. If there were in it anything hard to understand or perform, it would be removed from the capacity of the very souls who need it most. Sin has two marked effects—it both cripples the will and weakens the mind. Men sunk in sin are found to be not much above the beasts. God shows himself to be a gracious God by bringing salvation near to the least and the lowest. None are so bad as to be beyond hope, and none so feeble-minded as to be beyond understanding. Here, then, faith must be very simple, or it could not reach the most needy.

And the faith that saves does nothing, therefore, but *take God's free gift*. Several words are used, such as: "look," "hear," "taste," "take," "come," "trust," "choose." These words all convey the idea of some form of *reception*—with the eyes, ears, mouth, hands, feet, heart, and will. He who knows enough to throw away a worthless bauble and reach out and take instead a priceless treasure knows enough to give up his own hopeless efforts and accept the finished work of Christ.

Thus the child in years, or in understanding, may become the receiver of all the blessing implied in salvation. It takes very little knowledge or intelligence to accept God's free gift—eternal life.

(2) SANCTIFICATION is the experience of one already saved but desirous of being delivered from sin's *power* and *control* as well as penalty, and made godlike. This stage demands a higher exercise of faith because those who have learned the first lesson are further on than before and better prepared for the second.

In sanctification, the great word for faith is *"reckon"* (Romans 6:2)—a word which means to *count upon a thing as true.* The Lord Jesus seems to have the same thought in mind in Mark 11:22: count upon God's faithfulness. He assures you of his own presence with you and in you by his Spirit. Receive his assurance and reckon on his fidelity. Learn habitually to think of yourself as God thinks of you. Count upon his love and grace and power.

There are at least three grand representative experiences in which such reckoning faith proves the all-sufficient secret: *temptation*, in which we reckon on his power to resist and overcome; *trial*, in which we reckon on his power to strengthen and support; and *temper*, in which we reckon on his power to subdue and transform. Such reckoning on God is plainly a further exercise of faith's *receptive* power. It goes so far as to appropriate God's strength. It lays hold of omnipotence and finds his strength made perfect in weakness, and at the very point of weakness most manifesting its wonderful potency.

(3) The third sphere of faith is SERVICE, which expresses what is *rendered unto him*. In salvation and sanctification something is rendered unto us—received and appropriated from him; but in service the whole nature goes out in response to him, seeking to offer something that he can receive. Hence it represents the highest exercise of faith, and implies both the others. It represents the sphere in which the saved and sanctified soul seeks to do the will of God and glorify him by a surrender of spirit, soul, and body as a grateful offering.

Here the conspicuous Bible word is *"witness,"* and as we have seen in the great chapters, Hebrews 11–12, specially, the triumphs of faith and service are most fully set forth. In 11:39 we are told how all these heroes had *witness borne to them*, and in 12:1 they are presented as *bearing witness*. Those who have already "believed to the saving of the soul" are now put before us as bearing witness to God.

But let it be observed that this bearing witness to God always implies a *risk* or *venture*. There is an abandonment of self to God, and *in this mainly the witness consists*. Noah withstood a corrupt and unbelieving world and risked everything on God's being true. Abraham went out not knowing whither he went, and even laid his son of promise on the altar, trusting God to raise him from the dead. Moses renounced Egypt, with all its treasures and pleasures, and undertook to lead a vast host into a wilderness, depending on God to supply all needs. In 11:32–40 we have a brief résumé of the triumphs of faith, and the one great feature in all these lives of witnesses is the risk run, the venture of faith upon God—Gideon, with his three hundred and only lamps and pitchers; Daniel going unarmed into the lions' den, and the three Hebrew children into the fiery furnace; Jonathan and his armor-bearer daring to advance against a whole garrison; Joshua trusting God and taking Jericho without a blow struck or any dependence on carnal weapons. Every true servant of God accepts some such a venture for God. That is his way of witnessing, and God always honors such witnessing by proving his faithfulness.

In faith is found also the potent remedy for all the evils of materialism, secularism, rationalism, ritualism—whatever hinders individual or church development. It keeps the soul in the attitude of waiting on, and receiving from, God. It bends the energies of the saved soul upon that higher salvation found in actual likeness to Christ; and hence whatever is unlike him or hinders assimilation to him will be detected and detested. No believer can be absorbed in Godlikeness and at the same time engrossed in worldliness. He will see that some things divide attention, divert affection, and make spiritual duties and delights distasteful; and he will naturally turn from them. Godly people are always conspicuous for faith—for simple faith. They begin by the simple receiving from him of salvation; then they advance a stage further and learn the secret of reckoning on him for all he promises; and then they find it easy to advance to the point of risking everything for him, whom they find can be reckoned on to keep his word. His truth is his troth.

From first to last, then, faith is the secret. It makes salvation ours by appropriation; it makes sanctification ours by assimilation; it makes service ours by cooperation and identification.

Chapter 10

The Problem of Prayer

The supreme practical importance of this subject entitles it to more exhaustive treatment, and the biblical teaching upon it to the more prominence.

1. There are certain prominent *conditions* of prevailing prayer

1. Sin no longer cherished but forsaken.

If I REGARD INIQUITY in my heart, the Lord will not hear me (Psa. 66:18).

2. A forgiving spirit toward others.

When ye stand praying, FORGIVE, if ye have ought against any (Mark 11:25).

3. A spiritual, not a carnal motive.

Ye ask, and receive not because YE ASK AMISS, that ye may consume it upon your lusts (James 4:3).

4. Asking earnestly, importunately.

Ask, and it shall be given you;
Seek, and ye shall find;
Knock, and it shall be opened unto you (Matt. 7:7).

5. Asking in the confidence of faith.

What things soever ye desire, when ye pray, BELIEVE THAT YE RECEIVE them, and ye shall have them (Mark 11:24).

6. Asking according to God's will.

This is the confidence that we have in him, that, if we ask any thing ACCORDING TO HIS WILL, he heareth us (1 John 5:14).

7. Asking always in Jesus' name.

Verily, verily, I say unto you, whatsoever ye shall ask the Father IN MY NAME, he will give it you (John 16:23; 14:13–14).

2. The Bible addresses rich promises to praying souls

1. The possibilities of faith.

If thou canst believe, all things are possible to him that believeth (Mark 9:23).

2. The immediateness of help.

Before they call, I will answer; and while they are yet speaking, I will hear (Isa. 65:24; Dan. 9:20–23).

3. The unlimited supply of grace.

My God shall supply all your need according to his riches in glory by Christ Jesus (Phil. 4:19).

4. The power of abiding in Christ.

If ye abide in me, and my words abide in you, ye shall ask what ye will, and it shall be done unto you (John 15:7). Compare Rom. 8:26.

5. The perfect peace of prayer.

Be careful for nothing: but in every thing by prayer and supplication with thanksgiving let your requests be made known unto God. And the peace of God, which passeth all understanding, shall keep your hearts and minds through Christ Jesus (Phil. 4:6-7).

6. The abundant ability of God.

Able to do exceeding abundantly above all we ask or think, according to the power that worketh in us (Eph. 3:20).

7. The agreement of praying souls.

If two of you shall agree on earth as touching anything that they shall ask, it shall be done for them of my Father which is in heaven (Matt. 18:19).

3. Scripture history furnishes examples of prayer; especially of prevailing intercession

1. Abraham interceding for Sodom.

Gen. 18:22–33; 19:29.

2. Moses interceding for Israel.

Ex. 32:30–34; Num. 14:11–21.

3. Samuel interceding for king and people.

1 Sam. 7:5–12; 12:16–25.

4. Elijah interceding for fire and rain.

1 Kings 18:36–46; James 5:17, 18.

5. Daniel interceding for captive Hebrews.

Dan. 2:16–23; 9:3–23.

6. Paul interceding for prisoners and saints.

Acts 16:25, 26; Eph. 1:15–23; 3:14–21.

7. Jesus interceding for a lost world.

Matt. 26:37–46; Heb. 5:7.[25]

If faith belongs at the basis of all life in God, prayer belongs at the top. Faith is rudimental; prayer is monumental; one, a corner stone, on which all is built; the other, a capstone, in which all that is built reaches climax of completeness. Faith makes possible the highest achievement, and prayer *is* the achievement, beyond whose possibilities there seems to lie nothing more.

First of all, then, is needed a knowledge of *what prayer is*. The definition in the Westminster Catechism is: "prayer is the offering up of our desires unto God, for things agreeable to his will, in the name of Christ, with confession of our sins, and thankful acknowledgment of his mercies."

This definition is scarcely complete, for it contains no reference to that highest revelation of prayer which represents it as the very voice of the Spirit of God interceding in us and "for us with groanings which cannot be uttered;" and it takes no account of that highest mystery of prayer—as

25 Those who would still further study the promises to the prayerful would do well to examine carefully the following, among many others: Hebrews 11:6; James 1:5–7; Matthew 6:6–8; James 5:16–18; Luke 18:1–8; Matthew 9:28–29; Mark 11:22–24; Hebrews 4:14–16; Psalm 145:18–19; James 5:14–18; 1 John 3:21–22; etc.

communion with God, in which we not only speak to him but he to *us*—a privilege first hinted in Num. 7:89:

> When Moses was gone into the tabernacle of the congregation to speak with him, then he heard the voice of one, speaking unto him from off the mercy-seat that was upon the ark of testimony, from between the two cherubims: and he spake unto him.

The supreme triumph of the praying soul is not found in supplication to God but in revelation of God.

> In a vision and a voice divine
> Not a venture and a voice of mine.

This explains our Lord's all-night prayers—not so much all-night asking or interceding as a spreading out of his whole spirit before the Father, as Gideon spread out his fleece on the plains of Jezreel to get it filled with the heavenly dew. The closet is not an oratory only, but an observatory—a place of vision.

Our Lord therefore explicitly teaches, in his first great lesson on prayer, that the praying suppliant must, above all else, cultivate the habit of absolute *aloneness with God in the closet*, or closed chamber of communion.

> But thou, when thou prayest, enter into thy closet, and when thou hast shut thy door, pray to thy Father, which is in secret; and thy Father, which seeth in secret, shall reward thee openly (Matt. 6:6).

This brief sentence contains eight times the second personal pronoun, singular, "thou," "thee," "thy;" which is implied twice more in the verbs used—making ten times in all—something unique in the Word of God.

There is this intense emphasis on the singular number because the first lesson in prayer is that we must shut ourselves *in with God alone* in order to a vision of God. The greatest necessity of spiritual life is "to believe that he *is* and is a rewarder of those that diligently seek him." He can never be a reality to us unless we meet him habitually, when no one else is present. In that secret chamber where the human spirit is shut in with him alone, the believer learns to know God, and to "endure as seeing him who is invisible." The great danger is that, being invisible, he will seem *unreal*, while what is *seen* fascinates and absorbs attention; and for this tendency toward materialism the "closet" is the perpetual corrective, intended to bring heaven near and keep it near. PRAYER is therefore more than an asking; it is a receiving, a waiting, a learning of God, a converse and communion, in which he has much to say and we have much to hear and learn.

To know God as he is known only in this closed chamber is prayer's first triumph, and it is a continuous victory. To learn to make unseen things vivid and visible, and the invisible God indisputably real, actual and true—this comes nearest to solving all other spiritual perplexities and removing all other spiritual difficulties. It makes one go forth from the "closed" place to the "open"—the outside world of strife and turmoil, of unreality and unverity, of hallucination and temptation, illusion and delusion, in an all sufficient panoply.

Coleridge, referring to earlier and skeptical utterances on prayer, pronounced them folly, and solemnly said: "Prayer is the highest possible exercise of the human soul."

The following are some of the main points of Bible teaching as to prayer:

1. It may be offered "in the name of Jesus Christ," that is, by virtue of our identity with him (John 16:23–27).

2. By the inward moving and intercession of the Spirit of God (Rom. 8:15, 26–27).

3. It is inseparable from our calling and ordination to service (John 15:16).

4. It is often the only relief in deep distress (Psa. 130:1–2).

5. It is the natural resort of the child who realizes that he has a heavenly Father (Matt. 7:7–11).

6. It has the definite promise of unlimited power, where there is unlimited faith (James 1:6, 7; Mark 11:22–24).

7. It finds access with boldness in the mediation of the Lord Jesus (Heb. 4:15–16).

The prayer realm may be divided, like the earth, into three distinct zones: the torrid, temperate and frigid. If so, surely the frigid zone is ice-locked by the notion that God is amenable to no law, and controlled by no element in the life of the petitioner, but can and does answer earnest prayer, if at all, purely from the impulse of his own arbitrary will and power. Those who hold this view never know exactly where or how to find God, or in just what mood he will be found in reference to the special end desired, if found at all. This wrong view slanderously charges God's will, rather than the petitioner's life, with much of the failure to receive answers.

Of course, the *conditions of acceptable prayer* need to be carefully mastered. *All known sin* blocks prayer: as Bunyan says, the sinning kills the praying, if the praying does not kill the sinning. *Resentment* arrests prayer, for the platform of prayer is *grace*—favor to the undeserving; and to cherish an unforgiving spirit is to abandon the very attitude of dependence on mercy. *Carnal motives* hinder prayer, which is essentially the breathing of spiritual desire, and which fleshly lusts stifle. *Earnestness* and *patient waiting* are the tests of the depth of such desire and the sincerity of the seeking. *Unbelief* makes God a liar or at best a capricious promiser, and hence we must have confidence in his truth and faithfulness. There must be *harmony of wills* between God and the suppliant, otherwise prayer would only promote resistance and rebellion. And to ask in *Jesus' name* is the assurance of answer, since he becomes the real suppliant when we pray, pleading his merit as our ground of acceptance.

These are the main *conditions* and bear any amount of study.

So do the *promises*. The Word of God represents all the possibilities of God as at the disposal of true prayer. Help is at hand, and often comes before the prayer is yet complete, because he hears the unspoken sigh and groan. God's supplies are inexhaustible; his ability and willingness are both infinite; hence his answers often transcend all our requests or even imaginings. When the praying suppliant abides in Christ, as the branch in the vine, his supplications are but one form of the development and expression of the life of Christ in him, just as the buds, blossoms and clusters of the branch are expressions of the vine's vitality. Prayer brings peace by banishing care, transferring burdens to the great burden bearer. Special promises are addressed to those who *agree*—not the agreement of mutual sympathy only, but of *symphony* with God, brought first into accord with him, and so with each other.

The examples adduced in Scripture serve both to illustrate the principles of prayer and to encourage the habit, for the successful human intercessors were all men "of like passions as we"—even the Lord himself being "compassed about with infirmity" like ourselves; and because other believers have prayed and prevailed, so may we.

Certain great *facts* about prayer loom up before us, which need to be more distinctly seen and felt.

1. The *wealth of the assurances* addressed to praying believers. There are probably thirty thousand promises in the Word of God, and of them all the larger class pertain to prayer, more or less directly.

2. The *universal terms* used—all the unconditional phrases are applied to prayer: "whosoever," "whatsoever," "wheresoever," "whensoever," "all," "any," "every"—God means there shall be no mistake about this.

3. The *abundant testimony* to a prayer-hearing God—unimpeachable witnesses, sufficient in number, competent in judgment, trustworthy in character, varied in experience, and in all ages.

4. Yet, *shameful neglect* of prayer—nothing within the whole range of Christian duty and privilege so infrequent and inadequate, so empty, formal and heartless when done, and, with the average disciple, so dragged down from its divine elevation to a disgracefully low spiritual level.

Sixteen words deserve to be put before us in bold capitals as covering the whole problem:

> YE HAVE NOT, BECAUSE YE ASK NOT:
> YE ASK AND RECEIVE NOT,
> BECAUSE YE ASK AMISS (James 4:2–3).

Ten thousand gifts and blessings we fail to get, simply because we fail even to *ask* for them; ten thousand more we fail to get, because, when we do ask, we fail to ask as we *ought*. Either we neglect prayer altogether, or else in praying, we neglect to observe the conditions within which alone prayer can be acceptably or prevailingly offered.

Into this matter of asking amiss and asking aright it is our present purpose to enter with special care, inasmuch as here lie the very secrets of failure.

At the threshold of this theme, over against all this affluence of invitation and promise, we meet certain awful admonitions and prohibitions. In some directions there is a *closed door before prayer*. Even its boundless possibilities have a fixed limit, beyond which it is vain to attempt to go. God's restraints are not physical but *moral*. He can do anything that lies within the range of *power*, but he cannot deny himself or violate moral law. Because prayer pertains to the moral realm, it is subject to moral limitations, and these are its only boundaries. But he who would pray well, both believingly and prevailingly, must learn how far to go, and where to halt. It is of no use to knock at a door that cannot open, or beat our heads against a wall of adamant. We note some of these Scripture limitations:

1. *Man's barter is irrevocable.* Esau sold his birthright for a mess of pottage, and the birthright blessing went with the birthright heritage. Though Jacob got the blessing by fraud, behind his trickery lay the

permission of the God of the birthright. Jacob's crime of lying succeeded at his father's bedside, but Esau's crime of selling had forfeited what his brother fraudulently obtained. And, when the prophetic word had been spoken it could not be unsaid. Esau sought with tears a change of mind in his father, but in vain. However Isaac himself might regret both Jacob's deceit and his own mistake, he had spoken in the name of God, who had permitted the blessing to go to the brother who had, in Esau's deliberate bargain and barter, bought the right to the birthright succession and all that went with it.

There are many "profane persons" and spiritual "fornicators" like Esau, not a few of whom are in the church of God; who make a barter of spiritual privileges, opportunities and blessings—a barter which not even repentance will undo; a forfeiture which not even prayer will restore. Even God cannot give back a lost day or hour. While life is *before* us, it may be used for God and humanity or for self and carnality. If wrongly used, and so abused, how can the crime be undone! When life is *behind* us, it is no longer improvable, but irrevocable. We may repent of what is worse than waste, but the waste remains. This we believe to be the real point of our Lord's question: "What shall a man give in exchange for his life?" to buy it back, when once it is gone! If he would gladly give back the world for which he sold it, both the world and the life are gone together!

2. *God's decrees are irreversible.* When Moses, again and again, pleaded to be permitted to go over Jordan into the land of promise and so complete his work of leadership, God finally said to him, "speak no more to me of this matter, for thou shalt not go over this Jordan" (Deut. 3:25–27). He who was one of God's mightiest intercessors, ranking with such as Noah and Job, Samuel and Daniel, Elijah and Paul, was told by the very Jehovah whom he knew face to face as no other had ever known him, to *desist*. He had publicly dishonored God at Meribah by a second smiting of the once smitten rock—which was the type of him who was once for all smitten for us—and yet he had been expressly told to *speak* to the rock, and knew that he was in no respect to depart from "the pattern showed him on the mount." God, for that offence, which undoubtedly had a deep typical bearing, determined that he should not enter with the people into the land of their inheritance; and his decree could not be changed even at Moses' prayer.

3. There are *limits of fitness*—a time for everything. Prayer cannot take the place of obedience. Only what is seasonable is also reasonable.

Jehovah said, at the Red Sea, "wherefore criest thou unto me! Speak unto the children of Israel that they go forward!" It was not a time or place for mere supplication—asking was to give place to acting. The Lord had already given them assurance of their deliverance, and that he would fight for them and destroy their foes. It was not a time to breathe a prayer or cry aloud for help: that cry had been heard and answered; and prompt, courageous action and advance were now demanded. We may prolong our prayers unduly, waiting on our face before God when he is commanding us to be up, on our feet, and going forward.

4. *Discipline has its necessities.* Prayer cannot always avert a providential blow. David had sinned a great sin—and sinned publicly. He had taken another man's wife and, to keep her, had got that other man out of the way; and now the child born of that crime was dying. David went fasting and praying before the Lord to plead for the life of the child. But Nathan said—"it shall surely die." No prayer could avert that chastisement. God would not set a premium upon adultery, deception and murder. The fruit of that abominable and multiplied sin must not abide. It was doomed. The penitent sinner still needed the scourge, and the Father could not spare his rod because of the child's cries.

5. *Judicial penalties also set limits.* Temporal judgments are sometimes necessary as sanctions of God's law. Especially is this true of *nations*, which, as such, have no existence beyond this world and whose penalties must come within the bounds of time. There are times when a whole nation has been guilty of some great wrong, and righteousness in God demands retribution, as Lincoln sublimely said at Gettysburg. Though Job, Noah, Moses, Samuel and Daniel were together to appeal to God, his mind could not be toward his people to save them from judgment (Jer. 15:1; Ezek. 14:4).

6. *Intercession has its limits.* Sometimes the cup of human iniquity becomes full and overflows. When that is the case no plea is of any avail. There is nothing left but a deluge of water or a rain of fire. Sodom could not be saved even by Abraham's importunity, nor Jerusalem by prophets' pleading, when even chief priests and rulers had conspired to put the Son of God to death, and followed his crucifixion by Stephen's stoning. The bounds of God's forbearance were passed. Sin had transcended the limits of even divine patience. When the "three years" of letting alone, digging about and dunging the barren fig tree, had brought only new cumbering of the ground, the axe was irrevocably laid at the root of the tree.

7. Once more, *there is a sin unto death*—and John says, with awful suggestiveness: "I do not say that he shall pray for it" (1 John 5:6).

What this sin is we may not be sure, perhaps, but because there is such a sin, it behooves us to beware, for no prayer can pierce that death shade. Alford makes it an appreciable *act*, the *denying Jesus to be the Christ, the Son of God,* which willful deliberate denial John elsewhere accounts a sufficient ground for not wishing a man "Godspeed" or receiving him into the house. But the *state* of apostasy which makes such an act possible is undoubtedly included. This sin, whatever it be, is one that may be detected in a *"brother"*—a professed disciple—which makes the warning more terrible. And no fact is more significant than this—that, when a disciple has once radically departed from the faith and practice of godliness, and even goes so far as to deny the Lord that bought him and blaspheme his name, history may be safely challenged to produce one unmistakable case of restoration to his lost faith and love! If so, history may perhaps be a sufficient expositor in this case.

Planes of Answer:

4	Apparently Unheeded	Restful Faith.
3	Denied and yet Answered	Submissive Faith.
2	Delayed and Disguised	Importunate Faith.
1	Immediate and Obvious	Plane of Sight.

Acceptable Asking:

4	In the Power of the Spirit	The Holy Spirit as Intercessor
3	In the Name of Christ	Christ as Mediator
2	In a Filial Spirit	God as Father.
1	In Simple Desire	God as Giver.

Vain Asking:

4	In unbelief	Without Expectation.
3	As a form.	Heart Alien from God.
2	Asking Amiss	Selfish Motive.
1	In Sin.	Insult to Holy God.

9. Planes of Prayer and Answer

In the table are represented the *Planes of Prayer and Answer.* The lowest group of four represent vain asking; the next four above, acceptable asking; and the uppermost four, the various levels of divine answer; and the design is to convey the idea of a constant ascent from the lowest spiritual state or experience to the higher and more exalted.

Of *vain* asking, the first and lowest level is that of *known sin*—sin that is "regarded in the heart"—that is, cherished (Ps. 66:18). In such case one may as well not pray at all, for the suppliant who willfully and habitually sins against his sovereign only adds insult by such prayer. Hence "the sacrifice of the wicked is an abomination to the Lord" (Prov. 15:8). God does not demand sinlessness in a suppliant, but he cannot abide willful continuance in sin; there must be at least the *will* to obey.

James teaches that he asks "amiss" whose *motive* is carnal self-in-dulgence—to consume God's gifts upon his lusts; as when one asks for pleasure, money or position simply to indulge appetite, avarice and ambi-tion. At "Kibroth Hataavah," "the graves of the lusters," were buried the thousands who clamored for flesh, and it passed into a proverb that God "gave them their request, but sent leanness into their soul" (Num. 11; Ps. 106:15).

Again, mere *formal prayer* is vain. This is drawing near with the mouth, and honoring with the lips, while the heart is far removed from God (Isa. 29:13). The Pharisees, who paraded their long prayers on street corners that they might have glory of men while they were devouring widows' houses, only incurred "greater condemnation;" and it is useless to attempt to impose on God by a *show* of devotion. He sees not as man sees, judging not by outward appearance, but looking on the heart.

Even on the higher level, where there is no voluntary continuance in sin, no carnal motive, and no insincerity, there may still be an *unbelief* that forfeits blessing. James, whose epistle contains more hints on the causes of failure in prayer than any other, at the outset points out a *lack of faith* as the first hindrance (1:5–7). "He that cometh to God must believe that he is, and is a rewarder of them that diligently seek him" (Heb. 11:6).

Of all this vain, ineffective praying, one general word may be said: if God should grant all that men ask, in many cases it would be a curse rather than a blessing; it is often a mercy that he withholds. Agrippina, mother of Nero, besought her gods to spare her son and set him on the throne; but to his ascendancy she owed her own assassination. When Hezekiah was told to set his house in order, that he should die, he turned his face to the wall and begged for life. He had as yet no son and heir, and thought it a calamity to his kingdom to leave no succession. The Lord granted him fifteen years more, but those years added nothing to his glory or that of his kingdom. He incurred divine displeasure and excited man's cupidity by the ostentatious display of his princely treasures to the emissaries of Babylon; and though, during those fifteen years, he begat Manasseh, that son proved the Ahab of Judah, the greatest curse of that kingdom, and the main cause of Judah's captivity. So far as we can see, it had been far better for both Hezekiah and the kingdom of Judah had he died when he had warning, and not had that fifteen years of respite.

Even in *acceptable* asking there are degrees of prevailing power. The lowest plane of true prayer is that of genuine *spiritual desire*, or yearning, as when David, as God's servant, found it in his heart to pray a prayer unto him (2 Sam. 7:27). But if to such sincerity of heart there be added the *filial spirit*, the confidence of a child in God as a Father, we rise to a higher level. Our Lord makes much of this, as an argument and an encouragement, in that great exposition of prayer in Matthew 6, where he reminds us of God's care for the *sparrows* whom he feeds and the *lilies* whom he clothes. The birds of the air cannot appeal to him as Father, and the flowers of the field cannot even consciously feel their needs and appeal to him as creator; how much more then may his *children* who can recognize in him not only a creator but a Father plead with him in filial confidence. If he cares for his dumb creatures, and even his material creation, how much more his redeemed sons who combine in themselves all appeals in one.

We rise still higher when we pray *in the name of Christ*. In our Lord's new lesson on prayer, which is seven times urged in his last discourse on the eve of his death (John 14:13–24), he teaches disciples the power of *conscious unity and identity with himself*, which makes us even bolder than the sense of our sonship and God's Fatherhood. For it is plain that when we ask in Christ's name, *he* is the *real petitioner*. Whenever men use another's name as the authority for approach and appeal to a fellow man, and for a request that they could not urge without such sanction or warrant, it is obvious that he to whom the request is addressed *looks past* him who *presents* the petition to the party whom he sees behind the request, and for whose sake he grants the favor. Because our own name carries no weight, we use another's. So it is no irreverence to say that whenever we ask in the name of Christ, the Father looks past us and sees his Son as the real suppliant. This is emphasized as a new lesson: *"hitherto have ye asked nothing in my name."* No Old Testament saint, nor up to that time had any New Testament disciple, ever understood this high privilege, because the relation of Christ to his disciple had never been fully revealed.

If any level of prayer can be higher, it is when to all these—sincere desire, the filial spirit, and the claim of discipleship—is added a conscious *inward groaning of the Holy Spirit* (Rom. 8:26–27). In this case it is God, the Spirit himself, who is pleading in us. He guides our desires, he shapes our utterance, if indeed the yearnings he awakens do not transcend all language; he displaces carnal by spiritual motives; he teaches us, in conscious sonship, to cry "Abba, Father;" and himself practically *does the praying*. How mighty in prayer must the believer become when these fourfold conditions all meet in him! Then is that verse made real—the only one in which all three persons of the godhead are linked in relation to prayer: "*through him* (the Lord Jesus Christ) we have access *by* one *Spirit* unto the *Father*" (Eph. 2:18). We pray in the Spirit, for the Spirit prays in us.

As to the four planes of *answer*, their respective levels are determined by the measure of *faith* they demand. The lowest is where the answer is *immediate and obvious;* it comes at once and as expected, like that of Abraham's steward at the well (Gen. 24:14-15). This makes no demand on faith or patience. But sometimes the answer is *delayed, or disguised*, or both. When Elijah prayed for rain, seven times his servant reported "nothing;" and Daniel for three full weeks fasted and prayed before the answering vision refreshed him. Paul prayed for guidance in going to Philippi, but when he and Silas found only a scourge, a prison cell, and the stocks, it took faith to read God's answer in such disguise. Delays are not refusals. Many a prayer is registered, and underneath it the words— "my time is not yet come." God has a set time and way as well as a set purpose.

Sometimes the literal prayer is *denied*. But true prayer, though refused in *terms*, is always granted in *effect*. Paul thrice besought God that the "stake in the flesh" might be taken away. The Lord left it where it was, but he used Paul's weakness to display the perfection of his strength, giving such compensating grace that Paul gloried in his infirmity. Monica besought God not to let Augustine go to Rome lest he should be ruined. But when her son went to Rome, despite her pleadings, she consoled herself with the reflection that if the Lord does not give what we ask, he always gives something better. And so it was. Augustine's going to Rome proved his rescue, not his ruin. He met the saintly Ambrose of Milan, and, through his influence, he became not only a disciple, but a sort of new apostle; he brought the whole majesty of his intellect to the defense and confirmation of the faith; and no one man since Paul has wielded so potent a scepter on church life.

The late Dr. Moon of Brighton, while yet a young man, was threatened with total blindness. It seemed like a wreck of all his hopes and prospects, and he besought God to spare his vision. But the blindness proved chronic, a midnight that had no dawn. With a faith seldom surpassed for sublimity, he *thanked God for the talent of blindness*, and prayed so to use it as to bring profit to his master! Then he began to think how he could invest it, and developed that simple system for the millions of blind whereby they so easily learn to read that already it has been applied to about five hundred languages and dialects! God greatly widened his sphere of service by withholding the sight he craved.

The loftiest level of answer is where there is *absolutely no sign that God hears or cares*. With all the repeated, importunate call, there seems to be none that regards the cry, as with the Baal worshipers on Carmel. The hearer of prayer keeps silence. Unbelief would say that the throne of his glory is disgraced. Years pass by, and life's morning has reached noon, and noon has sunk to night, and there has been no sensible relief. When faith survives *such* a trial and still triumphs in God, it rises to the highest level of the sublime, resting calmly on the *changeless word* and *character of God*. It asks no sign, no voice, no vision; willing to wait for explanation, till the eternal morning dawns and all the shadows flee away!

I asked Mr. Müller, a little before his death, whether he had ever prayed for a long time for a blessing, with no answer. He replied with his wonted precision that, for more than sixty-five years and four months, he had besought God for the conversion of two men, yet in their sins. But he added: "I shall meet them both in heaven. My heavenly Father would not lay on me the burden of two souls for so many years, had he no purposes of mercy concerning them!" He died without the *sight*, but without the *doubt*, a rare example of a faith that could repose upon the immutable promiser, though more than three score years of apparently vain supplication had put both faith and patience to the test.

Before closing this discussion of this great problem of prayer, we refer again to the Epistle of James, which contains at least six or seven marked hints on what it is to *ask amiss*. In three places he refers to this practical question and in each case gives two reasons for failure (James 1:5–8; 4:2–5; 5:14–18).

The several grounds of unprevailing prayer which he suggests are: 1. Lack of faith. 2. Of patient holding on. 3. Of proper motive. 4. Of unworldly separation. 5. Of earnest resolve. 6. Of spiritual elevation. Only careful and thorough study could bring out these lessons in their force and fullness; but a few words may help to make the general instruction clear.

As to lack of faith and patience, the simile used is ludicrously striking. The wave, properly "the *surge* of the sea, driven with the wind and tossed." There are two motions when the sea is tempestuous, undulation, up and down; fluctuation, to and fro. Both are referred to—"driven with the wind," fluctuation; "tossed," undulation. The peculiarity of a wave is that *it stays nowhere;* and so of the double-souled man: he is unstable in all his ways. If he is impelled forward he falls back, and if he is lifted up he sinks down again. If he believes one moment, he distrusts the next; if he gets a little ahead he cannot hold on to any advantage. Unstable as water, he cannot excel.

The carnal and worldly spirit cannot triumph in prayer, for carnality prompts to ask for gratification's sake, and would make prayer only another avenue of selfishness. Worldliness allies the soul with the world—the enemy of God. All worldly alliance is spiritual adultery. And how can disciples who are coquetting with the very world that seeks to supplant the divine bridegroom in their affection and allegiance, go with acceptance to the very Lord whom these compromises dishonor to ask a favor!

In the last chapter of James, Elijah is held up as an example of one who "in prayer, prayed." We are reminded of that scene on Carmel when he who had commanded the fire from heaven now commanded also the *flood.* The details are significant (1 Kings 18:42–46). The prophet "cast himself down upon the earth, and put his face between his knees;" underneath his mantle he was able to see nothing, and he wanted to be undisturbed in communion with God. It is a parable of *faith and sight*— faith absorbed in supplication: sight taking observation and reporting "nothing." Unbelief, at such report, would have said, "just as I expected!" and ceased praying. But faith keeps on until the hand raised in supplication leaves its shadow on the sky, in the little cloud—hand-shaped—and then knows that the answer is already coming swift and sure.

One of the greatest hindrances to effectual prayer is the practical listlessness and indifference with which we approach this holiest of all and which makes such holding on to God impossible. "Prayer," says Dr. A. F. Schauffler, "is either a prodigious *force* or a disgraceful *farce*. If a farce, you may pray much and get little; if a *force*, you may pray little and get much." "If," said a plain, blunt, farmer, "any son of mine should ask a favor as tamely as that minister spoke to his 'Father in heaven,' I should give him a *stick.*"

It is significant that, in this acted parable of prevailing prayer, Elijah *kept his high level to the end.* How little we understand that *the prayer of faith is answered on the plane of faith.* Having got a vision of God and been emboldened to ask in faith, we must not go down to the low levels of sight for the answer; it will not follow us down, nor would we be able to recognize it there if it did. That mountaintop was the place to wait for the answer. It commanded the horizon, and the atmosphere there was clear. There are many valleys where but little of the sky is visible, and what is may often be seen only through a murky atmosphere. *Keep your high level* if you would receive or recognize God's answer.

It is of great importance that, having asked of God in faith, this attitude of faith should be carefully maintained until the divine answer is received.

Jehovah appeared to Abram in a vision and promised him a seed when it was a natural impossibility; but the "father of the faithful" rose to the occasion. With sublime trust in God, he "considered neither his own body now dead, nor the deadness of Sarah's womb, but against hope believed in hope, being fully persuaded that what God had promised he was able to perform" (Rom. 4:17–21). Yet, while this act of faith is recorded (Gen. 15:6) as an example for all time, in the very next chapter we read how Abram dropped to the lowest level of unbelief; and he who had sublimely hearkened to Jehovah's voice now hearkens unto the voice of Sarah his wife and actually resorts to carnal means to bring about the result. Seeing that his wife continued barren, he took her Egyptian handmaid, Hagar, as a concubine, that by *her* he might have seed. He succeeded, but Ishmael brought a curse, which still continues; for to this day his descendants continue the implacable foes of the faith and covenant!

We have a similar instance in *David.* In a crisis of his kingdom, when Absalom led a formidable revolt, and Ahithopel, whose sagacity was so proverbial that his counsel was compared to the oracle of God itself (2 Sam. 16:23) had joined the conspiracy, the king said, "O Lord, turn the counsel of Ahithopel into foolishness!" It was sublime to turn to the all-wise and ask him to defeat the conspirator by making him advise just what was most unwise.

How uplifting the thought that omniscient wisdom was more than a match for the subtlest human conspiracy and diplomacy! But no sooner had the king thus committed the matter to God, than, going further up Olivet, the mount where it is specially stated that "he worshiped God," he met Hushai the Archite and bade him play the hypocrite—pretend that he was also a traitor, professing loyalty to Absalom; that, as David said, "*thou* mayest for me defeat the counsel of Ahithopel" (2 Sam. 15:30–34). Blessed are the praying souls who, having laid their burdens on God, leave them in his hands and do not compromise the act of faith by the timidity of unbelief that cannot *hold on* to God and trust him to keep what has been committed to him.

Power in prayer, though not a condition of *salvation*, is a victory of faith.

"And this is the confidence that we have in him, that, if we ask any thing according to his will, he heareth us: And if we know that he hear us, whatsoever we ask, we know that we have the petitions that we desired of him" (1 John 5:14–15).

In London, an enterprising newspaper firm had a direct telegraph line to Edinburgh to secure the latest news from the Scottish capital for every morning's issue. Two clerks at the top of the building had charge of the Edinburgh wire, one of whom also collected the local news. One night after going his round of the city he found he had forgotten his night key. If he did not get in, the news would not get into the paper. He thumped, hammered and kicked, but all to no purpose—the man up in the fifth story could not hear. At last it occurred to him to wire to Edinburgh and get them to call up the man at the top floor; and presently his fellow clerk came down and let him in. This illustrates the fact that often our best way to reach men is by the *prayer that goes by way of the throne!*

Dr. Adoniram Judson, while laboring as a missionary to the heathen, felt a strong desire to do something for the salvation of the Jews. But his desire was not apparently gratified, and even to the closing fortnight of his life, in his last sickness, all his prayer in their behalf seemed a failure. Then at last came a gleam of light that thrilled his heart with grateful joy.

Mrs. Judson was sitting by his side while he was in a state of great weakness. From a newspaper in her hand, she read to her husband a letter from Constantinople which filled him with wonder. At a meeting of missionaries at Constantinople, it was stated that a little book, published in Germany, and giving an account of Dr. Judson's life and labors, had fallen into the hands of some Jews and had been the means of their conversion; that one of them had translated it for others who lived on the borders of the Euxine, and that a messenger had arrived in Constantinople asking for a teacher to be sent them to show them the way of life.

When Dr. Judson heard this his eyes filled with tears, there was a look of almost unearthly solemnity, and clinging to his wife's hand, as if to assure himself that he was not dreaming, he said:

> This frightens me. I do not know what to make of it. I have never been deeply interested in any object, and prayed sincerely and earnestly for anything, but, at some time—no matter how distant the day—somehow, in some shape, probably the last I should have devised, it came!

What a testimony! It fell from the lips of the dying Judson as a legacy to coming generations. The desire of the righteous shall be granted. Pray and wait. The answer to all true prayer will come, and supplication by way of the throne will reach souls that you never personally reach by direct contact.

Let us not forget what has been already referred to: the great value of *united prayer* when it is the agreement of those who have first learned the art of prayer by meeting God in secret (Matt. 18:19). "If two of you shall *symphonize* on earth as touching anything that they shall ask it shall be done for them of my Father which is in heaven." The word *symphonize* is a musical term, referring to the *harmony of notes in a chord*, which is possible only when each accords with the whole instrument. One note out of tune will turn accord into discord. So the power of joint supplication depends not on the *numbers* gathered but on the measure of real *agreement* of each with the mind and will of God. *One* out of accord with him hinders perfect harmony with the rest; hence the smallest number that can agree is specified, because there is more power when *two* pray, provided they truly agree, than when a larger number apparently unite, but such agreement is lacking. Numbers are of no importance, but perfect harmony is.

We may get a hint of why prayers often fail from the postal system and the dead letter office. Letters reach that big "waste paper basket" when they lack an address or any legible and intelligible directions, when they lack postage, or when they contain unlawful matter. And prayers go to the dead prayer office for reasons not altogether dissimilar. Some of them are hopelessly indefinite; others lack the authority of a divine promise or other essentials of acceptable prayer; others are from motives or for ends that God cannot approve.

We may get hints of how prayer may prevail from that common channel of communication, the telephone. Those who first use it find themselves awkward, until they learn to obey the rules which are often hung up beside a public instrument, such as "go in and shut the door," "call the central," "speak close to the mouthpiece," "put the receiver to the ear," "hold the wire," etc. Prayer to God is singularly subject to similar laws. You need to get alone with God and shut yourself in; to get contact with him and through him, with others whom you would reach; to get close to him so as to speak in his ear and hear him speak in your own, and to keep in contact.

Of all illustrations which the natural universe furnishes of the fact of supernatural contact and communion and its inexplicable mystery, none equals, certainly none surpasses, wireless telegraphy.

In May, 1902, on board the Campania, and by the courtesy of Captain Watt, I first saw wireless telegraphy in operation, being present when the message was sent to the shore, hundreds of miles away, and the answer was received and read. It was then explained that, in order to get a perfect circuit, the transmitter and receiver must be in *tune*, each with the other—the transmitter in vain setting in rapid movement the mysterious waves of ether unless the receiver was so adjusted as to respond to these vibrations. And I then had a vivid illustration of the fact that no amount of proof can either convince or, in fact, reach and touch a soul not adjusted to God's will and in harmony with his being.

Electricity depends for transmission upon *conductors;* a non-conductor stops the circuit and stays the mysterious current. The insulating stool is necessary if you are to be charged with electricity—the moment you touch the earth the current passes from you into the earth. At Northfield Auditorium the reports to the *N. Y. Tribune* were arrested by a wire that at one point failed of insulation, touching the ground. Answers to prayer belong to a lofty and unworldly plane. Contact with God is too precious to be sold in the world's market at so many pence per pound. It belongs to those valuable commodities which are offered only to the highest bidder, the man who is willing for their sake to sacrifice all else that is hostile to God.

But whenever such spiritual conditions are found, God, the hearer of prayer, finds us; and actual experience proves, beyond doubt, three grand facts:

First, that prayer is the most effectual way both to flood the Word of God with light and to put Scripture teaching to the test of experiment.

Second, that prayer is the most effectual way both to cultivate personal acquaintance with God and a holy walk with him.

Third, that prayer is the most effectual way to secure deliverance from all the foes of spiritual life and achieve the highest spiritual successes.

Argument, in such a realm, is like a bird without wings: it can walk on the earth, but it cannot soar toward heaven. It is only *experiment* that, as on eagle's pinions, leaves earth behind and below, in an upward flight that mounts beyond the level of mist and cloud to the regions of sunshine; and, instead of being stayed by the storm, actually outrides it in triumph!

Chapter 11

Fellowship With God

A gain we lay a biblical basis for our study:

Can two walk together, except they be agreed? (Amos 3:3).

Be ye reconciled to God (2 Cor. 5:20).

If a man love me, he will keep my words; and my Father will love him, and we will come unto him, and make our abode with him (John 14:23).

That which we have seen and heard declare we unto you, that ye also may have fellowship with us: and truly our fellowship is with the Father, and with his Son Jesus Christ. And these things write we unto you, that your joy may be full (1 John 1:3–4).

Therefore as the church is subject unto Christ, so let the wives be to their own husbands in every thing. Husbands, love your wives, even as Christ also loved the church, and gave himself for it.... This is a great mystery: but I speak concerning Christ and the church (Eph. 5:24–32).

Be ye holy, for I am holy (1 Peter 1:16).

These passages of Scripture teach: that the basis of all fellowship is mutual agreement, and that our starting point with God is reconciliation; that love, leading to voluntary obedience, secures the indwelling of God, developing and manifesting that fellowship; that in this highest fellowship with God is found the source and secret of all true fellowship among disciples; that the climax of privilege is found in the marital bond between the church and the heavenly bridegroom; and that holiness affords the only hope of perfect harmony with a holy God, whose holiness is also the supreme incentive and argument for sainthood.

Having seen that faith is the starting point in the believer's life, and prayer its mightiest force, we are now to consider how that life finds its supreme privilege and reward in fellowship with God.

To understand this fellowship we must first have right conceptions of that which makes it impossible, namely, sin. This constitutes at once

189

the damning guilt and desperate ruin of sin; and consequently it is the supreme triumph and glory of salvation from sin that it is a restoration of fellowship and makes it not only possible and real but intimate and indissoluble.

The most insurmountable obstacle to the successful preaching of the gospel is the low conception, generally prevalent, both of sin itself and of the ruin it has brought to the race. Sin is not only transgression of law but separation from God; and grace seeks to expiate guilt and change separation for union, and alienation for reconciliation.

Thoroughly to understand sin and its disaster we should examine more thoroughly its *natural consequences* as well as its *judicial penalties*, for there is a natural aspect to all spiritual truth which needs to be seen for a complete and correct view. The common conception of hell, for instance, especially a century ago, was that it is a sort of prison—a universal New-gate or Saghalien, for the confinement and punishment of culprits and criminals, with chambers of horrors and instruments of torture, which all symbolism has been taxed to express.

But few have ever thought of that other hell that is *within*—that is inseparable from sin and the sinner, and which even God himself could not abolish unless by the abolition of sin! A hell built out of the materials which every human being has in his own nature and whose fires are fed with the fuel he supplies! Hell, in the larger sense, is not of God's building—not the result of any arbitrary arrangement or decree on his part; but the natural, necessary, inevitable outcome of alienation on man's part. If God had provided no hell for incorrigible sinners, sin would build one and crowd it, and reason and conscience, imagination and memory would fuel and fan its fires.

In the apocalypse, the city of God which descends out of heaven has twelve gates which are never shut: yet "nothing entereth that defileth, neither worketh abomination or maketh a lie." What prevents the impure, idolatrous and false from going in through open gates? There is an invisible, impassable barrier—found in conscious repugnance to a holy God and a holy habitation—something within the sinner that says to God, "Depart from us! For we desire not the knowledge of thy ways!" There may be as many gates to hell as to heaven, and always open; and no external hindrance to prevent the inhabitants of either exchanging abodes: but God's metropolis and Satan's necropolis will always hold their own *because they are their own!* That which keeps saints from going out and sinners from going in the bridal city is not shut gates but a *state of character*—a restraint within, not without. Saints do *not want to go out*, nor is it far wrong to say that no inhabitant of hell would *wish* to enter heaven if he could! Its holy atmosphere would be stifling to a disobedient spirit. A misguided and sensational evangelist, standing by the pulpit balustrade, shouted, "if I were now standing on hell's battlements preaching this gospel, what a jubilee there would be in hell!" But he forgot that those who rebel against law rebel also against love! And that the fallen demons and lost souls in hell would accept no salvation which demands abandonment of rebellious self-will. Churches open their doors and ring their bells, but remain half empty; for though vice and crime and misery throng the streets, there is something more congenial in the companionship of sinners than of saints. So without a change of nature, no lost soul could enter "the general assembly and church of the first born" or would if he could.

Milton sagaciously puts these words into the mouth of Satan:

> Me miserable, which way shall I fly
> Infinite wrath, and infinite despair?
> Which way I fly is hell; *myself am hell;*

Milton's words do not imply that the self retributive power of sin exhausts the subject—neither does the judicial aspect of retribution. Both are needed, as the two sides of the same complex truths. But when "Judas by transgression fell, that he *might go to his own place*" (Acts 1:25), he obeyed the law of spiritual gravitation and affinity; and it is awfully true that every man *has* his own place and *makes* his own place; and though he may not always *find* it in this world, he is sure to find it in the next, and will feel it to be his own place when he gets there.

Such a view helps us to appreciate what a great *fall from God* it was when man first sinned, and what a *wreck of self*—so that fellowship with God and even the *desire* for it are gone. No more true is it that God's holy nature shrinks from contact with sin, and sinners as such, than that a disobedient, unregenerate soul repels God. The need for a new nature is found in the necessity of a fitness for companionship with a holy God and holy beings—a capacity to breathe heaven's air and enjoy heaven's bliss.

The basis of fellowship with God is *affinity for God*—capacity for heavenly employments and enjoyments—for association with heaven's society. Eternal life is inseparable from eternal sinlessness; and eternal death there could not be without eternal sin. Even in this world human beings often pass the limits of a radical change of character: they reach a point where, consciously or unconsciously, they become fixed in evil courses, holden with the cords of their own sins. Why should we stumble at the teaching of the Word of God that, beyond this life, there are changeless moral conditions? Character essentially makes condition: and if a man passes the bound between the two worlds with a character that has lost plasticity and settled into final hardness and impenitence, what is there beyond that should effect radical change?

This side of the truth we emphasize, not because it is attractive, but because it is true; and if the marvel of sin is the ruin it works, the miracle of grace is not so much that it brings sinners into heaven as that it makes sinners into saints. It would be a wonder if a fish could be removed from water into air, with gills changed to lungs, scales to feathers, and fins to wings, so as to be as well fitted for flying in the atmosphere as for gliding in the stream. But even this cannot adequately represent what it is for a human being to be so born again from above as to be actually lifted into an entirely new spiritual element, henceforth to live and move and have his being in God; to find that new element necessary to his vitality, activity and felicity!

All fellowship with God, therefore, begins with reconciliation, advances by daily and hourly obedience to his will, and reaches its perfection in conscious union and communion with him in glory. Hence a favorite biblical figure to represent it is that of a path, with its gate of entrance, its common route and direction, and its final terminus or goal.

"Can two walk together except they be agreed?" Agreement with God there must be if he and we are to walk together; and the agreement must reach to at least three matters: from what point we are to start, by what common path we are to travel, and at what point the journey is to end. As to all these particulars the Word of God leaves no room for doubt. The cross is the *starting point*, where alone he will meet any penitent sinner. Reconciliation is definitely declared to be "by the death of his Son" and specifically "by the *blood* of the cross."

There is danger in the current misconception that God and the sinner were mutually alienated until Christ died, and that then God was reconciled and now pleads with the sinner to turn toward him. In the purpose of God, Christ was from the foundation of the world the slain

Lamb of atonement; and the efficacy of the atoning blood was as old as the transgression that needed it. Expiation was needful in order to make possible for God consistently to accept reconciled relations to the sinner; we must not, therefore, make the worse mistake of minimizing the guilt of sin by making a holy God tolerant of it or lax in judgment. But there is a sense in which his attitude has *always* been that of reconciliation. The atonement was the common act of the whole Godhead, though each of the Trinity has toward it a specific official relation. So far as the sinner is concerned, in this dispensation of grace, God never *was* alienated: hence the sinner has nothing to do to reconcile him; all he needs is himself to *be* reconciled to God. Practically all the alienation is his, and therefore all the reconciliation must be. Hence, in the great central passage on this subject, it is not even said that God *is* reconciled, but, as though no change were needful *in him*, "God, in Christ, *was reconciling the world unto himself.*"

> All things *are* of God, who hath reconciled us to himself by Jesus Christ, and hath given to us the ministry of reconciliation;
> To wit, that God was in Christ, reconciling the world unto himself, not imputing their trespasses unto them; and hath committed unto us the word of reconciliation.
> Now then we are ambassadors for Christ, as though God did beseech *you* by us: we pray *you* in Christ's stead, be ye reconciled to God.
> For he hath made him *to be* sin for us, who knew no sin; that we might be made the righteousness of God in him.
> We then, as workers together with him, beseech you also that ye receive not the grace of God in vain (2 Cor. 5:18; 6:1).

Throughout this passage, not a word is found about any change of attitude as being necessary in God. Man is not coming to God to placate an offended deity. God's attitude is gracious, forgiving and even beseeching. But what strong emphasis upon the sinner's being reconciled to him, and not *receiving* the grace of God in vain! As the prodigal found, on his return to his father, that his father's face was toward him, and his arms stretched out; so the moment we turn toward God we find him already facing us and with a smile, not a frown.

The starting point, then, is the cross. There our reconciliation with God begins, and with it our walk with him.

The earliest object lesson given to man, on any elaborate scale, was intended to teach this great truth: it was the whole *Passover celebration* in Exodus 12. Here, for the first time, *the blood* is made conspicuous in connection with salvation. The ark, devised by God, built by man, suggests salvation from judgment, but there is no suggestion of atoning blood. But here the blood is everything. The lamb is slain that his blood may be sprinkled with the hyssop on the right and left and upper door posts, so that he who passes the threshold must be surrounded by blood. And when Jehovah, with his destroyer, passed through the land in judgment, he said, "When I see the blood, I will pass over you," and "not suffer the destroyer to come in unto your houses to smite you." This passing *over* is more than passing *through* the land, or passing *by* the bloodstained house. It implies passing *over into the house*. All Israel's passings over were into something beyond. They passed over the Red Sea into the desert, and over the Jordan into Canaan. So God passed *over the door* into the house; and, being in, would not suffer the destroyer to enter. This explains many other things, such as his claim on the firstborn as the special property of the new head of the redeemed house; and the psalmist's words, "I am a stranger and a sojourner *with thee*, as all my fathers were" (Psalm 39:12). It is a beautiful conception: Jehovah, seeing the blood, and himself passing over the threshold, to take the headship of the house, to become possessor, controller. Of course, where he was, the destroyer could not come. And he became a fellow pilgrim with his people, marching at their front in the pillar of his presence; and never had a settled habitation for himself till his people settled down in the land of promise. This gives new meaning to his message to David when he proposed to build him a house.

> Go and tell my servant David, Thus saith the LORD, Shalt thou build me an house for me to dwell in?
>
> Whereas I have not dwelt in any house since the time that I brought up the children of Israel out of Egypt, even to this day, but have walked in a tent and in a tabernacle.
>
> In all the places wherein I have walked with all the children of Israel spake I a word with any of the tribes of Israel, whom I commanded to feed my people Israel, saying, Why build ye not me an house of cedar? (2 Sam. 7:5–7).

This thought that, so far as *God* is concerned, reconciliation is an accomplished fact, and that nothing is needed but the sinner's change of attitude toward God, is very important, for it knocks the bottom out of all attempts at any good works as a means of salvation. All fastings and self mortifications, penances and pilgrimages, scourgings and privations—nay, even prayers and tears, in hope of securing favor with God, are a snare. Instead of securing salvation, they prevent it.

The English word 'reconciliation' carries the idea of *mutuality*. In all human alienations, the aversion is mutual, and so must the attraction be by which it is corrected. One party may turn toward the other, taking a reconciling attitude, but the reconciliation is only *partial* until there is a response, when it becomes mutual. We must be careful how we press this analogy in things divine. The Greek word *katalasso*, translated "reconciliation," *carries no such idea; moreover, it is remarkable that there is another word which does imply mutual change*, whereas this refers only to a change of one party from enmity to friendship.[26]

It is plain, therefore, that all the change necessary in order to perfect reconciliation with God, and so to fellowship, may be *instantaneous*. So soon as the sinner abandons his enmity and turns toward God, he finds the open arms and kiss of love. He is at once reinstated in the divine household as a son who was dead and is alive again, who was lost and is found (Luke 15).

Obedience, however, is *progressive*. The fellowship begun in reconciliation is thus continued and advanced, as every step in a common path advances travelers on toward a common stopping place. This is progressive *sanctification*. The first great question of the penitent believer is, "Lord, what wilt thou have me to do?" And every successive step must be taken in the same spirit—conformity to the will of God. The truest fellowship between any two intelligent beings is found in having *one will* as well as one *way*. There may be an outward walk together where there is inward antagonism: a culprit and a policeman, handcuffed together, have to walk together, but they are far from *agreed*.

One may enter a path in a moment by one step going in at the gate; but he cannot thus cover all the distance represented by the path. That is done by successive steps, following on to know the Lord by the progressive walk of a holy life.

Three little words in the New Testament carry great weight: *"stand," "walk," "sit."* The first represents the believer's judicial position, or standing in Christ, through faith. "Walk" expresses the change from place to place, advancing from one duty or trial, temptation or sorrow, to another, under divine guidance. "Sit" suggests the end of our walk, when the soul's quest for God is satisfied and we rest in him, as Christ "sat down" when his priestly work was done.

---

26 See Robinson's *Greek Lexicon of the New Testament*: *katalasso* and *dialasso*, p. 384.

To understand this progressive walk of sanctification, we need to remember that obedience is submission to authority, and that authority implies law. There is a very dangerous doctrine, working like a subtle leaven to corrupt even disciples, which is nothing less than *antinomianism*. It affirms that because we are no longer "under the law but under grace," therefore *all law is abrogated;* and this position finds a very plausible justification in sundry statements of the New Testament that the law imposed a yoke of bondage which neither our fathers nor we were able to bear, but that yoke is now broken and we are introduced into the liberty of the sons of God; and hence it is argued that even such a law as that of Sabbath rest is no longer in force.

Such views of obligation betray equally false exegesis of Scripture, and misleading notions of legal obligations. Law is not the ground of the sinner's *justification*, for "by the deeds of the law shall no flesh living be justified." But law is none the less the *rule of duty*. It is the expression of God's will and our guide as to what pleases him; and we are expressly told that "what the law could not do, in that it was weak through the flesh, God sending his own Son in the likeness of sinful flesh, and for sin, condemned sin in the flesh, that the righteousness of the law might be fulfilled in us, who walk not after the flesh, but after the Spirit" (Rom. 8:3-4).

The law of the Old Testament is both *ceremonial* and *moral*—the former part having to do with typical ritual that foreshadowed a coming dispensation; the other with immutable principles of ethics. One was temporary and transient—the shadow of things to come of which the body is Christ; the other is eternal and permanent, the embodiment in commandment of the moral will of God. Hence a portion of the law, known as the "ten words" of Jehovah, was twice graven on tablets of stone by the very finger of God—separated from all minor injunctions as a distinct and permanent code.

In the creation story in Genesis will be found ten creative fiats. "And God said" is the keynote to the narrative, the burden ten times repeated of this magnificent poem.[27] Here are certain immutable laws for the government of the material creation, such as universal motion and rotation, evaporation and condensation, cohesion, gravitation, revolution, affinity, growth and multiplication. There has not been a moment since when such natural laws have not been in operation.

---

27 Godet's *Old Testament Studies*, .p 133.

In Exodus we meet the *moral* tenfold code. He who before spoke as creator, here speaks as governor, and his commands are equally changeless. As the material universe would fall into ruin if natural laws should cease to control, so the moral order is dependent on these commands of the Decalogue.

This moral code constitutes an *organic body* of itself, every command of which is a member of the body, necessary to the completeness of the whole. Four commands relate to *God:* the first puts him as the supreme *head* of all authority; the second defines the mode of his worship as a spirit; the third forbids all careless trifling with his name, which expresses his nature; the fourth forbids trespassing on the time he sanctifies unto himself. Similarly the remaining six prescribe duties to man, putting the parent at the head as God's representative in the family—then guarding all human interests—life, chastity, property, reputation, and finally forbidding all wrong desire after what is another's!

It is plain that here is a complete code for man's guidance. There is only one way for it to pass away—when the perfect love that works no ill to God or one's neighbor so rules intelligent beings as that there can be nothing in conduct or even character that could mar the new creation; then and not till then will these "ten words" pass away, because all will be fulfilled.

Yet by some it is said that all *law is abrogated*, and that, among the abrogated things, Paul mentions to the Colossians, "the *Sabbaths*" (2:16). But the Sabbaths he refers to are not the weekly rest days commanded in the moral code, but the festival Sabbaths of the *ceremonial*—which therefore are in the same category with ceremonial meats and drinks and new moons and other festival days. The plural "Sabbaths" is commonly used in the Bible in this sense.

Few modern laxities work worse results on the whole social order, family, church and state, than the rapidly increasing and flagrant disregard of all Sabbatic law.

Undoubtedly this law of rest, one day in seven, has undergone some modification, but its essential principle survives. In Isaiah 58:13–14, curiously about midway between Moses and Christ, and in connection with significant blessings pronounced upon the "repairer of the breach, the restorer of paths to dwell in"—that is, one who rebuilds what is broken down and restores wanderers to forsaken ways of duty—we read, "If thou turn away thy foot from the Sabbath, from doing thy pleasure on my

holy day, and call the Sabbath a delight, the holy of the Lord, honorable;
and shalt honor him, not doing thine own ways, nor finding thine own
pleasure, nor speaking thine own words," etc.

It is most noticeable that while here all features of Sabbath observance
that were merely external and ceremonial are eliminated, the substantial
law of the Sabbath is not only preserved but lifted to a more sacred
plane. The Sabbath observance is modified but glorified—a new principle is enunciated, in accordance with which the day is to be regarded
not primarily as a rest day from labor, but as God's holy day—it is the
difference between man's holiday and God's holy day—and in it man is
to abstain from "doing his own ways, finding his own pleasure," or even
"speaking his own words." Before, it was a day fenced in as one to be kept
for physical rest; but now it is to be a day of mental repose and spiritual
refreshment. Even the tongue is to be under control, and selfish pleasure
to be curbed. It seems to be a sort of forecast of the permanent features
of the weekly rest day. Certain it is that wherever the day is thus kept,
every richest blessing comes to a community. The fact is, however, that,
on pretext of freedom from legal restraints, Sunday is fast becoming the
day of self-seeking and pleasure seeking, when even disciples find their
own pleasure and speak their own words freely. It is getting to be the day
pre-eminently of recreation—everything but the holy of the Lord, kept
as entitled to special honor. The enemy of God and man must rejoice over
such desecration of what the Lord has consecrated. Voltaire more than
a century ago declared, "There is no hope of destroying Christianity so
long as Sunday is kept as a holiday." Robert Ingersoll, discerning in the
Sabbath a strong defense and bulwark of the whole Christian system,
petulantly cried out: "Sunday is a pest! it must be taken out of the way!"
The oracles of infidelity all agree in a like verdict. Wherever the desecration of the Lord's day prevails, it weakens all the line of Christian
life and witness before the inrush of atheism and materialism. Finally
to abandon this sacred observance would be preliminary to a sure defeat
of the church of God, in all the campaign for righteousness and peace,
imperiling all the highest interests of men, both temporal and eternal.

If the Sabbath of weekly rest is abrogated as part of a law no more
in force, what of other commands of the Decalogue? Are we under no
obligation not to use graven images in worship, not to take God's name
in vain? And are the six commands of the second table abrogated? Is
there no longer an obligation on the believer to honor parents, to guard

another's life, chastity, property, etc.? This would be not antinomianism only, but anarchy, sanctioned by Christianity.

But it is said the Sabbath is a *Mosaic* institution—far from it, it is *Edenic*. It antedates not only Sinai but *sin*, and is the only surviving relic of man's innocence, except marriage. God saw, even before man sinned, that he needed a sacred season of time once in seven days. This is one of two institutions that come down from a sinless Edenic life—thus joined together by God—the Sabbath rest and the marriage tie—is it surprising that man cannot put them asunder without weakening both! Whenever the Sabbath is desecrated the family purity is diminished, if not lost.

Moreover, our Lord declared the eternal principle: "The Sabbath was made for man." It meets a need which will continue so long as man's earthly conditions continue. The weekly rest is needful to keep a normal balance between body and spirit. The night's sleep does not fully recuperate the exhaustions of anxiety and activity, and the weekly recurrence of a rest day is restorative and complementary. One of the greatest of British physicians warns his fellow countrymen of the rapid increase of insanity, and says that if this goes on, as now, it will not be long before the bulk of the race will be mentally unhinged; and it has been found that this insanity is largely due to the push and drive of modern life, for which the Sabbath is God's corrective.

The change of day, from the seventh to the first, does not affect the principle; for it is not any particular twenty-four hours that is essential, but one day in seven. In fact the whole human race cannot keep the same exact time, because the rotation of the earth makes the day different in different parts of the earth. So long, therefore, as the same proportion is preserved, with uniformity in each locality, all essential principles are conserved.

The historical argument is overwhelming. The logic of events is conclusive, that God brands Sabbath desecration with his displeasure. Who of us that are old enough to remember the days, not so long ago, when there were no public vehicles running on Sunday, no newspapers hawked in the streets, no shops or public places of amusement open, no railroad and steamboat excursions, very little traveling or private visiting and entertaining; and can recall the quiet of the hours, the full churches, the devout household habits, the general observance of the rest day, and contrast all these conditions with those now prevailing—can doubt that so far as man has trampled on God's decree of the Sabbath, he has worked harm to all individual, domestic and social life as well as ecclesiastical. The tradition in ancient Troy was that, if ever the statute of Pallas in Minerva's temple were removed, the city itself would be destroyed. The Sabbath is the Palladium in the temple of our Christian civilization, and if it falls in ruin, it means widespread disaster to church and state, and Satan knows it.

History warns us that the Sabbath was made for man—for the preservation of his physical, mental, moral and spiritual balance. The tendency of crowding all seven days with secular work is to crowd out even the thought of God, and paralyze the very powers by which we commune with the unseen and eternal. The effect of consecrating one day in seven is to give man time to recover from the secularizing influence of the rest of the week, or better still prevent the business of this world from dragging down his spiritual life. God's weekly rest recurs often enough to prevent the hallowing influence of one sacred day from being lost before the influence of another is felt, reminding us of the telegraph poles that are placed near enough together to prevent the wires, however they sag between, from touching the earth. Sabbath observance is a help to fellowship with God.

A few conspicuous witnesses might be heard on this great question in these perilous days.

"Quite apart from the religious aspect of the question, on social and economic grounds," says Dr. McLaren of Manchester, England, "the seventh day of rest is of the greatest importance to the well-being of the nation. The present tendency is to break down the day of rest, and is, therefore, I think, disastrous. The habit of attending public worship is decreasing in proportion to population. The old-fashioned habit of rigorously attending service twice a day is dead, the change being chiefly because of the indifference of parents. It was customary years ago for children, certainly on Sunday evening, to get Christian teaching at home from their parents. The child was taught gospel truths at its mother's knee; fitted for public worship. To some extent, no doubt, the custom still obtains; but not to the extent that it obtained in my own boyhood. Sunday school teaching is, of course, of the greatest value; but I look upon the Christian teaching of parents as infinitely better."

The echoes are still heard of Hon. Andrew D. White's recent utterance regarding the Sabbath, the occasion for which arose in the action of Bishop Luden, of the Roman Catholic diocese of Syracuse, in refusing

Christian burial to persons who died by accident on Sunday while culpably violating the duties and obligations of that day. In a letter to the bishop, heartily commending the stand he had taken, Dr. White said:

> I have, for some time past, watched with ever-increasing regret the tendencies in our large cities, and, indeed, to some extent in the country districts, toward a complete paganizing of American life as regards the first day of the week. The extremes to which our communities have gone of late in appointing every sort of game and amusement through the morning hours, and of making Sunday resorts less and less decent, are such as to create just alarm among all thinking citizens. It was under this conviction that I observed the very bold and noble stand which you have taken.

This is the view, not of an extremist nor a fanatic, but of a liberal, broad-minded man, who sees, as all must see who are clear-eyed, sound-minded, and morally erect, that the increasing Sunday desecration should be checked, not only in the interests of religion, but of law, order and public morality. The open, flagrant, defiant violations of the Sunday laws and of long-established and honored Sabbath customs and usages are sure symptoms of a spirit of irreverence for all laws and indifference to all moral obligations—a spirit fatal to the well-being of the family, the home, the state, and of every other institution which men hold sacred and dear.

All antinomianism is unscriptural, unspiritual, unchristian. Moral law can never be abrogated, as a rule of conduct or guide to character. The fact that we are not under law as a means of justification does not imply that we are not under law to Christ (1 Cor. 9:21) as to the regulation of life. This is to displace lawfulness by lawlessness, and obedience by apostasy. Abrogation of law can take place, even under a system of grace, only so far as the habit of voluntary and cheerful obedience makes all law unnecessary. Holy love can withhold nothing due to God or man, and this fulfilling of law is love's way of abrogating it. Habits of obedience imply law, for otherwise what is it that is obeyed, and what is the standard of obedience? Law transferred *within* by love, from the tables of stone to the fleshy tablets of the heart; this is the sublime method of doing away with legal bondage (Ps. 40:8).

It is sometimes said that obedience is impossible because the standard of law is impracticable, ideal, beyond reach. Does God then command impossibilities? Yes, in a sense, and partly to show that, to the natural man, obedience *is* impossible, and so to teach that a true obedience is spiritual and belongs not to the natural but supernatural; and so again to reveal the omnipotence of grace as the corrective of human impotence—how Christ strengthening me I can do all things. Obedience is possible therefore only so far as fellowship with God is maintained.

In 1 Cor. 1:9 we read those remarkable words, "called into the fellowship of his Son, our Lord Jesus Christ."

This word *koinōnia*, with its various kindred words, is used thirty-eight times in the New Testament, translated also "communion," "partaker," "companion," "partner," etc.

The dominant idea always is *partnership*, which of course implies *mutuality*. There can be no one-sided partnership. This thought pervades the whole Scripture, and especially the New Testament. We are by grace introduced into partnership with our Lord Jesus, and he enters into partnership with us. We enter into his sufferings, and he equally enters into our trials and temptations. This would be incredible were it not for divine teaching.

This explains many obscure hints in Scripture, and is the central mystery of grace. On the one hand, we read that Paul "filled up that which was behind of the sufferings of Christ in his flesh," and was a worker together with God. But with what amazement do we read of God, that, "in all their affliction, *he* was afflicted," literally, in all their adversity. *He* was no adversary. The verses following explain the meaning. He came to their help in the time of their trouble, the angel of his presence saved them, and he lifted them up and carried them. In Judges 10:16 we read: "his soul was impatient of the misery of Israel," literally, was shortened, or straitened. *He* so entered into their misery that he felt himself in straits, like his people.

In Zech. 2:8 he says, "whoso toucheth you, toucheth the apple," or better, "pupil, of my eye."

All this teaching is so remarkable that it taxes faith to receive it; but it is most significant and inspiring. It sets before a disciple a wonderful mystery of love. He is privileged to think of Christ himself as his *partner*, and, as such, associated with all his experiences of joy and sorrow, trial and temptation. He may count on his help and succor as an ally. He is not to indulge any thought, or aim, or pleasure, or engage in any pursuit, which he cannot ask him to share with him. That would be to insult his heavenly partner. But on the other hand, when he finds himself in sore straits and knows not how to save himself from moral or spiritual bankruptcy, he may look confidently for his interposition, as in business one man might count on his associate in the firm. Reverently we may say that the disciple and his Lord are embarked in a common venture with common risks. Each comes to the other's aid. There is some work for doing which he counts on the disciple, without whose cooperation it will not and cannot be done, as the work of witnessing to a dying world. But there is other work which cannot be accomplished without the Lord. He is so necessary that, unless he comes to our aid, defeat and disaster are inevitable. Nay, we may say more than this, we shall be absolutely helpless and hopeless. Satan is more than a match for the strongest disciple. In the crisis of a mighty temptation or an insupportable sorrow we must hear him saying: "Ye shall not need to fight in this battle, for the battle is not yours, but *God's*."

Here is the grand solution of all problems of spiritual life. When in any respect we are at our wit's end, and our wisdom or strength—or both—utterly fail us, instead of giving way to despair or despondency, it is our privilege and right to count on God in proportion to the greatness of the emergency and, in a sense, involve him as a joint partner in our difficulties. He is not a partner for fair weather only, resigning his connection with the firm when serious complications arise. When insolvency threatens is the time when his fellowship with us in the business is of most value. This is not a "limited liability" company, where he seeks to evade failure by setting a legal limit to responsibility. Never does he so delight in his fellowship with us as when we most feel our absolute inadequacy to act, move, or attempt to live without *God*. And it may safely be added that, in no circumstances will God be found more a present God and a mighty helper than when the crisis is most intolerable. We may well have had experience of darkness unrelieved, prayer unanswered, sin for the time triumphant, and affliction insupportable, if at last we have learned that he is for us when even he has seemed against us. In the crisis of his passion in the garden our Lord besought his disciples, "tarry ye here and watch with *me*." May we not in our crises confidently ask him to watch with us?

Fellowship with God is the secret of *resistance to the Devil*. There are some difficulties and foes that even the believer is incompetent to deal with. He must "stand still and see the salvation of the Lord" (2 Chron. 20:14–26).

In one of David's inspired songs, he refers to the sons of Belial as "thorns which cannot be taken hold of with the hands; the man that would touch them must be fenced with iron and the staff of a spear." Thorns must be burned, not handled. We all find out that in conflicts with the Devil, he is too wily for the wisest saint and too mighty for the strongest. Michael the archangel durst not contend with him, far less durst Joshua the high priest; both could only say, "the *Lord* rebuke thee." We can do no more than put on the whole armor of God, and *stand*, and let the Lord defend and protect us, and defeat and vanquish our adversary. And, as the British soldiers used to ask on the eve of an engagement, "is Wellington here?" feeling confident that the winner of forty battles was invincible; so, infinitely more must the disciple rely upon him who was manifested to destroy the works of the Devil and cannot be defeated even by the arch enemy.

Ulysses is fabled to have defeated the Sirens by causing himself to be bound to the mast, his ears and those of his sailors being stopped with wax lest they should hear their seductive song; but it is said that Orpheus followed another and wiser device: he took aboard his lyre and drowned their song in the melody of his own hymns of praise. We need a *positive* method to make us proof against Satan's wiles.

Such fellowship explains what it is to "abide in our calling with God."

Mrs. Garfield, in a letter written to her husband some years previous to his election to the presidency, gives us a glimpse of how humble household service may be illumined by the spiritual uplift of such fellowship. She says: "I am glad to tell you that out of all the toil and disappointment of the summer just ended I have risen up to a victory; that silence of thought since you have been away has won for my spirit a triumph. I read something like this the other day: 'There is no healthy thought without labor, and thought makes the labor happy.' Perhaps this is the way I have been able to climb up higher. It came to me one morning when I was making bread. I said to myself: 'Here I am, compelled by an inevitable necessity to make our bread this summer. Why not consider it a pleasant occupation and make it so by trying to see what perfect bread I can make?'

"It seemed like an inspiration, and my whole life grew brighter. The very sunshine seemed flowing down through my spirit into the white loaves, and now I believe my table is furnished with better bread than ever before; and this truth, as old as creation, seems just now to have become fully mine—that I am not the shrinking slave of toil, but its regal master, making whatever I do yield to me its best fruits."

We see the force of that New Testament expression "IN CHRIST JESUS."

The highest point to which New Testament revelation carries us is this conception of fellowship with the Lord Jesus Christ in life and service, suffering and glory.

Christ was made sin for us. He becomes the representative sinner, even to the point of dying in the sinner's behalf and going into the grave bearing his sin and its penalty; but in the resurrection his humiliation ends and his exaltation begins; and by as much as he was identified with the sinner, the sinner is now identified with *himself.* Henceforth the Lord Jesus Christ is the representative *saint.* In awaking from the death sleep and sloughing off the discarded wrappings of the sepulcher, he shows himself the prince of life and that it is not possible that he should be holden of death. He puts on the new man, the incorruptible body of the resurrection and its new celestial attire, miraculously provided, and begins his forty days' walk in newness of life, a resurrection life of new experience even to him as the incarnate God-man. Then he arose and took his seat at the right hand of God.

Now the wonder is that *all this* the believer is represented as also *doing in him* as his representative. The two are regarded and treated as *identical.* In him the believing and penitent sinner dies; it is as though the believing thief on the cross where he was suffering the due reward of his deeds had by faith been transferred from his own cross to that of the Lord Jesus Christ, and in him died a painless death, all his merited suffering transferred to that vicarious sufferer—he becoming so one with him as to be from that moment identified with his whole future in paradise.

To abide in the will of God is to abide in absolute *safety.* David said to Abiathar, "Abide thou with me. Fear not; for he that seeketh my life seeketh thy life; but with me thou shalt be in safeguard" (1 Sam. 22:23). So speaks God to the humblest believer. Is not this the true interpretation of that ninety-first Psalm, that to all commentators seems such a mystery? Is not that secret place of the most high, where one abides under the very shadow of the Almighty, covered with his feathers and hiding trustfully under his wings—simply the *will of God?* There abiding, in vain does the fowler spread his snares for our feet or the adversary hurl at us his darts of death. Into that sacred chamber of the divine presence neither the pestilence that walketh in darkness nor the destruction that wasteth at noonday can find entrance. Here we tread upon the young lion and adder and trample under foot even the dragon.

In such fellowship there is security from all approaches of false doctrine and the uncertainty of doubt. At one time when inroads of heretical teaching were feared in Britain there was a movement in favor of multiplying creedal statements, and one prominent brother urged it on the ground that a few additional "guideposts would be helpful, especially when there was a little mist about." But Baldwin Brown, then chairman of the Congregational Union, quietly rejoined that more "guideposts would be of little use when there was a competent and living guide."[28]

Fellowship with God is the all-sufficient antidote to anxiety—the cure of *care*. Anxious thoughts are not only useless, but worse, for they burden us with the anticipation of troubles that never come, while they avert or avoid no real and inevitable troubles and only double them by anticipation.

It is no wonder if, when once the consciousness of such fellowship is enjoyed, even death loses all terrors and becomes nothing but the messenger, not of the king of terrors, but of the King of glory. Stephen's death, though by stoning—the first recorded death of a believer after our Lord's resurrection—seems to be intended as *typical*. His perfect calmness, his radiant face lit up with solar light, his entire absence of resentment—"Lord, lay not this sin to their charge"—his vision of the risen Christ, and his quiet falling asleep—all seem to hint that henceforth even a cruel death loses its horrors and terrors to one who is in fellowship with God. And with the fear of death vanishes the fear of judgment, "because as *he* is, so are *we* in this *world*" (1 John 4).

We can understand why saints have forbidden survivors to mourn. "I particularly request and direct that at my death those who love me will put on no sign of mourning, but that they will think of me as promoted to a higher school, where I shall meet my Lord, and know even as I am known."[29]

The great essential truths about fellowship are illustrated, if not intentionally taught, in the tabernacle as by an object lesson. The outer court emphatically teaches the *terms* of fellowship, in the *altar* and *laver*, as conditioned on two things, the blood and the spirit—the blood to atone, the spirit to regenerate. Then the holy place teaches the *forms* of fellowship—how we are to walk with God: as stewards holding all property in trust; as witnesses, holding all truth in trust for testimony; as supplicators

---

28 *Life of Jos. Parker*, p. 129.
29 Will of Mrs. Emma J. Parker.

and intercessors, holding the privilege of access to God in trust as the greatest of all means for promoting his kingdom. Then, if we would learn the very goal of all fellowship, it is represented in the holiest place where we meet *God himself*, abiding in his very presence, and united with his very person in the Lord Jesus Christ.

The astounding teaching of the New Testament is that by faith every penitent sinner is taken up into Christ's personality, so that in him he dies for sin and to sin, in him is buried by baptism into death, and at once acquires in him an entirely new standing—a permanent position, justified and accepted with the Father as himself a son of God; then in him a new attire of heavenly tempers and manners and outward conduct, henceforth enabled to walk in wisdom toward those who are without—an essentially heavenly walk on earth. Then, still in him attaining the privilege of a seat at God's right hand—satisfaction in God as his supreme joy, strength, hope, trust, and eternal reward. This revelation of the believer's fellowship with Christ is so absolutely unique—so entirely original, so peculiar to the New Testament, and so manifestly superhuman, that it is enough of itself to stamp the Bible as incontestably a divine book.

Such fellowship with God is a privilege open even to a *child*.

One most marvelous feature of the Bible is that it is emphatically the *children's book*. This we should not expect, and it is unique. No other book ever written that dealt with such profound mysteries has had also any such adaptation to children. And moreover, note the marks of design. Every particular phase of child-life is touched somewhere and somehow once for all, and without repetition. Just enough examples are given to illustrate all needed lessons, and no such lesson is left out or emphasized out of proportion. Samuel's childhood is recorded to teach us that, in the person of a little child, the Lord may, after centuries of silence, unseal the lips of prophecy and restore the open vision. Solomon's youth is portrayed for the purpose of exemplifying how a mere lad may please God by a request that reveals supreme wisdom. John Baptist's childhood showed how even from birth a child may be filled with the Holy Spirit. Timothy's early history proves how from a child one may shew an aptitude for piety and know the Holy Scriptures. Daniel's youth reveals remarkable power of self-restraint, even over the appetites that in most children have control. David is an example of early faith and courage, daring in God's name to attack even a giant.

Perhaps no more notable examples can be found than the two cases of nameless children—one the girl who waited on Naaman's wife; the other the lad that had the five barley loaves and two small fishes. We know nothing about either except this one thing: one was a mere servant maid and she simply told her mistress that there was a prophet in Israel who could recover Naaman of his leprosy; in the other an unknown and poor boy, who had a few small buns and fishes, barely enough for one hungry child, gave up his whole supply to the Lord whose blessing used that little measure of provision to satisfy five thousand hungry men beside women and children.

How plain the lessons are, how they match each other and fit human need! One teaches us that a little girl may do great good to a distinguished general by simply telling what she knows of God's power, and the other that a mere lad may give what he has got and so feed a hungry multitude. And we cannot forget how she who told what she knew, knew no less for the telling and helped others to know; and that he who gave what he had, got back as much as he gave and fed all others who had nothing.

Then, of course, the climax of all this sublime teaching is in the childhood of our Lord himself, who, by being born as a babe and living as a boy in a family, subject to parental authority and learning a trade, forever taught boys the beauty of obedience and the dignity of labor.

This fellowship finds its supreme expression in the *marital bond*, for nothing so conveys the idea of perfect mutuality as ideal wedlock. Bride and bridegroom are partners in a common family life and home, each forsaking father and mother to cleave to the other. They share a common name: Adam called Eve, "Isha, because taken out of Ish." They share a common experience: the mathematics of love adding to and multiplying joys, and subtracting from and dividing sorrows by such sharing. They have common interests and occupations, co-workers for common ends and by joint methods. They hold property and possessions in common. They have essentially one history and destiny.

In every one of these respects the New Testament represents the Lord Jesus Christ and his church as identified. To cite textual proofs would be both impracticable and needless, as the whole inspired scroll is a heavenly marriage contract and certificate in which, with the golden pen of inspiration, all these privileges are recorded as the dowry and heritage of the redeemed church!

Chapter 12

The Problem of Service

The Word of God supplies sundry maxims on this subject that deserve to be emblazoned on the banners of the church and written on the door-posts of our houses and on our gates, to be kept ever before us.

SERVE AND WAIT.

> Ye turned to God from idols to *serve* the living and true God, and to *wait* for his Son from heaven (1 Thess. 1:9–10).

To EVERY MAN HIS WORK (Mark 13:34).

BY LOVE SERVE ONE ANOTHER (Gal. 5:13).

DOING THE WILL OF GOD FROM THE HEART (Eph. 6:6).

SHE HATH DONE WHAT SHE COULD (Mark 14:8).

WHOSE I AM AND WHOM I SERVE (Acts 27:23).

I AM AMONG YOU AS HE THAT SERVETH (Luke 22:27).

These are sublime mottoes, couched in few words but full of deep meaning. They hint at the true attitude of a disciple, serving his Lord and waiting for his reappearing; they suggest that the master has called every one of us to some form of work and only asks of us to do what we can; that we belong to him and that service is his due, to be rendered in love to all men for his sake, and from a hearty purpose to fulfill the will of God; and that the master himself has set us an example of unselfish service.

Among the hundred words which stand most prominent in the Bible, this word SERVICE is very conspicuous, and more so the conception it represents. Here is the ultimate end toward which all else properly tends—the true goal of salvation and sanctification. No man lives to himself. He is saved that he may be sanctified—conformed to the image of God's dear Son; but even such conformity reaches its highest result in helping others to a like destiny, and so all culminates in glory to God. How plain it is that those who are content to be saved from ruin themselves, and do nothing to rescue others, are "blind and cannot see afar off"—so shortsighted in spiritual vision as to lose sight altogether of the grand final purpose of their own redemption!

The whole Bible is *saturated* with this conception of service; it is like Gideon's fleece when the least pressure brought out drops of the heavenly dew. Or it is like the temple waters that ran underground, appearing at intervals in the pools like those of Siloam and Bethesda, but even when not coming to the surface, always there and flowing. The idea of service is pervasive, and the forms of expression and illustration frequent and varied. First and last and all the way through, the Holy Scriptures summon disciples to serve God and man. Some of the more conspicuous ways in which this challenge is conveyed and enforced we shall now examine.

1. The Parable of Nature

In the first chapter of Genesis marked stress is laid on the fact of *capacity for reproduction as the sign and proof of perfect development of life*. When God created the first plants and animals, in each was its "seed according to its kind," and God saw that it was good. In no case did life find its perfection without this power of reproduction. Nothing is accidental or insignificant in God's Word, and this emphatic repetition, "whose seed is in itself after his kind," nine times occurring, cannot be without a purpose. It is God's primary lesson on service.

How constantly we meet such words as "*field*" and "*seed*," "sower" and "reaper," "seed time" and "harvest time"—applied to service! The Lord Jesus Christ interprets the parable of nature by the parable of grace. "The field is the world," and the seed is of two sorts: "The good seed is the *Word of God*," and "The good seed are the *children of the kingdom*" (Compare Matthew 13:19; 38). The meaning is not obscure. It is God's way of bringing men to the knowledge of himself to use his inspired word together with his believing children—his truth on the one hand and their testimony to the truth on the other. Truth is always most convincing, not in abstract but concrete forms, and believers are to be, like their master, the word made flesh and dwelling among men—every child of God a sort of new incarnation of the truth, witnessing to others.

The field is the world—the whole world; "every creature" the subject and object of effort; and every believer a seed of God, necessary for the sowing of the world field and the final harvest for the garner.

This parable of nature teaches lessons of supreme value:

First, that, unless divinely implanted by the Word of God, there is no life in us. By no "spontaneous generation" can spiritual life produce itself. Lord Kelvin, president of the Naturalist Society in England, said in 1871, in his famous opening address:

> A minute examination has not, up to this time, discovered any power capable of originating life, but life itself. Inanimate matter cannot become living except under the influence of matter already living. This is a fact in science as well ascertained as the law of gravitation. And I am ready to accept as an article of faith, in science, valid for all time and in all space, that LIFE IS PRODUCED BY LIFE AND ONLY BY LIFE.

Infinitely more true, if possible, is it that divine life in the human spirit comes only from divine seed. "He that soweth the good seed is the Son of Man." What was the good seed he sowed? The *Word of God*, which he not only spake and taught, but lived and WAS. Until his teaching finds in us a place, as seed in the soil, we have no life in us (John 6:53; 63). His teaching, containing vital truth about salvation and enforced, illustrated, incarnated in his own life and work, is life-giving to human souls. This is the first stage—*implantation*.

Then comes the second stage. The seed of truth must "take root downward and bear fruit upward." It must find a reception in the heart, room and root, if it is to develop into blade and ear. Down deeper than mere outward hearing, or even intellectual understanding, it must penetrate to the heart and conscience and lay hold of affections and will. This is the stage of *germination*.

But even germination has its stage of perfection: "first the blade, then the ear, then the *full grown corn* in the ear." There may be a growth—such as is indicated in the third sort of soil (Matt. 13:22), when the blade attains a certain length of stalk, but forms no ear, or if so no kernel. But this is not growth into perfection. True normal development produces the seed in itself after its kind. This is the third stage, *fructification*.

Our Lord reminds us that even yet there must be a *death* of the seed if it is to attain its divine destiny. "Except a corn of wheat fall into the ground and die it abideth alone; but if it die, it bringeth forth much fruit" (John 12:24). It is God's will that no believer abide alone. Even our Lord himself had a horror of such abiding alone, and welcomed the cross, that, dying, he might bring forth much fruit. What is this *death*? In the case of the seed it is not absolute but relative; it dies *as a seed* to live *as a crop;* nothing really perishes except the original form of the seed. In the disciple's case, death is the voluntary sacrifice of self-interest. He dies to self that he may live to God. But as in the case of the seed, it is not a final and absolute loss even of the self-life. Like his master, his cross and tomb have a resurrection after them. He loses life now to find it hereafter. Self-interest is sacrificed in this world to be found in a higher sense in the world to come. Present self-indulgence, self-seeking, self-advantage are laid on the altar of service; but no self-denial is a final forfeiture, only a temporary postponement. He that loseth his life in this world keeps it unto life eternal. This is the fourth stage—self-abnegation in order to *dissemination*.

Then follows the grand result—the harvest. And our Lord suggests its possible magnitude—"some thirty, some sixty, some an hundredfold." This language simply follows the figurative form of the truth he presents—a part of the drapery of the parable. The ordinary ear of grain contains not less than thirty kernels; but Isaac's sowing at Gerar yielded an hundredfold (Gen. 25:12), which doubtless suggested this high measure of fruitfulness in this parable.

But let us consider what hopes this language inspires, construed literally. If we roughly estimate at five hundred millions the professed number of Christians now living, and reckon only one in ten of them all as truly regenerate, what a harvest would be possible even with an average increase of thirty-fold! Suppose every disciple of these fifty millions to be the means of multiplying himself or herself thirty-fold—being the instrument of saving one soul each year for thirty years—at the end of that time the number of disciples would equal the entire present population of the globe—fifteen hundred million! And should each multiply an hundredfold—which supposes only about three souls saved a year, as the fruits of every disciple's tillage, the Christian population would at the end of a third of a century be more than three times the whole human family now living! So easy would it be, humanly speaking, to people this globe in the course of the lifetime of one generation with disciples of Christ. This suggests the fifth and last stage—*multiplication*.

We are quite aware that the problem of a world's evangelization and salvation cannot be solved arithmetically. Yet our Lord's own words have suggested this numerical calculation and estimate, and it is but too obvious that most of us live an essentially selfish life, even as Christians, content to abide alone, and practically heedless of the world field.

It is hinted in Genesis that God's plan is to subdue the world by this multiplication of the good seed of the kingdom. To our first parents he said, "be fruitful and multiply, and replenish the earth and subdue it." This suggests that he purposes that the higher forms of life shall predominate, and so dominate the lower. It is the triumph of mind over matter, brain force over brute force, spirit over flesh. Sometimes the farmer plentifully sows a vigorous sort of grain that its stronger vitality may crowd out and displace noxious weeds; and often in the animal realm, breeding strong types of animals in due time does away with the weaker and diseased. God has ordained that there shall always and everywhere be left virtue, intelligence, industry, honesty and integrity enough to cope with vice, ignorance, indolence, fraud and crime; the only necessity being a proper *application* of the better elements to the social corruption—as a little salt may arrest the decay of a whole mass. The divine way of subduing the evil in this world is by multiplying the good and securing right contact. And every evil doer, turned into a doer of good, both decreases the forces of evil and increases those of righteousness. Here, then, we find a sixth principle: *subjugation*.

The same lesson in Genesis hints a *succession of crops*. Every harvest furnishes "seed for the sower as well as bread for the eater," and so rapidly does seed multiply in geometrical progression that a single grain of wheat, multiplying through twenty successive crops, might yield enough seed to plant every square foot in the solar system! He who sets in motion a good word or work, who by speech or example starts what is good, is first in a series that multiplies infinitely and eternally.

The mother of John Newton by her prayers and tears brought her profligate boy to Christ. He in turn was blest to Thomas Scott; then the great commentator to William Cowper, and the poet to William Wilberforce, and the great emancipator to Leigh Richmond, whose tract, *The Dairyman's Daughter*, has probably been the means of saving millions. But think what fruit will ultimately be found to be due to that agonizing mother's pleadings for her wayward son!

When Saul of Tarsus, at the vision of the crucified, gave up his own will and way for his newfound master's, how little he imagined the final harvest of that self-abnegation. He died daily that he might live eternally in souls saved. That one man planted churches all through Asia Minor and founded at Philippi the mother church of all Europe and America. He left fourteen epistles and we are today reading, studying and preaching from them. That seed fell into the ground that day to die, and already there is no measure big enough to estimate the crop. Here then is the last of these seven thoughts on service suggested by the seed sown in the field—increase by a series of crops in indefinite *perpetuation* and *succession*.

2. The Example of Stewardship

A second marked stage of teaching on the subject of service is reached when we first meet with an example of *stewardship*.

This proves to be another of the pervasive ideas of Scripture, and here again we shall be much helped by observing the first mention of a steward, in Genesis 15:2. "The steward of my house is this Eliezer of Damascus." The literal rendering here is: "the son of possession"—that is, the possessor of my house or personal property. "This son of Mesek is Dammesek—Eliezer." There is an alliteration and play on words in the original not seen in English but apparent in the Septuagint. Eliezer is probably the same man referred to in chapter 24:2 as Abraham's eldest servant, whom he sent to Padan-Aram to take a wife for Isaac. It is significant that in this first "steward" mentioned in the Bible its author has given all needful hints as to what stewardship involves. It is expressly stated that "all the goods of his master were in his hand" (24:10); that his master was "become great, in flocks and herds and silver and gold, men servants and maid servants, and camels and asses" (35). The steward was content to be known as his master's "servant," and in his visit to Laban's home he does not even appear to have revealed or used his own *name*, but is known throughout the narrative simply as Abraham's servant. Though all the goods of his master are in his hand, he never calls them his own, treats them as his own or uses them for his own purposes. They are always his master's goods, in his hand only for his master's uses. Our Lord hints that stewards should be "faithful and wise," and Eliezer well exemplifies these two qualities uniformly represented as pertaining to an ideal steward: faithfulness in always using what he held for his master; wisdom in studying how to make them most profitable in promoting his master's ends. As we follow his course, we see how remarkable were his zeal, fidelity, sagacity and unselfishness—the last amounting to absolute self-oblivion. Nor is it any accident that, in presenting this Scripture portrait of the ideal steward, the name given him, "*Eliezer,*" means *my God is my help*—the highest lesson of all; for how can I as God's steward be a help to my master if my master himself is not, at every step and stage, my help?

This conception of divine help is, with exquisite beauty, set forth in the narrative in Genesis. As he started on his errand, he sanctified it by a solemn vow of fidelity. He is to go forth as Abraham's confidential servant with authority to act for him in one of the gravest matters possible—bringing back a bride for the son of promise and heir of all things. In the customary way, he made oath as to the matter in charge and then went forth with blessing. At every successive step he sought and received new divine guidance. Arriving at the well by Nahor, he made his camels kneel down to rest while he knelt to pray. With the simplicity of a little child, he put into the hands of the Lord the whole commission he was to execute, even venturing to suggest the form of the sign he desires, and he receives the exact providential aid he asks. Every subsequent step is taken in a like spirit, under the same guidance. The jewels of his master are displayed, but only to win the bride for Isaac. If he is impatient of indecision and delay, it is only because his master's business requireth haste, and it is his master's interests that he always pleads and urges.

Whether the steward here portrayed in such clear lines and glowing colors is the Eliezer of sixty years before or not, we have here a complete outline of what stewardship means and involves; and this narrative, like so many other first things in the Word of God, sets the key to all teachings on the same subject that follow.

There are at least four cardinal ideas necessary to this scriptural portrait of stewardship.

First and fundamental is that of an *entrustment*. The steward of God is not an owner but a trustee. The goods in his hand were originally, and continue to be inalienably his master's goods.

Then follows, naturally, the idea of *investment*, or *employment*—the goods are in his hand to be used, invested, employed for his master's service, not as in a bank, to be kept, however safely, but, like current coin, put into circulation for good uses and increased values.

There is implied, of course, an additional idea of *opportunity*, for if there were no errand and commission there could be proper use of the goods: and, in this case, the exact way to discharge the trust is made known.

The other necessary idea is *responsibility;* the trustee is to be called to an account for his stewardship.

As the Word of God is studied, it reveals certain other minor peculiarities of stewardship.

Its *universality*. It includes all *men*, for the master of all commits "to every man his work." Whether the entrustments be equal, as in the distribution of the pounds, or unequal, as in the case of the talents, no one of all the servants is left out in the distribution. Again, all *work* is assigned. No sphere of activity is left unoccupied. Again, all *ability* in the workers is fitted with its corresponding activity—"to every man according to his several ability." The entrustment implies enablement. God calls on no man to work without furnishing the means. But all things belong to God.

Stewardship is all embracing in its *variety* and comprehensiveness. *Life* itself is an entrustment—the possession of vital energy allies us to the living one, and we are to study to develop and direct vital force, that first and most solemn of all entrustments. Then the *powers* of life— thought, love, will—are divine entrustments. Thought is the life of the intellect; love, the life of the heart; choice, the life of the will. Who shall measure the possibilities of thinking, loving, choosing! The gift of *speech* is of vast value. It distinguishes man above all animals, even those that imitate and mimic human utterance. Between the prattle of the parrot and the language of a thinker the gulf is almost infinite. Speech may be employed for God in a measure that only eternity can reveal or infinity measure. Hobbes therefore said that man differs from other animals "*rationale et orationale*—by reason and speech."

Property—money and all material possessions—form so conspicuous a trust that we principally but mistakenly think only of these when we speak of stewardship. Our worldly calling, trade or profession, the Scripture teaches, is an assignment of God (1 Cor. 7:20–24). It is therefore not a human business only, but a divine vocation; in the workshop, every tool is branded with the name of God. Jesus has forever made the carpenter shop as sacred as the temple. Our whole position and influence among men should be looked upon as God-given and constituting a part of the trust committed to us.

A valuable hint is found in the word "*exchangers*" (Matt. 25:27). These were bankers, parties who studied the investment of money as a science. If the steward distrusted his own ability to make his one talent yield profit, and feared he might lose the talent itself as well as all gain from its investment, there were others who undertook safely and profitably to invest, and he might have employed their intelligence and sagacity in lieu of his own. The exchangers—*trapezitae*—received money on deposit and paid interest for its use.

Have we not here a valuable divine suggestion? There is no excuse for a useless life. This "unprofitable" servant was "wicked and slothful." His plea of fear lest he should lose his master's goods was a pretext, and out of his own mouth he is convicted. His master's argument is a refutation of his own plea, which his own conduct shows to be fictitious. Had he really been moved to bury his talent by a timid apprehension of the risk of trading on his own account like his fellow servants, there was another way of realizing at least a moderate return of interest, by putting out the talent he had buried to usury in the hands of those more competent.

Here is a direct lesson on the duty and privilege of *helping one another*. More timid and less gifted people, who feel themselves unfitted for independent action on behalf of the kingdom of God, may so associate themselves with others, wiser, stronger, more experienced and more capable, as to make their ability a substitute for their own. There are others whom God has lifted to responsible positions of authority and opportunity, whose counsel and help one may use so as to increase his own usefulness. It is the old fable illustrated, of the blind man carrying the lame man—he became legs to the cripple while the cripple became eyes to him—and thus both reached the goal that neither could reach alone.

Bible students will observe that there are three parables which turn upon the same general pivot, of a divine call to service and a final settlement in wages and rewards: the parables of the *talents*, the *pounds* and the *pence* (Matt. 25:14–30; Luke 19:12–27; Matt. 20:1–16). Only by taking the three together do we learn the complete lesson. In the first, the distribution is unequal, but the improvement equal, and the reward the same. In the second, the distribution is equal but the improvement unequal, and the rewards proportionate. In the third, the opportunity is unequal, but the readiness to make it available even when it comes at the eleventh hour causes the compensation to be the same as to those called at the earlier hours. Thus the parable of the talents teaches that *ability* differs; and the parable of the pence that *opportunity* differs; but all unite in the lesson that these differences are of God and need not affect the final result, if whatever our measure of ability, it be improved to the utmost; and whatever the lateness of our opportunity, it be promptly and diligently used.

We are not to compare ourselves with others; it is unwise. There is no denying the fact that all are not alike highly endowed, and that to all opportunities are neither equally early or frequent; but all that God asks is that whatever he gives in trust, though but one talent, shall not be buried in uselessness, or spent in wastefulness, but put out to usury; and that opportunity, whatever he gives and whenever he gives, may be at once laid hold of, even at the last hour. Then he will see that we suffer no loss in the final award. He will equally approve all who are equally faithful. "If there be first a *willing mind*, it is accepted according to that a man *hath* and not according to that he hath not" (2 Cor. 8:12), one of the profoundest principles ever enunciated as to service.

How immensely important these suggestions connected with stewardship! All we have is God's, and not ours, save to use for him. It is all to be invested and so improved, not like money hoarded, even though not lost, but like coin "current," running about in circulation and gathering increase as it runs. If one lacks ability or opportunity for wise and safe investment, let him seek advice, and by association and cooperation with those who are abler and wiser, promote his own usefulness. Society is organized for mutual helpfulness; and particularly in the church, with its experienced boards and committees, its philanthropic schemes and missionary societies, even the poorest and humblest believer may find channels for abundant increase.

No man need lack for large service and reward. The prayerful use of life with its golden hours; of powers of mind, thought, reason, imagination, memory; of the grand weapon of influence, the tongue; of the heart's rich capacities of sympathy and unselfish affection: who shall measure these possibilities!

Every secular calling is a gift from God, and even a workshop may become like the shoe shop of John Pounds, a schoolmaster's college, and the tools of the workman the tongues of witness. If only our business be our vocation—not an avocation, calling us away from our true service to God and man—we shall find that we have been in partnership with God. The great principle is to be an outlet as well as an inlet; to get in order to give, and receive to impart; to regard everything that comes to us as from God, to flow into and through us, leaving blessing behind, yet carrying blessing beyond; and that to cease to scatter is to decrease rather than increase, to become a stagnant pool instead of a living fountain.

3. Sharing and Giving

A third conspicuous lesson in service may be found in the *holy place of the tabernacle* (Ex. 30:1–10; 37:10–29; Heb. 9:2).

To this we have referred before,[30] but the subject now under consideration would hardly allow an omission of a further mention of what seems divinely meant to forecast the whole possibilities of Christian service. For consider that, in the nature of the case, there are only three ways of honoring God and serving men: first, by consecrating all *property* to unselfish purposes; second, by *witnessing* to the truth and to Christ by anointed lips and a transformed life; and third, by *praying* without ceasing for every good gift for ourselves and others. These three forms of service are all inclusive; outside of the spheres they embrace and the possibilities they suggest, there are no other ways of rendering service. To live unto God, first of all, so that the testimony of the tongue is not annulled but enforced by that of the temper, and character and conduct, speaking in their mute but mighty manner of the God-life within; then to distribute freely, humbly, conscientiously and constantly of all God's entrustments, counting all as his, so that there is no room either for pride or perversion of gifts; and to crown all by that holy prayer life that learns to prevail with men by prevailing with God, and to reach the greatest results on earth by way of intercession at the throne of grace—surely this is the perfect ideal of service.

It would be a coincidence—far more marvelous if by chance rather than by design—that the three articles of furniture between the first and second veils so singularly suggest exactly these three comprehensive forms of service: the table of shewbread, with its supplies weekly renewed, naturally reminding us of the duty of laying by in store on the first day of the week for all the purposes of benevolence, according as God hath prospered us; the golden lampstand, with its seven lights, illustrating the fact that we are the light of the world, witnesses to compel others to believe; and the golden incense altar, nearest the second veil and the mercy seat, standing so obviously for that closest approach to the divine presence found in devout communion with him who styles himself the hearer of prayer.

One of the most beautiful lessons in service is found in the very *simplicity* of it all. Here is nothing impossible or impracticable to the most

---

30 See chapter 4, page 72 ff.

ungifted and unlettered. A child can understand all this and do it. Yet there is no department of this threefold service that is not shamefully neglected.

Giving is still confined to the few, and here lies a stupendous mistake, that we so often measure by the aggregate sum instead of the proportionate distribution of the offerings—by the amount given and not by the number giving and the sacrifice involved. We forget that the greatest benefit of giving is felt in the giver not the receiver, and hence the fewer the givers the less the blessing. God and his poor may have need of our bestowments, but not half as much as we of bestowing.

In voltaic or galvanic electricity to increase the force of the current it is necessary not to enlarge the *size* of the cells but to increase their *number*. So, in order to increase the power of gifts in God's kingdom, we must not enlarge the individual gifts so much as increase the number of givers. If one man could and would give everything that is needful for missions, it would be the greatest possible evil for all the rest. It is not colossal individual benefactions that are needed so much as a great aggregate of individual gifts that are small, but which blend as rills to form a great river. It is an awful thing indeed when people lose sight of the *individual* responsibility of giving. We need such giving as makes every believer a constant and conscientious giver, giving in proportion as God prospers, and cheerfully—giving as a steward of God, who does not regard anything as his own, but everything as *his*, and, therefore, pours it back in the lap of God, as having first come from God—this is the giver that God will own.

To serve effectively, we must serve *intelligently*. If witnessing, giving and praying are God's appointed forms of service, surely knowledge must fit for all.

These are days when there is an attempt to promote intercession for missions, and one finds everywhere memoranda meant to stimulate prayer. But we must beware of making our helps too mechanical. There is a great deal of praying that effects nothing because it affects the suppliant so little. Some of our supplications are so general, so unsympathetic and formal that even the mention of particular fields or workers carries no real effectiveness. To study the wants of a mission station, to know the needs of the natives and the exact condition of the work; to keep informed of the progress of events and trace the history of the Lord's dealings—to put one's self into the place of the missionary—this makes both praying and giving a mighty force in the kingdom. Then to abide in the presence of God until even knowledge of facts is saturated with passion for souls, until the burden of a dying world rolls on us so heavily that the only way to bear it is to bear it with him who bore it up to the cross—that is to find a whole night of prayer a rest and a relief. Mr. Finney was but converted when he began to feel this load upon him, and he spent a night in pleading with God; but before the dawn broke, there was another dawn within—he had a vision of God and a revelation that his prayer had prevailed.

As to proportionate giving, Rev. Joseph Brown, D. D., of Glasgow, says that men who, with different and increasing incomes, continue to give the same amount—"bolt over simple proportion into vulgar fractions."

IV. The Body Corporate

One more great lesson on service is found in the *body of Christ* (Rom. 12, 1 Cor. 12, Eph. 4, etc.).

Here all disciples are incorporated in one organism, Christ being the head and every one members one of another. To each member is assigned a sphere and a work, by the indwelling Spirit, for the service of the body generally.

No more suggestive metaphor is found in the Word of God. A few of its many lessons may be indicated:

There is neither room nor reason for an unprofitable life, for God has provided for each a place of service.

There are many members, so there is plenty of work for all.

All have not the same office. So there is plenty of scope for all varieties of ability and adaptation.

All are alike necessary though not alike important; so that none can afford to be neglectful.

All are mutually dependent. None, therefore, can work alone, but in cooperation with all the rest.

All are assigned to their respective places by God, and so there is no room either for boasting, envy or discontent.

All receive their power from the head. Hence none need despair of success or can afford to be self-confident.

All are united to the one head. Hence all share the same dignity, honor and privilege.

All belong to one body, so that weakness in any one is supplemented by the strength of others and by the vital force that pervades the whole.

The providence of God is, in our day, as with special trumpet call, summoning the whole church to service as never before. No period in all history has ever presented such facilities and opportunities, and we may add invitations, to serve. In this respect God seems to have exhausted himself.

There is in his bestowments a regular succession and progression. The great first step, after the fall, was the calling out of an elect family to be conservators of the truth. Then he gave his Word orally, and later in written form, till the Old Testament was complete. Then his Son came to fulfill and exemplify the Word and guide his people. Last of all, the Holy Spirit was given, and God's last gift is always his best, for it includes all that went before. The Spirit illumines the written Word, magnifies and glorifies Christ the living word, and beside all this, regulates and sanctifies the believer. So that we may reverently say that God has exhausted himself. He has added the New Testament to the Old; in the Lord Jesus Christ he has fulfilled prophecy and founded Christian history; and the Holy Spirit, resident in believers, individually and collectively, throws light on the Scriptures and radiance into the face of Christ, and becomes the personal guide in holy living. What could even God do more!

With all these gifts, he has in the most wonderful way thrown open the whole world to Christian effort. All nations are, as never hitherto, an open field for witness. New methods of transportation and communication have made the world a neighborhood, where nobody is afar off. Modern invention has made the Bible so cheap and plentiful that, at trifling cost, it may be scattered everywhere; and scholarship has already made it available in five hundred dialects. Moreover, within about eighty years God has successively called out his reserves: first, women, as such, in the Zenana work, and later in organization for all mission enterprise; then young men in Christian associations; then young women in similar associations; then young people as a whole in Christian endeavor, student volunteer and like societies. He has no reserves left but the cradle roll, and he is beginning to call *that* also. Surely the providential summons is emphatically to serve in a new and peculiar sense.

V. Reward

No study of service is complete that leaves out *reward*, and in nothing is Biblical teaching more unique: its originality and sublimity form a new argument for the divine authorship of the Scriptures. In all the literature of the ages there is nothing approaching the system of compensation unveiled in the sacred page. We can only sketch this in outline, but the dominant principles which govern God's administration of rewards should be indicated.

(1) First, it is not the *sphere* but the *spirit* which he recognizes and rewards, not position but disposition. As he himself assigns to each his work as he wills, all spheres of service are lifted to one common plane of dignity; and all he asks is that we shall be content wherever he puts us, and humbly do his will in whatever sphere or at whatever work. Hence those words:

> He that receiveth you receiveth me, and he that receiveth me receiveth him that sent me.
>
> He that receiveth a prophet in the name of a prophet shall receive a prophet's reward; and he that receiveth a righteous man in the name of a righteous man shall receive a righteous man's reward (Matt. 10:40–41).

The Jews thought the prophet outranked priest and king because, as Jehovah's mouthpiece, he instructed and rebuked both; and as his office was highest, so his reward. Yet our Lord startles his disciples by announcing that to *receive* a prophet, in his capacity as such, entitles one to share *his* reward, because to help to make the prophet abler to do his work is to take part indirectly in that work.

Elijah was "received" by the woman of Zarephath when she gave him her last handful of meal and last drops of oil; and she received a prophet's reward in the miraculous increase of the meal in the barrel and the oil in the cruse. Elisha was "received" by the woman of Shunem into the little chamber in the wall, with its bed, table and candlestick. She also found the oil miraculously increase; and both these women who ministered to the prophets of their substance had a prophet's reward in the resurrection power which wrought in their own homes and upon their own sons (1 Kings 17, 2 Kings 4).

(2) Again, rewards depend not on *endowment* but *improvement;* not on how much property, but how much profit. It is not of importance how much we have but how much use we make of what we have, as we have

seen in the comparison of the three parables of the talents, the pounds, and the pence.

(3) God regards the *quality*, not the *quantity*, of the work done; not how much but how well. Never once is stress laid on *numbers*. Our Lord was as ready to meet one man, Nicodemus; or one outcast, like the woman at the well, as to preach to the throngs; and Philip was ready to leave crowded Samaritan villages to guide one inquirer on the desert road. The poor widow's two mites were more in the Lord's eyes than all the rich sums cast into the treasury because of the spirit behind them.

(4) The *least* act done for Christ is as sure of reward as the *greatest*.

> Whosoever shall give to drink unto one of these little ones a cup of cold water only in the name of a disciple, verily I say unto you, he shall in no wise lose his reward (Matt. 10:42).

Perhaps you cannot afford to give the *cup*, but you can give what is in it: *that* costs you nothing but a trip to the spring and a dip in its waters. But as the altar sanctifieth the gift, the purpose to relieve thirst makes the deed noble.

(5) The whole *performance* is judged by the *purpose*.

> If there be first a willing mind, it is accepted according to that a man hath, and not according to that he hath not.

David did well that it was in his heart to build a house for God, though he was not permitted to build it; and he was rewarded as if he had carried out his heart's desire. It is your part to desire and design, but it is God's part to determine how far you are to fulfill both. But inasmuch as he sets your limitations, he rewards your intentions. If he sees that, if you had much to give you would give it, in his eyes you have given much. If he sees that you would do much if you were strong enough, in his eyes you have done much.

(6) Hence *dependence* not *independence* pleases him. Men are proud when they can "take the initiative," and count it great honor to be able to lead. But the Lord reserves to himself the initiative and leaves to us to follow his lead. We are too prone to plan for ourselves instead of letting him plan for us. Hence the energy of the flesh so often displaces the energy of the Spirit. Hence also the needless and sinful "worry" even "in the Lord's work." Cannot he take care of his own work? If "the eyes of the servant were always looking unto the hand of the master;" if we always

waited for his leading and depended always on his providing, we should cease to be at the mercy of circumstances, and rejoice even in bonds and imprisonment, like Paul at Philippi.

(7) *Surrender* not *success* is what he compensates. Duty is ours, results are his. We are to "cast our seed beside all waters, knowing not whether this or that shall prosper, or whether they both shall be alike good." Fidelity cannot ensure fertility, but it will assure divine approval. What is in our eyes a dismal failure may, in his, be a glorious success. Stephen purposed preaching and got stoning; but he died in unspeakable peace, and his death gave the church its greatest apostle. No steward is required to be successful but only to be faithful. Patient suffering is as much rewarded as active serving.

(8) But, most astounding of all, to be one with Christ in *serving* entitles us to be one with him in *reigning*.

> If any man serve me, let me follow me; and where I am, there shall also my servant be: if any man serve me, him will *my* Father honor (John 12:26).

From the footstool to the throne! From slave's apron to king's robe! Where before, in any scheme of religion, have the humblest servants been raised to the seat of sovereignty?

> Not outward sphere but inward heart;
> The love wherewith we do our part.
> Not how large gifts we hold in trust,
> But how far used, or left to rust;
> Not how much done but how well done,
> Faithful to many souls, or one:
> Seeking the Master's will to find,
> And lean on him, with peace of mind;
> Content to fail, in human eyes,
> His smile, the one reward we prize;
> In any sphere serve him alone,
> Till cross is left for crown and throne.

Chapter 13

The Problem of Suffering

Five texts suffice to indicate the lines of Biblical teaching:

By one man sin entered into the world, and death by sin" (Rom. 5:12).

Receiving in themselves that recompense of their error which was meet (Rom. 1:27).

Whom the Lord loveth he chasteneth, and scourgeth every son whom he receiveth (Heb. 12:6).

We glory in tribulations also: knowing that tribulation worketh patience; and patience, experience; and experience, hope (Rom. 5:3).

Choosing rather to suffer affliction with the people of God, than to enjoy the pleasures of sin for a season (Heb. 11:25).

Unto you it is given … to suffer for his sake (Phil. 1:29).

Next to sin, suffering is the most inexplicable enigma, and its mystery is threefold:

First, millions suffer, not in consequence of their own sins but of those of others before them; millions more are victims of a depraved, perverted social system that they did not frame but cannot escape; and in many cases, whole nations suffer from the temporary triumph of might over right, kept in bondage under systematic tyranny.

Again, a vast amount of suffering seems out of all proportion to individual sins or needs. There is apparent lack of equitable apportionment and administration. Sometimes the victim's whole life is one of torture, and often calamity is age-long, prolonged through generations, without either relief or hope.

Worse than all is the apparent silence and indifference of God. No merciful judge seems to administer the moral universe; or, if there be a God, he acts as one who neither knows nor cares, either unable or indisposed to interpose.

Those who have had no help from divine revelation in solving this problem have come at best to one of *three* conclusions: atheism, fatalism, or dualism.

The atheist says there is no God; that men are tossed to and fro by blind chance; that there is neither moral order nor moral government, nor any personality behind the universe. The fatalist conceives God as, like himself, held in the grip of an inexorable necessity—unable to interpose to save or help because himself but part of a universal machine, absolutely soulless, and moving with mechanical regularity and uniformity; so that whether one is crushed or exalted by it, there is no sovereign power to determine. The dualist recognizes in the universe two opposing forces— one benignant, the other malignant; one that seeks human welfare, and another that delights in man's misery, it being always uncertain which will have the ascendancy.

From all merely human theories we turn to see if there is no clear light upon this inscrutable mystery in the Word of God; and we find here a unique solution of the whole problem, which puts to shame the wisest system of human philosophy.

It is of primary importance, in studying this problem, to draw some clear lines of discrimination as to the different kinds of suffering, for the term is very comprehensive.

There are six sorts of experiences all falling under this general term, and which are worthy of a more extended study than can here be given to them:

I. Organic and hereditary (Jer. 31:29, Ezek. 18:2, Ex. 20:5, Rom. 5:12).

II. Penal and judicial, a form of retribution (Jer. 31:30, Ezek. 18:4, Num. 32:23, Prov. 5:22–24).

III. Corrective and reformatory, meant to restore to righteousness. This is paternal (Heb. 12:5–13, 1 Cor. 5:5, 11:31).

IV. Disciplinary and educative, preparatory for greater sanctity and service (Heb. 5:8, 2 Cor. 4:17, 18, 2 Cor. 12:1–10, 1 Peter 2:19, 4:13).

V. Permissive and vindicative, designed for the vindication both of God and saints (Job 1, 2, Ps. 34:17–22; 35:17–28).

VI. Voluntary and vicarious—one of the great laws of the kingdom (2 Cor. 1:5–9, Col. 1:24, Phil. 3:10).

To discriminate between these is necessary, that we may know both the source of suffering and its object and what should be our attitude toward it, whether to accept it as inevitable or recognize it as avoidable;

whether as inflicted in judgment or mercy, to be patiently borne or penitently got rid of; whether it is a penalty from a judge, a preparation for higher blessing from a father, or a privilege to be welcomed as part in the larger scheme of promoting the glory of God in the final triumph of righteousness.

I.

First, there is suffering which is *organic and hereditary*. It is due to organic connection with the race, not only to immediate but remote ancestry, much of it traceable as far back as Adam, in whom we all died, so that "death reigned even over them that had not sinned after the similitude of Adam's transgression" (Rom. 5:14).

God has solemnly said that he "visits the iniquity of the fathers upon the children unto the third and fourth generation" (Ex. 20:5–6). The leprosy of Naaman was judicially inflicted upon him and his children (2 Kings 5). This hereditary suffering is an unquestionable fact. Organic penalties follow violations of organic law and affect all who are in the social organism. Somebody does wrong, and the effects individuals have to endure, in body and mind, because of their connection with the race. "In Adam all die." We may dispute that statement theologically, but it is one of the most patent facts. No man can transmit to his posterity any better conditions than his own. When our first father sinned and fell from his high estate, he broke up the symmetry of his being and contracted the taint of sin; he lost communion with God and the capacity for fellowship with all holy beings. It was inevitable that his children should inherit his moral likeness; and though they had not sinned after the similitude of his transgression, they could not escape the consequences of his fall. It entailed not only suffering but the taint and tendency of a sinful nature. Whatever be our philosophy, the facts are obvious and indisputable.

To see the proofs, on a terrible scale, one has only to visit the slums of great cities, such as were once found in the Five Points at New York and the Seven Dials in London, where, before the sanitary broom had swept away the social filth, might have been seen the awful relics of generations of sin and crime. Fifty years ago, scores of adults and little children were there whose bodies were marked and marred with the features of vice, deformed and crippled, whose aptitude for drink and propensity to crime were inborn, to whom life was one long drawn out curse. But the most respectable of us all inherit evils for which we are not personally responsible.

What is to be our attitude toward such organic and hereditary suffering? We must, of course, submit, for it cannot be helped. It is part of the penalty of being born into this world and being members of the body politic, where, if one member suffers, all the members suffer with it. There is an organic bond between parent and child, and the offspring reap the harvest of the sins of not only the immediate parents but of the more remote ancestors.

There is a tendency to complain of this organic law—to find fault with the creator because "the fathers have eaten sour grapes and the children's teeth are set on edge," as Jeremiah recorded long ago as heard by him. God has been arraigned as unjust because parental transgressions have transmitted to their children abnormal tendencies and aptitudes, like the fabled eagle that in stealing the sacrificial victim from an altar, bore with it a live coal that set fire to its nest and burned up its young. But such complaints have found an answer in the arguments of an infidel scientist who, from the scientific point of view, vindicates this law of nature as just and wise and good, on the whole, notwithstanding the incidental suffering it often causes. The design of his fable is to show that we *cannot have a law in operation for good which may not become a source of suffering when perverted.*

He represents a young man as complaining to Jupiter that in consequence of his father's debaucheries he is pierced with severe pangs and is unjustly punished for sins not his own. Jupiter replies that, in accordance with the very law of which he complains, he has also received from his father delicate nerves and vigorous muscles, senses that are inlets of joy and many noble capacities and faculties of mind and heart. Jupiter offers, in his case, to *suspend the offensive organic law,* but warns the young man that, in losing his pain he shall lose all advantages and blessings coming to him through the same law of hereditary descent; and he further reminds him that even his pain is a messenger of mercy, a monitor to warn him from the vicious paths trodden by his father. The sufferer withdrew his complaint, resigned himself to his suffering, grateful in view of the many blessings which had likewise come down to him in consequence of his parent's better qualities and resolved to be himself obedient.[31]

---

31 G. Combe, *The Constitution of Man Considered in Relation to External Objects.*

The fable teaches a plain lesson. The same law that works evil when perverted, works good when obeyed. For, while God threatens to visit to the third and fourth generation the iniquities of the fathers upon the children, in accordance with the *same method or law of dealing*, he promises to "show mercy unto *thousands of generations* of them that love him and keep his commandments." While the consequences of disobedience thus reach to the fourth generation, the rewards of obedience reach to the remotest time. And so, however awful the penalties of evildoing, the blessed results and rewards of well-doing are even greater.

The creator originally meant and adapted heredity as a channel of blessing; sin turned it, in part, into a channel of cursing; but he is not to blame for its perversion. Nor has the law ceased to have its beneficent side. It acts as a sentinel, warning against similar violation or neglect of organic law. Temperate and virtuous habits of life may not only convey blessing to those after us, but relieve, if not remove, the hereditary evils from which we suffer, promoting health and happiness. We may thus be stimulated to such a pure and upright life as may help future generations to rise to a loftier level.

II.

A second department of suffering is *judicial and penal*—a visitation of *retributive penalty* upon the evildoer himself. It is due to the demand of a righteous law and an inflexibly just judge. It marks the perfection of God's government that no evildoer escapes. "Every transgression and disobedience receives a just recompense of reward" (Heb. 2:2). God himself would become a partner in sin were it otherwise.

The Bible teaches us that there are *three or four qualifications* which modify the working of this law.

1. Judgment covers *two realms*, here and hereafter. The scope of retributive and penal suffering extends both over time and eternity. The great white throne is beyond this world. There is constant working of retribution even here, but it is designedly incomplete, because this life is *probationary*, and affords opportunity for repentance and reformation, and all sinners here are under suspended sentence for the time; and, because perfect adjustments of both reward and penalty are not possible here, there is a larger plan of God's providence that finds its outworking in eternity. Should every transgression at once be visited with penalty, all

probation would cease with the first voluntary sin, and the world would be depopulated by God's judgments.

2. A perfect adjustment is impossible in this world because of *incompleteness;* much of man's evil doing goes *on to the very end;* and there can be no proper compensation or recompense for either right or wrong until both are complete. Acts must be committed before they can be compensated, and the larger plans of retribution must take in the life beyond.

3. God's administration also recognizes in dealing with man the principle of *substitution.* Grace has provided a voluntary and vicarious substitute for human offenders—a marvelous scheme of love whereby a broken law shall be vindicated and all the great ends of the divine government answered without the visitation of penalty upon the sinner himself. Meanwhile, judgment is suspended until it is seen how the transgressor will treat the proffer of salvation—whether he will accept or reject the offer of amnesty. But, either in himself or his substitute, the equivalent price of sin must be paid (John 11:49–52). Obviously, much penal suffering is avoidable. "Sin no more, lest a worse thing come upon thee."

4. There is a further modification of this law, that it must be so administered that even *mercy* shall not imperil *justice.* A forgiven sinner sometimes has to suffer in part the judicial penalty for his sin, lest indiscriminate laxity set a premium upon transgression. *Eternal* penalties are abolished, while *temporal* penalties remain. After David's confession of his great sin, Nathan the prophet said, "The Lord also hath put away thy sin; thou shalt not die. Nevertheless, because by this deed thou hast given occasion to the enemies of the Lord to blaspheme, the child that is born to thee shall surely die" (2 Sam. 12:14). And a further penalty was visited upon this public crime, in permitting the king's own son to commit a worse crime with his own father's concubines, and in a public manner. Even divine forgiveness, while sparing David final condemnation, taught all men that he who mercifully deals with sinners is nonetheless a just and righteous judge.

Our attitude toward such sufferings is to be one of glorying in the perfection of the divine administration. If, because of such perfection, I myself suffer, I must lose sight of my own discomfort in the larger interests of the moral universe; while I am lost in the infinite grace that provides for the entire abolition of eternal judgment in my behalf because of my faith in the Lamb of God, who beareth away the sins of the world.

Surely it is more than a relief to the dark shadows of retributive penalty that grace has planned such a scheme of mercy as that God can be just and yet justify the believing sinner. The ends of punishment are all met in the sacrifice of Calvary; God's law is upheld, his government vindicated, his own character exhibited as abhorring sin, transgressors themselves reformed, and it may be that others are prevented from similar sins in other spheres of the universe.

III.

Yet other suffering is purely *paternal, disciplinary, corrective*. It is meant to remedy our faults by measures as mild as possible. It is a sign not of God's holy displeasure but of his love. "Whom the Lord loveth he correcteth" (Heb. 12).

There are *two applications* of this method: first, to sinners, to bring them to repentance; and second, to saints, to refine, purify and sanctify. So long as there is hope of transgressors, mercy stays judgment, and the Lord chastens them in his longsuffering, to lead to true repentance and newness of life; then, when by faith they become his children, he still follows them with the rod of correction to make possible greater attainments in holiness and usefulness.

Such disciplinary suffering it would be disastrous to escape or avoid, except by that constant self-scrutiny that corrects also the faults and follies God would remove. Hence, "if we would judge ourselves, we should not be judged. But when we are judged, we are chastened of the Lord, that we should not be condemned with the world" (1 Cor. 11:31-32). Here a principle of great importance is enunciated: that there is a conscientious self-judgment which makes much divine chastening unnecessary. But in some cases, results are so precious that without suffering they are unattainable, as only fire can remove dross from silver and gold.

There is a tradition that by a disastrous conflagration in the Pyrenees, which destroyed vineyards and threatened the people with dire distress, rich veins of silver were disclosed that more than compensated for all the loss. Many a seeming disaster to a child of God proves the disclosure of new veins of experience and fellowship with God. Sorrowing saints discovering these mines of consolation and compensation in God have learned to comfort others with the comfort wherewith they have been comforted of God; and such deep experience has been the means of enriching others far beyond all that could have been imagined.

"Our God is a consuming fire." But while sinners have reason to fear this consuming fire as one of judgment, the saint rejoices that the same fire burns up what he desires to be rid of forever. We all learn in the trials of housecleaning that some accumulations of rubbish are never finally disposed of till they are consigned to the flames—the broom only sweeps them into some corner to be scattered again, and nothing but the fire will finally get them out of the way—so there is rubbish in our lives that only the consuming fire of God can remove. True heart cleanness is a costly product, and blessed be he who cheerfully submits to the divine discipline, leaving himself in the hands of a faithful Father.

IV.

This prepares us to consider a fourth form of suffering, close akin, but on a little higher plane: that which is *preparatory* and *educative*—which fits for closer fellowship with God, revelation of God, or service for God. Some experiences of suffering are times of spiritual uplifting, like the dawn after a dark night of unbelief. It is a fine saying of President Patton that "as the night grows darker the stars of prophecy come out."[32]

Our Father who seeks to perfect his saints in holiness knows the value of the refiner's fire. It is with the most precious metals that the assayer takes most pains, and subjects them to hot fires; because only such fires melt the metal, and only molten metal releases its alloy, or takes perfectly its new form in the mold. The old refiner never left his crucible, but sat down by it, lest there should be one excessive degree of heat to mar the metal, and so soon as, skimming from the surface the last of the dross he saw his own face reflected, he put out the fire.

How beautifully are we told that the redeemer "shall sit as a refiner and purifier of silver" (Mal. 3:3). Being determined to perfect his saints, he puts his precious metal into his crucible. But he sits by it and watches it. Love is his thermometer, and marks the exact degree of heat; not one instant's unnecessary pang will he permit; and as soon as the dross is released so that he sees himself reflected the trial ceases.

To be specific, God's object is not only to remove alloy, but to develop all the possibilities of the precious metal of character. There are three graces that outrank all others in Christian attainment: *patience, humility,*

---

32 Francis Landey Patton, elected President of Princeton University in 1888.

and *unselfishness* or *love*, all of which depend for development on suffering.

Obviously, patience is the direct fruit of trial, for it is the *faculty to endure*, and there must be something to be endured. How can we suffer patiently if we do not suffer at all? Patience is the night-blooming cereus in the Lord's garden, the flower that comes to fullness of bloom in adversity, and the greater the trial the more signal the beauty.

Humility, the lowly grace, generally implies an experience that brings down pride and self-sufficiency to the dust. With man, it is commonly born of defeat and disappointment. He naturally likes to strut like a peacock, displaying his feathers, and imagining that he has something to boast of; and the great majority learn to be humble only by being first humbled. When the collapse of our own plans, the defeat of our schemes, the loss of our self-confidence brings us prostrate, in our true attitude before God, we learn humility.

A merchant prince has said that the greatest quality in a successful merchant is "to know how to recognize his losses and deal with them;" and few attainments are of more value in a disciple than to find his own limitations and organize success out of defeat and failure. Only when we have got to the end of self have we got to the beginning of God! Human biographies generally magnify a man's successes, but when God writes biographies in Scripture, he shows how his saints have learned quite as much from their failures, as in the case of Job. Praise feeds pride, while rebuke helps to humility; and suffering is usually the precursor of a humble spirit.

As to unselfish love, whoever learned that lesson without trial! Whoever yearned over others without having passed through sorrow! It is in the furnace of tribulation, where self is consumed, that we learn how to sympathize with the tribulations of others. Poverty teaches us to relieve the poor, bereavement prepares us to console the bereaved, and self-loss is the very seed of an unselfish harvest.

Even the great captain of our salvation was made "perfect through suffering," and "learned obedience by the things that he suffered." If even he, the perfect man, reached his complete equipment for his work of leadership through a soldier's endurance of hardship, his followers should not be reluctant to undergo a similar training if they aspire to approximate, in any measure, a like result.

The Rev. Howard W. Pope tells the story of a Christian blacksmith who had a good deal of affliction, and being challenged by an unbeliever to account for it, gave this as his explanation:

> I don't know that I can account for these things to your satisfaction, but I think I can to my own. I am a blacksmith. I often take a piece of iron and put it into the fire and bring it to white heat. Then I put it on the anvil and strike it once or twice to see if it will *take a temper*. If I think it will, I plunge it into the water and suddenly change the temperature. Then I put it into the fire again, and again I plunge it into the water. This I repeat several times. Then I put it on the anvil and hammer it, and bend it, and rasp and file it, and it makes some useful article that I put into a carriage, where it will do good service for twenty-five years. If, however, when I first strike it on the anvil I think it will not take a temper, I throw it into the scrap heap and sell it at a halfpenny a pound.
>
> I believe that my heavenly Father has been testing me to see if I will take a temper. He has put me into the fire and into the water. I have tried to bear it as patiently as I could, and my daily prayer has been: "Lord, put me into the fire if you will; put me into the water if you think I need it; do anything you please, O Lord; only, for Christ's sake, don't throw me into the scrap heap!"

God puts so high a value upon "the riches of the glory of *his inheritance in the saints*" that, in order to perfect that inheritance, he subjects his saints to sorrow and suffering as a proprietor plows up his land and pulls down his homestead, that he may beautify the estate, which is his inheritance.

Suffering is not always a *penalty*, either judicial or organic. It often has for its end the purifying, beautifying and glorifying of character. Every form of figure is used in Holy Scripture to set forth this divine idea of sorrow, and yet we are such half-pagans that we think of suffering, practically, as though it were an expression of divine anger and not love.

What a solace would God's sorrowing saints pluck from the very boughs of trial could they but feel that he is purifying and perfecting them by the discipline of sorrow! Capt. Lott used to say that a little headwind is good, and favors progress; it makes the furnaces draw!

As we have seen, there are virtues and graces which depend on sorrow for growth. Unworldliness is learned only by the process that weans us from temporal and perishable things. If the wine is not poured from vessel to vessel it will settle on the lees and taste of them. The assurance of hope comes only when the anchor of hope has been tested by holding us in the gale. And how shall we get capacity to comfort others until we are ourselves comforted of God?

In the paper mill, what a contrast between the heap of filthy rags at one end and the pure and spotless white paper at the other! What a trial the rags go through before they emerge in this new form! Torn to pieces and ground to pulp, bleached with chloride of lime till all stains are removed, washed over and over; submitted to another bleaching by the action of chlorine and alum; washed again till the levigated pulp or stuff is white as cream or snowflakes; caught upon a wire cylinder, after the severe shaking by the Fourdrinier process, which crosses the fibers and gives compactness and firmness to the fabric, and then passed between and around the hot surfaces which makes the paper smooth and even; how like the divine discipline by which our filthiness is cleansed away; how like the tribulation out of which all they come up who have washed their robes and made them white in the blood of the Lamb!

In the preparation of ornamental pottery, how much depends on the *fire* of the *furnace*. The decorations are comparatively repulsive until the heat gives character and quality to the colors. The substances used in painting the pottery must be fused into glass, becoming soft in the furnace and at white heat melting into and incorporating with the substance of the vessel itself. Nor must the pottery *cool too quickly*, or the labor expended on it may be lost. And even after all this "experience," the dead surface must be polished by the blood-stones until the burnishing gives radiance and brilliance!

And yet how many Jacobs are there that cry in sorrow's hour, "All these things are against me" while "all things work together for good!" How many Rachels, bowing over the grave of their little ones, weeping for their children, *refuse to be comforted*, because they are not! Blessed are they who in the seeming shipwreck of worldly joy and temporal good, cast out of the stern the four blessed anchors of faith and hope and love and patience, and then, waiting, *"wish for the day!"*

Lift up your heads, sorrowing saints! Glory in tribulation, for it worketh patience, and patience experience. And what is *experience?* It is the approval of God—the stamp of the divine assayer, who, having purified the precious metal, marks it, *"approved."* When the Lord rejects the metal, he stamps it "reprobate;" when he releases it from the alloy so that it mirrors his own face, he stamps it "approved." Such "experience" prepares for that *hope* that maketh not ashamed and for that shedding abroad of his love in our hearts which is, above all other, the earnest and foretaste of heaven, the peace which passeth understanding!

> So, sorrow is the furnace fire,
> The fuller's soap, the vale of tears;
> Yet sorrow works my deep desire;
> His image in my soul appears!

V.

There is another sort of suffering that is *voluntary and vicarious*. It may be avoided; by all who do not enter deeply into fellowship with Christ it is escaped. This suffering is that into which we voluntarily enter for the sake of such intimate fellowship with the Lord and abundant service to men. The Lord himself need not have borne the cross of pain and shame; his life no man took from him; he had power to lay it down or keep it. But human sin needed a great salvation, and it could be secured only at the cost of his self-emptying.

There are many passages of Scripture that refer to a similar and voluntary sacrifice of self on the part of the disciple. He may avoid it and yet not forfeit his own *salvation*, but he *will* forfeit the closest union and fellowship with his Lord and the largest service to men.

For example, "If any man will come after me, let him deny himself and take up his cross and follow me" (Matt. 16:21–27). This, if we may trust both the context and the general teaching of Scripture, is not a condition of salvation but of service. It was spoken to *disciples as such*—to those who by believing had already come into a saved state, and is one condition of *coming after the Lord*, that is following him—that we do as he did and take up our cross as he did. To make this a term of *salvation* is to produce confusion, for we are repeatedly and emphatically taught that the simple, single act of *receiving God's free gift of eternal life in Christ* makes salvation our own. To make eternal life, therefore, to hang on any good work or heroic self-denial is to obscure grace by legalism. The lesson taught here is rather that if, being saved by the acceptance of the Lord Jesus Christ, we desire to follow him closely, such consistent discipleship is impossible without a voluntary assumption of that cross of self-abnegation which was the badge at once of his glory and shame. It is a question not of salvation but of coronation—voluntary assumption of the cross as the way to obtain the crown. A similar lesson is taught in John 12:24–31.

The "corn of wheat" may be laid up in a granary and preserved, but it will "abide alone;" the condition of producing a crop is its burial; it must die, as a seed, if it is to live in the harvest.

Scores of like Scripture teachings may be found, all conveying the same essential lesson. There is a voluntary assumption of "the sufferings of Christ," joining him in a vicarious work—that is in sacrifice for others' sakes. One may be saved because he has built upon the one foundation, even though the structure built upon it is as worthless and unenduring as wood, hay and stubble. But if the *work* is to last and be rewarded, it must be like the master's work. We must choose to go outside the camp and bear his reproach (Heb. 13:13). We must consent to the inevitable antagonism of the three great foes—the world, the flesh and the Devil. If we are of the world, the world will love its own; if we live as he did, a separate life, the world will hate us as it did him. A disciple may give way to the carnal, or resist it and yield to the spiritual; and he may resist the Devil and fight the good fight of faith.

Here is another territory of truth worthy of investigation: a soul may be saved and the life work lost. Heaven may be entered but with no reward. Many who are redeemed by blood will be uncrowned. The highest identification with a suffering Savior in glory will be reserved for those who have filled up that which is behind in his suffering, in their own flesh, for his body's sake, which is the church" (Col. 1:24).

This is a distinction that is oftener overlooked than clearly seen. The New Testament is especially clear in distinguishing gifts and rewards. Salvation is always represented as a free *gift*, with no condition save *acceptance*, which is the only condition attached to any gift. But there are works which, being done by the saved, are recognized and rewarded. Hence the same chapter in John which so grandly teaches that to those who ask Christ gives the living water, also teaches that "he that reapeth receiveth wages, and gathereth fruit unto life eternal" (verses 10, 13, 36). To shirk work does not forfeit the gift of salvation, but it forfeits the wages of service.

Hence, we repeat, this suffering for service's sake is not imposed on us but assumed by us. We choose it, and it is the fact of such voluntary entrance into such fellowship with the crucified which constitutes its charm and beauty. God does not *force* it upon us; it must be a free-will offering, not a compulsory or obligatory one. Gratitude for a free salvation and love for the Savior must prompt it. We elect to undergo this sacrifice, not like the Romanist to secure salvation, but to identify ourselves more closely with him to whom we owe salvation, and for the sake of hastening his triumph and the satisfaction of his travail. We consent to die to self that we may live to him. It is not our safety but our fruitfulness that is the ruling motive; and because it involves self-oblivion, comparatively few are willing to accept it; but the reward of it is great and can only be understood "in that day."

VI.

One more aspect of suffering remains to be considered—what we have called the *permissive* and *vindicative*.

Of this we should have known nothing, apart from the inspired volume; but it is especially unveiled in the book of *Job*. That great epic is a *theodicy*, or *justification of the divine government*, and only as such can be rightly read. The problem is to show how God's justice can be harmonized with the multiplied sufferings of a perfectly just man. The being arraigned before the bar of judgment is really not so much Job as Jehovah.

The name Job is typical: from the same root as the word "adversary" or "enemy," it means *one who is assaulted or persecuted by an adversary*; the very name is therefore the key to the book. In the prologue, three persons occupy the stage of action: Job, Satan and the Almighty God, the author, judge and rewarder of good in the universe, who, before the heavenly assembly, declares his satisfaction with Job's uprightness. Satan, the adversary, skeptical of all *untried* virtue and of all *unselfish* piety, challenges God's estimate of his servant; but, having no ground for impeaching his *outward conduct*, assails his *inward motive:* "Doth Job fear God for nought?" He boldly hints that if all the temporal rewards of his good behavior were withdrawn, his virtue would prove easily assailable—that his external prosperity was the hedge that fenced out temptation.

The thoughtful student will see that this blow was really aimed *at God himself*, for to deny that even the best of men loves God for his own sake, apart from his benefits, is to insinuate that he is not worth, or is unable to inspire, such love! To tell a manufacturer that, but for his wages, not a workman would have any respect for him, or to hint to a father that all that keeps his household from abandoning him is food and clothing, is, most of all, to humiliate the business head or the parent. To be incapable of winning disinterested love is to lack the highest virtue; and if Job only served God for what he got by it, God must himself be deficient in all that attracts true devotion.

Satan's hatred of God prompts him to charge God's model man with being a mere mercenary, that he may indirectly charge God with being himself lacking in perfection; for, as Godet says, *"no one is honored except so far as he is loved."*[33]

This assault on God explains the book. God vindicates his own honor by permitting Satan to attack this servant, to sweep away the hedge about him, and successively strike at his property, his family, and finally himself. The rich man suddenly becomes a beggar, the father childless, and the vigorous man is hopelessly smitten with leprosy, which, beside its terrors as disease, was a walking parable of death and divine judgment. Even his wife's faith turns to ashes, but Job still holds firmly to God.

Then comes the last form of Job's trial. His three friends turn against him and practically side with his wife and Satan. They argue that, as God is just and awards both virtue and vice righteously, Job's extraordinary and multiplied trials prove *secret* guilt, and urge him to confession. They see no clue to such suffering save that the God of recompenses is requiting evil doing; and that he by whom actions are weighed with exact justice is adjusting so much sorrow to so much sin.

Job is plunged into the deepest trouble, for he cannot answer such arguments. In default of help from reason, he appeals to conscience. He knows not what to do; if he vindicates God, he must accuse himself; if he vindicates himself he must accuse God. In despair he can only hold on to God, believing that at some time, it may be after death, his own vindication will come and in that the vindication also of his maker.

Elihu's voice is heard, toward the end of the book, as V. F. Oehler says, "indignant with Job, because he could only justify himself by accusing God; and with Job's friends because they could justify God only by accusing Job." He suggests a partial solution of the enigma: that suffering is not always retributive, but, as we have seen, purgative and educative, correcting faults and preventing lapses into sin. But this is not a complete explanation, which is reserved for Jehovah himself, who alone can explain his own ways.

Twice he overwhelms Job, in his first address challenging him to explain the mystery of the universe, and in the second to govern it better than his maker. While he scorns to justify himself in man's eyes, he thus

---

33 A. Vinet, *Old Testament Studies.*

reminds Job that he must trust infinite perfection and accept the veil of mystery that hides him, winning in the trial of patience by faith, not sight. And Job, having held out to the end, however imperfectly, has a double crown of prosperity.

All that we care now to emphasize is that some suffering, and that which is the most inexplicable, may be, as seen from heavenly summits, our highest honor, in that we were permitted to be assaulted of the Devil, *in order to the vindication of God;* that our pains and losses were not retributive of our sin, but vindicative of his perfection; that it was given us as a high privilege "to suffer for his sake," to show that he was so infinitely lovely that he could win and hold our affection and allegiance when only *himself* was left.

We close this imperfect study of the problem of suffering by suggesting a few grand reliefs to the darkness of what would otherwise be despair.

1. "*God is love.*" This is the last revelation of his character. Long before, in his Word he had been presented as righteousness, fountain of life and light, the holy one. But it is given to John, at last, to give this new name, and to declare not that he is lovely or loving, but IS LOVE—the incarnation of unselfish benevolence. We are therefore dealing with one who is too wise to err in judgment and too good to err through malice. In his hands we may safely trust ourselves, welcoming his discipline and confident that in doing as he pleases, he will please to do only what is the very best.

2. *Trial is the school of trust.* Faith gets new purity, temper and tenacity in furnace fires. It is in the deepest darkness of the starless midnight that men learn how to hold on the hidden hand most tightly and how that hand holds them; that he sees where we do not, and knows the way he takes; and though the way be to us a roundabout way, it is the right way and leads to the city of habitation.

3. The sweetest songs are "*songs in the night.*" Praise is easy when we are prosperous. There is a *natural* gratitude that says "God, I thank thee that I am not as other men are," but it takes a *spiritual* gratitude, in everything to give thanks, even when self-indulgence is turned into the endurance of pain. On sunny days, when blessings are plenty, there is an outpour of animal spirits that may easily be mistaken for joy in God. But would you be as joyful *in God* if there were less to be joyful for *in yourself and in your surroundings?* You say, "he has been very good to me," and you mean, in

your prosperity. Was he any less good to Job in his adversity? Can you bless him like Job, when he takes as when he gives? Yet he is sometimes more considerate of us in withholding or withdrawing what we love and crave than when he gives. Bestowments are sometimes worse for us than deprivations.

There is a hymn of Benjamin Schmolke's whose true beauty can be understood only by knowing the circumstances in which it was written. This Lutheran pastor first suffered from a fire that devastated his parish; then from a bereavement that emptied his home; then from a paralysis that left him a blind and helpless cripple. It was on his bed, after these accumulated afflictions, that he dictated that hymn, in which, by italicized lines, we indicate the references to all these forms of sorrow. How exquisitely pathetic, yet how gloriously triumphant!

> My Jesus, as thou wilt!
> Oh, may thy will be mine;
> Into thy hand of love
> I would my *all resign;*
> Through sorrow, or through joy,
> Conduct me as thy own,
> And help me still to say,
> My Lord, thy will be done!
>
> My Jesus, as thou wilt!
> Though seen through many a tear,
> Let not my star of hope
> Grow dim or disappear;
> Since thou on earth hast wept,
> And sorrowed oft alone,
> If I must weep with thee,
> My Lord, thy will be done!
>
> My Jesus, as thou wilt!
> All shall be well for me;
> Each changing future scene
> I gladly trust with thee:
> Straight to my home above
> I travel calmly on,
> And sing, in life or death,
> My Lord, thy will be done!

Thus the most precious fruits in character and life are the results of sorrow—the highest sanctity and the noblest service. It is worthwhile to have gone through tribulations as many as Paul's to have learned like him two lessons: how God can comfort us in all our tribulations, and how he can prepare us with a like solace to comfort others (2 Cor. 1:4-5). Our highest success is to be one with him, absorbed in his will and plan, so as to be absolutely confident in him when all seems against us.

A lesson on "the hardness of God's love" has been left for us by one who was for years laid on a couch of suffering:

> I kept for nearly a year the flask-shaped cocoon of an emperor moth. It is very peculiar in its construction. A narrow opening is left in the neck of the flask, through which the perfect insect forces its way; so that a forsaken cocoon is as entire as one still tenanted, no rupture of the interlacing fibers having taken place.
>
> The great disproportion between the means of egress and the size of the prisoned insect makes one wonder how the exit is ever accomplished at all, and it never is without great labor and difficulty. It is supposed that the pressure to which the moth's body is subjected in passing through the narrow opening is a provision of nature for forcing the juices into vessels of the wings, these being less developed at the period of emergence from the chrysalis than they are in other insects.
>
> I happened to witness the first efforts of my imprisoned moth to escape from its long confinement. Nearly a whole forenoon, from time to time, I watched it patiently striving and struggling to get out. It never seemed able to get beyond a certain point, and at last my patience was exhausted. I thought I was wiser and more compassionate than its maker, and resolved to give it a helping hand.
>
> With the points of my scissors I snipped the confining threads to make the exit just a very little easier, and lo! immediately, and with perfect ease, out crawled my moth, dragging a swollen body and little shriveled wings. In vain I watched to see that marvelous progress of expansion in which the wings silently and swiftly develop before our eyes; and as I traced the exquisite spots and working of divers colors, which were all there in miniature, I longed to see these assume their due proportions, and the creature appear in all its perfect beauty, as in truth it is one of the loveliest of its kind.
>
> But I looked in vain; my false tenderness had proved its ruin. It never was anything but a stunted abortion, crawling painfully through that brief life which it should have spent flying through the air on rainbow wings.
>
> The lesson I got that day has often stood me in good stead. It has helped me to understand what the Germans call 'the hardness of God's love.' I

have thought of it often when watching with pitiful eyes those who were struggling with sorrows, suffering or distress, and it has seemed to me that I was more merciful than God, and I would fain have cut short the discipline, and given deliverance. Short-sighted fool!—how know I that one of those pains and groans could be spared? The far-sighted, perfect love of God, which seeks the perfection of its object, does not weakly shrink from present transient suffering. Our Father's love is too true to be weak. Because he loves his children, he chastens them, that they may be 'partakers of his holiness.' With this glorious end in view he spares not for their crying. "Made perfect through suffering," as Christ was, the sons of God are trained up to obedience and brought to glory "through much tribulation."

4. *Suffering sometimes is the summit of privilege.* Nothing is more perilous to a disciple than a self-centered life; our danger lies in self sparing, not self denying. The Devil is always bidding us to spare ourselves, while the Lord as constantly bids us deny ourselves. Perhaps the transfiguration which immediately followed this injunction, this revelation of the life of suffering, was meant to teach the blessedness of voluntary self-emptying. From that mountaintop, doubtless, he might have ascended, had he chosen, to the true "delectable mountains" of his heavenly home, straight into the glory. And when Peter proposed the three tabernacles, in a double sense he knew not what he said; for, had the Lord chosen to abide in the glory, the world would have been left to abide in sin and sorrow. He descended from those marvelous glories to the shame of the cross. And thus he taught the disciples to *postpone the coronation and accept the crucifixion.*

We cannot atone for sin, but we may share the spirit of the atoning Savior. We may, like him, suffer for others' sakes; and to all such he says:

> Ye are they which have continued with me in my temptations, and I appoint unto you a kingdom, as my Father hath appointed unto me, that ye may eat and drink at my table in my kingdom, and sit on thrones judging the twelve tribes of Israel (Luke 22:28–30).

When Catharine of Siena used to stretch out her hand in agonizing intercession, and implore: "Promise me, dear Lord, that thou wilt save them! O, give me a token that thou wilt;" the Lord seemed to clasp her outstretched hand, and she felt a piercing pain, as though a nail had been driven through her own palm! She felt the grasp of the pierced hand of her Lord.

Who of us are willing, for the sake of saving souls, to share his pangs! Yet is there any power to win and save until we have felt that agony—until in some measure we have entered into the fellowship of his sufferings!

Here then is another great solution of a great enigma. The blind cannot lead the blind, except to the common ditch of a despairing perplexity. But he who follows scriptural leading finds a divine light cast into the darkest chambers of this problem of suffering.

Chapter 14

The Problem of Providence

The Scripture basis may be laid in a few leading texts:

Abraham called the name of that place, JEHOVAH JIREH—the Lord will provide (Gen. 22:14).

In all thy ways acknowledge him, and he shall direct thy paths (Prov. 3:6).

The Lord is a God of knowledge, and by him actions are weighed (1 Sam. 2:3).

The Lord God of recompenses shall surely requite (Jer. 51:56).

For this cause have I raised thee up, for to shew in thee my power (Ex. 9:16).

Surely the wrath of man shall praise thee: the remainder of wrath shalt thou restrain (Ps. 76:10).

He calleth his own sheep by name, and leadeth them out (John 10:3).

It marks the poverty of human language that even the rich English tongue supplies no word to express exactly what is meant by divine *"providence."* The word literally means pre-vision, a foreseeing, and so pre-vision comes to mean provision—preparation for that which is foreseen, and then to convey a larger conception of superintendence over creation, in all parts of the universe, through all ages of time, and in all matters, great or small. But no such fullness of meaning is suggested by the word itself.

The texts above quoted outline teaching that pervades the whole Bible, and which no isolated passages can properly represent. But a cursory glance shows that in them God is represented on the one hand as a *provider,* and on the other as a *recompenser;* that obedient souls may look to him for individual guidance, even in small matters, confident that in his general supervision of all, the individual is not forgotten; and that he constrains even his foes to fulfill his designs, restraining their violence within fixed bounds; and shewing himself a God of perfect knowledge and justice, by weighing with precision all human actions and with certainty requiting both good and evil.

No grander metaphors can be found, even in this inspired book, than those used to convey this conception of God's providence. He is represented as seated in heaven as on a throne, resting his feet upon the earth as his footstool; his raiment, the light; lightning the flash of his eye and thunder the voice of his indignation. He rides on the clouds as his chariot and flies on the wings of the wind. He takes up the waters in his palm and the isles as a very little thing. He touches the hills and they smoke as volcanoes; he speaks and the earth trembles and quakes. What magnificent conceptions, expressed in what overwhelming affluence of poetic imagery!

This, then, is the biblical doctrine of divine providence. God, the creator, is the administrator of the material and moral universe. He personally fills all time and space, ever present and everywhere present. He controls all creatures and all events. Foreseeing all crises and emergencies, he provides against them and for them in infinite wisdom, power and goodness. Yet, with all this majesty, terrible in power and might, is combined gentleness and tenderness equally infinite, so that there is not a being, a creature, or an atom too small and insignificant to be under his loving care. He calls the stars by name and each of his sheep; the odd sparrow that, when two farthings' worth were bought, was thrown in as not worth mentioning, he does not forget; nor does a lily of the field or a blade of grass escape his notice.

This doctrine of God's superintendence and control of all creatures and events implies a higher hand behind all the shifting scenery of this world and the developments of history—infinite knowledge—nothing being hidden from his eye, and the future being as the present; infinite wisdom, all things being guided as, by a master pilot's hand on the helm, a vessel is steered through stormy seas and past dangers, rocks and whirlpools to the desired haven. There is also infinite benevolence, so that all things, even the most seemingly adverse, work together for ultimate good; and infinite care of details, so that nothing escapes supervision as outside God's thought and plan.

But divine providence, properly understood, implies also *action*— actual *administration*—efficacious government, continuous, universal, irresistible; and inasmuch as for the time being many things are wrong and work harm, God's providence cannot be complete without a final and perfect *adjustment* of all issues. He who is the God of providence must be the final judge. Though the word providence literally means only *foresight*, divine foresight implies fore-planning and fore-acting, a comprehensive prearrangement for the securing and accomplishing of all desirable ends.

So considered, this truth is one of the great peaks in the mountain range, which, as the Cordilleras in the American continent are the backbone to the whole Western hemisphere, constitute the sublime elevations of Scripture. Based on the bedrock of God's omniscience, omnipresence and omnipotence, this superbly grand truth rises to the loftiest level, its stern sides bathed in the light of his love and converging in one crystal cone of eternal glory beyond all the clouds, storms and mists which belong only to lower levels.

But every great peak of truth has its earthly and heavenly altitudes and must be studied from two aspects—the *here* and the *hereafter*, for neither alone explains the whole mystery. It was from looking at the earthly and temporal aspect unduly that Job, Asaph and many others like them stumbled till their steps had well nigh slipped into the fatal abyss of atheism (Job 21, 24; Psa. 37:35; 73).

Of this doctrine one book in the sacred canon is the exposition and illustration—the *book of Esther*. In all its ten chapters not once is found the *name of Jehovah* or any other title of God, nor any clear reference to a divine being. Yet careful study can trace the planning and working of God throughout. Amid many striking incidents there are no accidents. The story reminds us of the strangely beautiful and symmetrical way in which particles of mineral or metal take shape on a surface when a magnet is held on the underside. We feel, as we read, that an invisible power is behind all the changes of events; and here, as in no other one book in the canon, all the great leading truths of divine providence are illustratively set forth, so that not one needs to be added to make the whole complete.

The conspicuous figures and actors in this drama are a Persian king, Ahasuerus—probably, Xerxes; Vashti, his queen; Esther or Hadassah, chosen to succeed Vashti when she was put away; Memucan, the king's counselor, and Hatach, the king's chamberlain; Haman, the Jews' enemy, who plotted their ruin, and Mordecai, Esther's uncle and adopted father, whom Haman hated because he refused to do him homage. About the events here recorded, covering perhaps in all ten or twelve years, revolves the whole mystery of providence, every grand feature of it set forth as in pictorial and concrete form and better, perhaps, than any abstract study of the doctrine is this illustrative historical example. This complete teaching may be outlined:

1. First, divine providence presents a present paradox

Here is the first factor in the problem: the good suffer; the bad prosper. Vashti is divorced because her modesty and virtue forbid indecent exposure of her person before courtiers inflamed with wine. Mordecai and innocent Jews are under the ban and in danger not only of robbery and outrage but of death. Ahasuerus, a licentious despot, occupies a throne and wields a scepter; and Haman, a demon in human form, coolly plots the massacre of an entire race out of simple hate and malice.

This is the mystery of the ages. Things here and now are not right; so much is wrong that one feels tempted to think at times that there is no God to hold the balances with an even hand. Justice is represented in Scripture as blind, to indicate impartiality; but what if justice has no eyes to see that the scales do not hang evenly and that there is no proper weighing of human character and conduct?

The superficial observer hastily infers that there is no God, or that he is practically too far off. Froude reminded Carlyle that there is a God, but he grumbled, "he *does* nothing!" The silence of God—his apparent inaction and indifference, while wrong goes on and right is under foot, has stumbled the faith of many and wrecked the faith of not a few. Tyrants trample on helpless subjects, and malice plots against innocence and builds gallows for the just. Wholesale massacres are planned and perpetrated, as in Armenia, till blood flows in rivers—and yet God pays no heed and seems more indifferent than man! "If there be a God," men say, "either he *cares not* or he *cannot.*"

2. The real *solution* to the problem of providence *is a future judgment*

The book of Esther shows light ahead. For a while all went wrong, but there came a time, even on earth, when wrongs began to be righted. Positions were reversed; victims became victors; Haman was hung on his own gallows, and the persecuted Jews slew their persecutors.

Both evil and good have their *ultimate* awards, according to desert. There are grand principles that cannot be upset in the moral sphere until, as Dr. Parkhurst says, "Eternity ends and God dies!" The prosperity of evil doers is, like the pleasures of sin, only for a season—at the longest short lived, and eventuates in adversity; the adversity of the good eventuates in prosperity. When Asaph went into the sanctuary of God, then understood he the "end" of evil doers; though their strength seemed firm, their feet were set in slippery places and slid in due time (Luke 16:22–25). The prosperity of the wicked is unsafe and unsatisfying even while it lasts.

Lowell wrote of an ever "present crisis,"

> Careless seems the great avenger: history's pages but record
> One death grapple in the darkness, twixt old systems and the Word.
> Truth forever on the scaffold; wrong forever on the throne:
> But that scaffold sways the future; and, behind the dim unknown,
> Standeth God, within the shadow, keeping watch above his own.

Those who wait long enough will find all wrongs will be righted—if not here, then hereafter. There is obvious moral disorder and disarrangement, but there will be an entire reversal of all abnormal conditions, and, either in this life or the life to come, an exact adjustment of awards. The story of Esther shows how, within the compass of one human life, and even of a very short period, such reversals may take place; but right and truth are sure to prevail ultimately. The great providential administrator can afford to be patient because he is eternal.

3. Divine providence provides, as well as foresees

God is equal to every emergency. He provides *for* every coming need and *against* every coming disaster. To him there is no real crisis; all history is *his story*. He controls all actors and actions, times and events. To him is due all triumph of truth and right; by his permission all falsehood and evil run their course. What of the wrath of man and of demons he can use, he uses; the remainder he restrains. His curb bit is in the mouth of every mad steed trampling in fury over human rights. Pharaoh and Moses were alike raised up to show his power, and Cyrus was as truly his anointed and appointed one as Daniel. He had as much the control of Ahasuerus and Haman as of Mordecai and Esther.

In this short book, some ten or eleven actors are the personal factors in the history: Ahasuerus, Vashti and Esther, Mordecai, Haman and

Zeresh, Memucan, Hatach and Harbonah, Bigthana and Teresh. Five are conspicuous, the others not; but all are named and brought into the plot to show that, whether obvious or obscure, human agency forms a necessary part of the universal scheme. All details in the worldwide, age-long drama of history, God manages. The actors appear on the stage and retire at his pleasure, and their conduct he controls. Through all these complicated events and various lives and the strange course of things, he is supremely guiding—the great actor and mover, to whom all is ultimately traceable. Whatever is good he ordains and decrees; whatever is evil, he permits and restrains. Men, when most self-willed, are unconsciously fulfilling his will; and the moment they have come to the end of his purpose they come to the end of their course.

4. This divine providence is *special as well as general*

The vast host of stars is not too countless to be called by name; nor the blades of grass and flocks of sparrows too many to be noticed individually; nor the hundred thousand hairs of our head too numerous to be all "numbered," which means more than *counted*—suggesting that each has its own *number*, like the mystic "man of sin" in the Apocalypse. All events, however seemingly trivial and trifling, are woven into the fabric of his purpose upon his loom. He works not only through the extraordinary and supernatural, but through the ordinary and natural, dignifying common life as the sphere of his working, so that whatever occurs is part of his plan. His providence is microscopic. What would be thought beneath his notice he not only notices but thus dignifies and exalts by embracing it in the warp and woof of his universal providence.

In this book of Esther, minute events are not only inwoven into the larger plot but constitute the conspicuous features in the pattern, as single, colored threads often outline figures in tapestry. Great crises, like doors, turn upon small hinges. Vashti's refusal to attend a banquet, and the king's arbitrary temper; the caprice that fancies Esther, the trifling circumstance of her kinship with Mordecai, and his Jewish reluctance to pay homage to Haman; the accident of the king's sleeplessness, and his fancy for having the chronicles of his reign read to him, and the other accident of the reader's stumbling on the record of the attempted assassination, and Mordecai's information; the chance of the king's favorably receiving Esther when she came *to him unbidden;* the accident of a courtier's having noticed the gallows built by Haman and mentioning it at the exact time when the king was meditating vengeance on Haman; such are a few of the apparent trifles upon which hang all the greater issues of the story. They remind us how, in God's sight, nothing is small. When he makes history, it is a mosaic of ten thousand little fragments; but each bit of stone helps to complete the design and is essential to its completeness.

5. Divine providence is *not to be confused with fatalism*

But again, divine providence is *not to be confused with fatalism,* nor construed as interfering with human freedom. God's sovereignty and man's liberty co-exist; his decrees do not imply an inevitable doom from which there is no escape, or even a fixed destiny to which we blindly come at last whether we will or not. However we may be unable to find the point of convergence, the two lines of God's action and man's action are not parallel; they come together in harmony somehow and somewhere. In this book a providential plan is, from first to last, wrought out; yet all parties follow unhindered their own choice, whether for good or evil. When the grand crisis comes Mordecai reminds Esther that for just such a time as this she may have come to the kingdom; but we see her weighing the whole question of opportunity and responsibility with all the risks of failure and disaster, and calmly resolving to go in unto the king, uncalled: "If I perish I perish!"

Our Lord declared as in one breath *both* facts as to his own betrayal and crucifixion: "The Son of Man goeth as it is written of him; but woe unto that man by whom the Son of Man is betrayed."

Nothing is more certain than that our Lord's death in all its details was foreseen and foretold by prophets; yet, at every step the chief priests and Judas planned and plotted; the traitor made his own bargain and had his own way. Men, whether servants of God or slaves of Satan, are bound by no inexorable necessity. God controls, but does not compel. He leaves all to their own choice, so that they act without undue constraint. Their acts are their own. Mordecai uses arguments; he sends word to Esther that danger impends and may engulf her with her people; that it may be that God has put her on the throne to sway events at this crisis, and that if she does not interpose, he will find some other deliverer. But it is plain that she calmly, prayerfully makes her decision and carries out her own purpose as freely as though there were no sovereign God.

6. Again, God's providence is *exact in its awards*

> The Lord is known by the judgment which he executeth; the wicked is snared in the work of his own hands (Ps. 9:16).

> The Lord is a God of knowledge, and by him actions are weighed (1 Sam. 2:3).

Here are two comprehensive statements: one is that God holds the scales of judgment, in which, with infinitely accurate discrimination, all actions are weighed. This sublimely awful thought reaches its climax in the handwriting on the wall of Belshazzar's palace: "Tekel: thou art weighed in the balances and found wanting" (Daniel 5:27). Omniscience discerns all human activities, even to the thoughts, and with exactness weighs them in just balances of judgment. The other passage teaches that God, in judgment, exactly balances *crime* and *penalty*. A singular phrase is commonly used to express this—"poetic retribution." As in poetic lines there is a close correspondence in rhythm and rhyme, the metrical feet and even the sounds of words responding one to the other, so there is a rhythm and rhyme between the movements of men in history and the movements of God in judgment. In this life poem man writes a line with the pen of action; God writes another with the pen of retribution, and the two exactly and awfully correspond. The wicked is snared in the work of his own hands. He digs a pit and is the first to fall into it.

This law and fact of judgment is singularly illustrated in this book of Esther. No one object stands more conspicuous in the narrative than the huge gibbet that Haman built for Mordecai (5:14). In his malice and hate he could think of nothing too humiliating and disgraceful for the Jew he hated; and he erected a gallows tree, fifty cubits high (about eighty feet), the height intended to intensify the disgrace and publish it to all observers; and Haman counted his power to be equal to accomplishing his enemy's ruin so speedily that he could venture to build the gallows one day and hang him on it the next. Yet God so timed the tide of events that the first culprit that hung on that gibbet was the man that built it, and, shortly after, his ten sons, who undoubtedly were his abettors in his foul plot, were suspended from the same tree of shame.

The Jewish scribes especially struck with this instance of poetic retribution, in transcribing the book of Esther, have left a curious trace of their discernment. The ten names (in chapter 9:7, 8, 9) are written on *three perpendicular columns of respectively three, three and four*, like bodies strung up on three parallel cords, one above another; and in the Targum of Esther, in Walton's *Polyglott*, a minute account is published of the exact position of Haman and his sons on the gallows, Haman at the top, and his ten sons in one line below, at intervals of half a cubit, and so their names are printed in the Hebrew Old Testament; at the right of the page and on ten successive lines thus, reading from left to right and then back again from right to left:

And	
And	
And	Parshandatha,
And	Dalphon,
And	Aspatha,
And	Poratha,
And	Adalia,
And	Aridatha,
And	Parmashta,
And	Arisai,
And	Aridai,
	Vajezatha.

Another example of this poetic exactness in retribution is seen in the way in which Haman fell into a second snare. Just as he was come into the King's court to obtain the decree for Mordecai's hanging, the king asked him what would be a fitting way to honor the man whom he delighted to favor. And thinking that he himself was the king's favorite, he prescribed a grand program—the favorite, mounted on the king's own charger, robed in royal apparel and even crowned with the royal diadem, should be marched in procession through the streets by one of the noblest princes of the realm with a proclamation: "thus shall it be done unto the man whom the king delighteth to honor!"

"Make haste," responds the king, "and do thou even so to—MORDE-CAI!" This is one of those instances in which the providential award is so exact that it strikes one like a stroke of grim humor and reminds of those words in Psalm 2, "the Lord shall have them in derision!"

7. This providence of God is not *always an apparent fact*

Last of all, this providence of God is not *always an apparent fact;* God is not always a *visible* actor, but always at work.

Much has been said in objection to this book that it does not contain once the *name* of God nor any direct reference to him. Some Jewish commentators account for this by the fact that the book was intended partly for *Gentile* readers; but a far more satisfactory reason is that it is designed to remind us that, in providential working, he always moves in *secrecy and mystery;* the hand that guides is a *hidden hand.*

Power, however commanding and controlling, does not always visibly operate. The stage manager and scene shifter in a theatre are not seen, but in the drama the effects of their activity appear. In this short narrative, in nearly two hundred cases the king is referred to, and in thirty his name appears. Twenty-six times his kingdom is spoken of; but while the name of God is not found from beginning to end, the agency of God is obviously back of the whole movement of affairs. He uses the natural working of the minds of men, and the natural course of events, to accomplish a supernatural design. Without any ostensible interposition the hidden hand is moving and shifting everything.

Some have found the name of Jehovah in the book of Esther, curiously inwoven in the fabric of the story in *acrostic form* four times and at the pivotal points in the narrative. In each case the words whose letters furnish the acrostic are consecutive, though in construction unlike; two of them form the name by *initial* and two by *final* letters; in two cases the name is spelt *backwards*, and in two *forwards;* even these minor peculiarities corresponding to the movement of events; in some cases the events are initial, and in others final; in some the movement is onward, and in others backward, and the acrostics in every case correspond.

Dr. E. W. Bullinger, at a congress of orientalists held at Stockholm, read a paper in which he recited the above facts. The Massorah has a rubric, calling attention to the four passages, and in three ancient manuscripts the letters forming these acrostics are written large, so as to be conspicuous. We construct four couplets, in which the capital letters of the word L-O-R-D may show how the four letters of the Hebrew name for Jehovah are curiously embedded in the very structure of the narrative.

> Due Respect Our Ladies, all
> Shall give husbands, great and small (1:20).
> "Let Our Royal Dinner bring
> Haman, feasting with the king" (5:4).
> "GranD foR nO avaiL my state,
> While this Jew sits at the gate" (5:13).
> "ilL tO feaR decreeD, I find,
> Toward me in the monarch's mind" (7:7).

These are the *only* such acrostics in the book, and cannot be there by accident.[34]

But it will be plain that no such acrostical arrangement could ever be the result of chance.

Nevertheless, no careless, cursory reader would ever find this hidden name, just as such never would detect other rich suggestions concealed in the Scriptures which, like veins of gold and silver, disclose their wealth only to those who devoutly search as for hidden treasure.

8. Conclusion

The grand conclusion is: *divine providence excludes all mere chance*. This is the supreme lesson of this book. These events are celebrated as the *Feast of Purim*, and Purim means *"Lot,"* because Haman had cast the *lot* in connection with the plot for the Jews' destruction. But, as the issue shows, though "the lot is cast into the lap, the whole disposing thereof is of the Lord" (Prov. 16:33), and so they kept the Feast of *Purim* as the Feast of *Providence*. What to men was *chance*, to God was *choice*.

In the accompanying diagram (10) the leading facts and truths concerning the providence of God are presented in successive sections, each showing a double truth with its seeming paradox:

7. Final conclusion:	{ No Chance—Behind all is choice of GOD. { No visible control. A HIDDEN HAND.
6. Ultimate reversals:	{ The GOOD in Prosperity. { The BAD in Adversity.

---

34 If anyone tries to construct sentences with such acrostics hidden in them, he will find it requires unusual study. I tried thus to incorporate the word "Rome" in a supposed telegram from a man who has bought a villa on the Thames and invites his brother to come over on Easter Monday and have a row with him on the river. The four recurrences of the acrostic will be noted by the capitals. "Run Over Monday Evening. Enjoy Morning On River. takE traM tO dooR, numbeR twO durhaM terracE."

5. Perfect administration:	{	Exact Reward to Human Virtue.
		Poetic Retribution to Evil Doers.
4. Providence resistless:	{	Benevolent Plan Steadily Advancing.
		Malice of Foes turned to His Ends.
3. Comprenensive plan:	{	Embracing all Agents, Acts and Ages.
		Weaving Minutest Threads into Plan.
2. A second paradox:	{	GOD controlling as Sovereign.
		Man a Self-determining Free Agent.
1. The present paradox:	{	The GOOD in Adversity.
		The BAD in Prosperity.

10. The problem of providence

First, the present mystery: the good often in adversity, and the evil prosperous, triumphant and arrogant. Next, the perplexing contradiction: God as a sovereign, working as he will, and man as a free agent, choosing and acting for himself. Then, a third marvel, the comprehensiveness of the plan of God, embracing all history with all its actors, actions and ages of time; making even the most minute details tributary to its ultimate completion. Still, beyond this, the purpose of a wise and loving God marching on toward its goal, despite all opposition, and with divine skill turning to good even what men and demons mean for evil, so that even the malice of foes works final victory for God. Again, the exactness of divine awards is exhibited in the poetic precision with which both evil and good receive their retribution and reward, according to their deserts. And so we reach that stage of final adjustment where there is perfect harmony between condition and character. The grand conclusion is that, while there is no visible interposition of God, his hand, though hidden, holds the helm of affairs, and there is no such thing as CHANCE.

That is a sublime truth, not always clearly vindicated in this world, that "God is no respecter of persons" (Acts 10:34). Inequities and inequalities there are, but all of them will have ultimate judicial adjustment. Many things which make the ways of the Lord seem unequal are due to human perversity, the inequalities being of man's making; and many others may find a remedy in grace. All disadvantages have doubtless natural off-sets as well as gracious compensations, as in the case of the deaf saint who thanked God that for twenty years she had not *heard* a malicious, uncharitable or impatient word! If there are different allotments and measures of endowment and opportunity, so are there different degrees of reward, determined not by what we have but how we use it, so that the great question is not one of entrustment but of improvement. God asks only that we do our best and wait for the end of all things, for our reward and his vindication. The judgment seat of Christ and the great white throne will finally solve all problems, right all wrongs and adjust all that is unequal and inequitable.

Some important facts belong to this revelation of providence:

1. The present age is confessedly one of *mystery*. In a sense, men are designedly *left to themselves*. God practically withdraws from the scene, that the experiment of man's self-guidance and self-failure may be complete. In Eden he gave man dominion over all the visible world, and his own intimate and personal fellowship, on but one condition, that he should submit to divine control. The prohibition as to the tree of knowledge was in a sense arbitrary—no reason for this one restriction being given that it might be the more a test of man's willingness to accept the will of God for his guidance even where he could see no adequate ground for the command, and where reason might argue that it was a restraint on his truer liberty. Man then chose *his own will*, and ever since then God has been trying him on the old issue; and all approaches to Eden, even on the part of disciples, are hindered by the same old *self-will*. This trial is to go on until the will of man completely and finally bows to the will of God—and in order to a fair experiment, God meanwhile keeps silence and seems inactive—for if at once judgment followed evil deeds, fear would restrain man's liberty. "Sentence against an evil work is not executed speedily" (Eccl. 8:11). There is a mystery of *delay*, but it is in order to the present result—the unfettered action of man, and the final result—the ultimate blending of man's will with that of God.

2. Consequently the future alone can be the *final and full solution* of the mystery of providence. After man has carried his rebellion against God to the full, and the experiment of self-will has demonstrated its insane folly; when man has shown even to himself and his fellowman his incapacity for self-government, God will proceed to reveal his own judicial character. He will take his seat on what now appears to be a *vacated throne of judgment*, and then will begin the ultimate assizes. Of course that will be a day of terror to the wicked, who will meet exact, impartial, inevitable and irreversible judgment. Retribution will be poetically *exact;* "whatsoever wrong" any man has done *"that same"* will he receive of the

Lord, whether he be bond or free, and there is no respect of persons." The Lord God will then be seen to be a "God of knowledge by whom actions are weighed;" and "the Lord God of recompenses who will surely requite." The judgment of Belshazzar was typical of this last day—every man "weighed in the balances," and woe to him who is "found wanting;" for his kingdom, though world-wide, will be divided and given to others; God will number his kingdom and finish it.

But terror is not the only aspect of that day. It is even more a day of supernal glory, as expressed in the great white throne; for it will be the final vindication of God. He will come out of hiding and shew himself strong in behalf of him who has waited for him. That will be the *righting of the wrong of the ages*. The church that, like a widow pleading vainly before an unjust judge, has suffered from long deferred hope, will find an avenger who will rid her of her adversary speedily and finally. Every drop of martyr's blood, all the centuries of slavery's unredressed horrors will be compensated—the feet of the oppressed will be on the necks of their oppressors; the victims of the inquisition will see their torturers on the rack; the rich plunderers will be reduced to eternal beggary and the beggars be made princes. That day will explain God's long silence and hiding of himself; his inaction was not due to indifference. God was not *dead*.

3. The last day will also reveal how God has been speaking even in the silence and working even in apparent inaction—that even the present age is the scene of a judicial providence. All future retribution and reward have their forecasts and foretastes in this life, not completely and fully, but partially and by way of anticipation. In Eph. 6:8 and Col. 3:17 are two statements which, being combined, express a full truth, that whatever good or wrong thing any man doeth that same shall he receive of the Lord whether he be bond or free, and there is no respect of persons.

The operation of this double law may be seen even now. Who that leads another astray does not go himself astray? Who teaches another to lie or deceive without sinking lower in lying and treachery? No one can debauch another's imagination without finding his own becoming a chamber of horrors; or tamper with another's purity without becoming the prey of his own passions. To eat at the vitals of another's life and virtue is to feed a vulture that shall gnaw at one's own heart, and he who forges a chain for another's neck fastens the other end of the chain about his own. Just as truly, he who seeks to uplift the fallen becomes strong himself to stand alone; he who teaches the ignorant himself learns wisdom; he who guides another in perplexity sees his own way better; he who strengthens another's weak purpose is mixing iron with his own blood. *Whatsoever* good or wrong, that *same* he receives. Call it natural law or divine decree, as you will, it is *so* and the Spirit of God says it is *"of the Lord."*

Before dismissing this great theme, there are a few instructive and consolatory lessons which its study suggests:

1. *There is a divine and sovereign ruler.* He supervises all worlds and creatures. Beings of all grades and ranks are subject to his control, and the blind forces of nature are guided by his all-seeing and far-seeing eye. Psalm 104 represents him as the God of nature, using light as a garment and the clouds as a curtain; winds and waters, fire and flood, lightning and tempest, his obedient servants. In that inspired song some thirty features of nature, animate and inanimate, are presented as subserving his ends. Isaiah 54:16 tells us that he has created even "the *waster* to destroy;" the destructive as well as constructive elements and agents in the universe are his creatures and execute his behests. Joel grandly makes the insect world an army marshaled in detachments and marching under his generalship: "The locust, the cankerworm, and the caterpillar, and the palmerworm, my great army which I sent among you" (2:25).

2. *His universal providence includes all particulars.* All general supervision implies specific and minute oversight. The book of Jonah incidentally teaches this lesson of special providence. The Lord is represented as sending out a great wind into the sea, so that there was a mighty tempest; as preparing a great fish to swallow Jonah; as speaking unto the fish so that it vomited him out upon the dry land; as preparing a gourd, and preparing a worm to smite the gourd; and as preparing a vehement east wind so that the sun beat upon his unsheltered head. Nowhere else is such pains taken to trace such natural occurrences to the special act of God, "sending," "preparing," "speaking."

3. *God is indifferent to no concern of his people.* He gives to every hair its number and to every drop of blood its value; he who forgets not the odd sparrow or the lily of the field calls by name his own sheep as an oriental shepherd calls every one of his thousands of sheep by name as the flock passes the watering trough or the door of the fold. Jesus "loved Martha and her sister and Lazarus"—what lovely individualizing! It was not enough to say, "he loved the family at Bethany," but each member of it must be specified.

Psalm 103 beautifully records that, "like as a father pitieth *his* children, *so* the LORD pitieth them that fear him. For he knoweth our frame; he remembereth that we are dust."

As an intelligent father studies the peculiarities of his children, knowing their weaknesses, and having regard to them in the food he gives each and the burdens he lays on each; so the Lord who made us and knows our "frame"—how we are put together, all the weak points in the framework—will, in all his dealings, remember and regard all our inabilities and incapacities.

4. *God's providence assures the supply of every want* (Phil. 4:19). The only thing we need to care for is the supreme object: "Seek first the kingdom of God and his righteousness." Not only are we not *bidden* to seek the lower good, but we are *forbidden* to seek it. We are to be anxious about nothing, but, seeking the higher trust, for the lower. There are but few who dare thus to depend; but those who do, find it more restful and joyful than to depend on stocks in the most prosperous business or hoards in the safest bank vaults.

5. *Providence includes also protection.* Duty never involves real danger; the only risk is in not doing duty. "Who is he that will harm you if ye be followers of that which is good?" (1 Peter 3:13). The ninety-first Psalm is the triumphant song of immunity from peril of all sorts, and its only explanation is that the secret chamber of this security is the *will of God.* To him who simply accepts that will as his strong tower of refuge, there is no risk and can be none. "According to your faith be it unto you;" but, as Robert Brown says, he that searches his Bible will find that in effect God also says, "according to your *unbelief* be it unto you." Dr. Baedeker, in his frequent journeys among European prisons, exposed to countless dangers for forty years, tested that Psalm and found it literally true.

6. *Personal direction is also implied.* To many a child of God those words have been at once compass, rudder and anchor in sailing out upon life's treacherous sea:

"Trust in the LORD with all thine heart; and lean not unto thine own understanding. In all thy ways acknowledge him, and he shall direct thy paths" (Prov. 3:6).

That text was given to the writer by his father, in boyhood, as a life motto; and since then no important step has been taken without waiting for divine leading, and never in vain. We can afford to wait as long as he can, for it is his work, way and time that are of all consequence. If, therefore, guidance does not at once come, it is safer to wait till it does; a step taken too soon may be a step taken amiss.

7. *Personal vindication is also involved.* When wrongfully assailed, one has only to keep quiet and commit the whole matter to God instead of undertaking self-defense. He may have to wait some time for God's vindication, but it will come if the cause be committed to him; for whenever his saints are falsely accused, *he is*, and their defense is his own. The Psalmist describes the snares set for his feet and the mischievous slanders uttered about him; but he tells us he was as one deaf and dumb—he acted as though he neither saw nor heard anything; and his reason was:

For in THEE, O LORD, do I hope (Ps. 38).

A venerable saint recently departed gave as the sober retrospect of eighty years mostly spent in public life, "I have often been wrongfully attacked but have never attempted to defend myself. I have borne in silence and committed my cause to God; and there has never been a wrong done me that has not been rectified, nor a blow aimed at me which has not recoiled on him who dealt it."

8. Once more, *providential compensations often follow even in this life.* Even here, as in the story of Esther, there is a striking reversal of conditions, so that, out of calamity, blessing is born.

In a public discussion, G. J. Holyoake challenged Dr. Joseph Parker to show any "providence" in Stephen's death. He promptly answered, "he enabled Stephen to say, Lord, lay not this sin to their charge." He might have added that it was that death which gave to the church the apostle Paul, and in so doing perhaps contributed more to the permanent blessing of mankind than any other single event of like character in all history. In a true sense they knew not what they did who stoned Stephen. The light on his face as he fell asleep left such impression on Saul of Tarsus that he never forgave himself for his part in that transaction, and this first sight of the Lord Jesus in the face of the martyr, and through the martyr who solemnly affirmed, "I see heaven opened and Jesus standing on the right hand of God"—prepared Saul for the revelation of the Lord Jesus in the way. Moreover, the death of Stephen became the key to a new interpretation of *death*. Henceforth the word passed from the vocabulary of the early saints—witness the six million tombs in the Catacombs. Stephen's death began the new era!

Missionary history reveals this compensation on a large scale, as when John Williams was clubbed to death on Erromanga's beach in 1839, and fifty years later the son of his murderer unveiled his monument; or as when Bishop Hannington was shot by Lubwa, and his son afterward baptized the son of Lubwa. But more astonishing was the series of events between 1871 and 1885 in African missions. Within those fourteen years there passed away some of the greatest of all modern missionaries: Patteson, Livingstone and Krapf, Moffat and Hannington—three of them martyrs. But there never were such years of marvelous progress. Patteson's death aroused all Christendom to stop the crime of kidnapping and other forms of slave trade. The death of Livingstone prompted heroic effort to heal that open sore of the world and cover the dark continent with a chain of missions. The old slave market at Zanzibar became the site of the Universities' Mission, and where the whipping post stood the Lord's table now stands.

Read with open eyes, history is aflame with God; and the undevout historian, like the undevout astronomer, is mad. Columbus was heading for North America until driftwood in the sea and parakeets in the air diverted him to the south and saved North America from the blight of papacy. One more day's delay and Mormonism would have spread its curse over California in 1847. A few hours' delay in the arrival of the "Monitor" in 1862 and the navy of the United States would have been destroyed in Hampton Roads; and the war for the Union never turned successfully until the man at the White House got right with God about the freeing of four million slaves.

Britain escaped the Spanish Armada in 1588 because "the stars in the heavens fought against Sisera," so that out of one hundred and fifty vessels and thirty thousand soldiers and seamen, fifty shattered ships and eight thousand men found their way back.

When Napoleon was reminded by Madame de Stael, as he started for Russia, that "circumstances might be against him," he boastingly replied, "I *make* circumstances." But when out of his vast host scarce a tenth found France again, he discovered that there is one higher than man who can marshal the snowflakes and ice crystals to do his bidding. "Who can stand before his cold?"

Believer, yours is a sublime peace! Psalm 99:1 should read:

> Let the people tremble: The Lord reigneth!
> Let the earth stagger: He, between the cherubim, sits firm!

The Epic of Esther

Back of all that foes have plotted;
    All that friends of God have planned;
Human schemes, or work of demons,
    Moves a higher hidden hand!
Man's horizon is but finite;
    Present mysteries ensnare:
Wrongs in vain seek an avenger;
    Hope is tempted to despair.
But, in God's eternal future,
    The exact and full reward
Will reveal the even balance
    In the judgments of the Lord.
Through the mystic fabric, woven
    On the great historic loom,
Runs one golden thread of purpose,
    Not the iron thread of doom.
Warp and woof are heaven's making,
    All the pattern, good and wise;
On the earth side, strange, perplexing;
    Perfect to celestial eyes.
Every act and every actor,
    Great and little, foe or friend,
Like converging roads of empire,
    To one golden milestone tend.
Nothing too minute to enter
    Into God's complete design,
Perfecting the forms and colors
    In the outline so divine.
Yet all agents act with freedom,
    Choosing, whether love or hate,
Close alliance, bold defiance—
    None are helpless slaves to FATE.
Yet the hand that guides is hidden,
    Moving secret and unseen,
Managing, in life's great drama,
    Every act, and shifting scene.
Nothing *happens*, accidental,
    All that men ascribe to chance,
Choice of God has first determined;
    Nothing can escape his glance.

Mortals cast their lot, and gamble
   With their deeds, as with their dice;
Reckon to caprice of fortune,
   All their virtue or their vice;
But the wrath of man, unconscious,
   Serves one all-controlling will;
Man proposes; God disposes;
   All things his design fulfil.
This, the goal of all the ages;
   Hither, highways, byways tend;
So, despite all foes and factions,
   God proves victor in the end.
Man's high festival of *Purim*,
   Read by faith's illumined sense,
Shall be kept, in realms eternal,
   As the feast of PROVIDENCE.

Chapter 15

The Mystery of History

This is a profound mystery, but upon it the Word of God throws a flood of light.

1. The beginning of all history.

In the beginning God created the heavens and the earth (Gen. 1:1).

2. The beginning of *man's* history.

God created man in his own image (1:27).

3. The *second* beginning of human history.

And Noah went forth, and his sons, and his wife, and his sons' wives with him (8:18).

4. The beginning of the *Christ's* earthly history.

Unto you is born this day in the city of David a Savior which is Christ the Lord (Luke 2:11).

5. The beginning of the *church's* history.

The Lord added to the church daily (Acts 2:47).

6. The beginning of the *millennial age* of history.

When the Son of Man shall come in his glory ... then shall he sit upon the throne of his glory (Matt. 25:31).

7. The beginning of the *final age*—the end of history.

Then cometh the end, when he shall have delivered up the kingdom to God, even the Father (1 Cor. 15:24).

This mystery of history can be understood only in the light of four other mysteries: (1) that of the *dispensations;* (2) of the *ages;* (3) of the *kingdom;* (4) of the *two advents*. In order to make the presentation of the theme as complete as practicable each of these will have brief treatment, as subheads.

1. The ages

How august and majestically mystical the biblical conception of God's eternity hinted in that untranslatable name, "Jehovah," which so blends all tenses of the verb *to be* as to suggest a *being who*, as to all ages of time, can equally say, "I AM," as one to whom there is properly no succession or duration, taking in all ages, as the ocean does the drops of water, which yet form an insignificant part of the limitless whole.

Another and kindred conception is that all the ages are his *creation*—the worlds of time, or duration, as much as the worlds of matter or space, and the worlds of life, or being. God was, when as yet there were no created orbs, beings or ages. Hence, we read that he "made" and "framed the eons" (Heb. 1:2; 11:3), the word being *aion*, and, as Dr. Upham suggests, should be rendered "time-world." The creator made and put together as in a structure these time-worlds, framing them into his plan as stones and timbers in a building, or bones and muscles in a body. Architectural *form* implies architectural *plan;* a foundation age, an order of succession and mutual fitness; and a final age in which all culminate. Where else, save in God's Word, can such a conception be found?

ETERNAL AGE Ω	GOD the FATHER	GOD ALL IN ALL KINGDOM IN RESTORATION	{	UNDISPUTED UNDIVIDED UNIVERSAL
AGE to COME	Transition: final revolt. Last judgment. New heavens &c.			
	GOD the SON	KINGDOM IN MANIFESTATION	{	EXTERNAL PERSONAL & visible EXTENSIVE
PRESENT EVIL AGE	Transition: apostasy. Man of sin. Restoration Israel. Second advent			
	GOD the SPIRIT	KINGDOM IN MYSTERY	{	INTERNAL INVISIBLE INDIVIDUAL

PAST	Transition: rejection of Christ. Cross. Resurrection. Pentecost.			
AGE	THE GOD	KINGDOM	⎰	RACE IN BONDAGE
B.C.	of	IN	⎱	ISRAEL APOSTATE
	THIS WORLD	USURPATION		MESSIAH REJECTED
ETERNAL	Transition: revolt of angels. Temptation. Fall of man.			
AGE	GOD	KINGDOM	⎰	UNDISPUTED
A	TRIUNE	IN	⎱	UNDIVIDED
		PERFECTION		UNIVERSAL

GOD ALL IN ALL

11. The plan of the ages

The mystery of history is naturally linked with that of prophecy. He to whose eye all time is a present reality touches the eyes of his servants and they become seers, whose backward and forward look commands the past, however remote, and the future, however distant. Prophecy becomes the mold of which history is the medallion; the same image appears in both and they fit together.

The accompanying diagram (no. 11) outlines this program of history, its five sections corresponding to the five "ages" hinted at in New Testament epistles: "before the foundation of the world," "from the beginning of the world," "the present evil age," the "age which is to come," and the age after "the end." These are both scriptural divisions and designations (Eph. 1:4, 21; 2:2; 3:5, 21; Gal. 1:4; Heb. 9:26, etc.).

First, an eternity past, before time began; then a second, third and fourth ages, together constituting "the times;" then a future eternity—the omega, corresponding to the alpha. Thus what we call "history" has three periods, reaching from the first man, Adam, to the Second Man and last Adam; then spanning the interval between the two advents of Christ, and last, the kingdom age or millennium.

The ages are all associated with a *kingdom:* first, that of the triune God, reigning with absolute, undisputed authority. Then, at man's creation, he was given a kingdom, with dominion over the earth; but when he fell, Satan seized his scepter and by right of conquest became the "god" or "prince of this world." Then, in turn, the Second Man wrested the scepter from him and holds it in behalf of redeemed humanity. During this age, the kingdom is in mystery, the spirit of God ruling in all true subjects, and through them working upon men. In the coming age, the kingdom will be in manifestation, Christ being visibly on the throne. Then in the eternal age, the kingdom will be in restoration, as in the eternal past, with the added glory of a glorified church.

Every historic age *opens* with a new *advent* and *closes* with a new *revolt:* the first, with the advent of man; the second, with the advent of Christ as Son of Man; and the third, with his advent as King of Glory. The revolt which ends one age marks the transition to the new age that follows: Satan's and man's introduce the age before Christ; Israel's, the present age; and the final revolt of the nations, the millennial. Minor details on the diagram briefly hint at the truths referred to in this and preceding chapters; and the most cursory glance at the whole scheme shows that to be one with God is to move steadily on to final and eternal victory over all foes.

It is plain also that in God's plan of the ages is the key both to the locked chambers of Scripture and of history. However wrapped in mystery still, the main outline is clear: the beginning of time; certain marks that distinguish the ages; the imposing march of events from creation to the incarnation, crucifixion and Pentecost; the unutterable splendors of the coming age; and the yet greater glory of that final period, which the Scriptures can only refer to by a titanic piling of word upon word, like heaping up mountains—"unto all the generations of the age of the ages!" (Eph. 3:21.)

2. The dispensations

"Dispensation" means a method of dispensing or dealing, inadequately intimating that in the various periods of history God has dealt with men with a definite purpose and upon principles having a definite relation to his governmental administration. "The dispensation of the fullness of times" (Ephes. 1:10) suggests also the complete *fulfillment* of his purpose in every age, so that nothing anticipates or retards it.

God's dealings with man have been a series of new experiments on his part, and with new failures on man's. It is curious and significant that the main features of the first dispensational period have in every succeeding one been *reproduced*, so that the first proved a pattern for all that follow.

For example, in the period from Adam to Noah we note seven marked developments:

First, a *new revelation of truth.* The fall was at once followed by the first promise of the victorious seed of the woman and the institution of sacrifice. New light shone in the darkness.

Second, *a spiritual decline*. Salvation is promised but does not prevent the first murder and martyrdom, a godless civilization under Cain, and polygamy under Lamech. As the race grows, so does apostasy.

Third, *a carnal compromise*. The "sons of God" and the "daughters of men"—probably followers of Seth and Cain, respectively, mix in marriage; believers and unbelievers lose all true separateness.

Fourth, *a worldly civilization*. It develops giants in stature, mighty men of renown, but is neither God-fearing nor God-honoring. Its success is its failure, for it neglects, if it does not defy, Jehovah.

Fifth, *a parallel development*. Good and evil grow side by side like the tares and wheat, the good neither uprooting the evil nor the evil utterly crowding out the good—they grow together until the reaping time of judgment.

Sixth, *a general apostasy*. God's verdict is, "the wickedness of man is great in the earth, and every imagination of the thoughts of his heart only evil continually." But one man, just, perfect in his generations, who walked with God!

Seventh, *a judgment crisis*. All flesh had so corrupted his way upon the earth that a wholesale destruction of the race was a mercy, for mankind was rotting in its own vices and dying by a slower suicide.

Let these features in the Scripture portrait of the antediluvian age be compared with those of every age succeeding—for example, this present age.

It opened with a new flood of light in Christ and the Spirit, but the apostolic times show a marked decline in doctrine and practice; and under Constantine compromise with the world reached its climax in a state church. The civilization of which giants were born, in prowess and intellect, was and is godless. The growth of tares and wheat goes on side by side, the world more rapidly than the church; and when even professed teachers in the church deny an inspired Bible and an atoning Christ, it looks like the last falling away. If so, but one of the seven features is lacking—the crisis of judgment!

This uniform history of dispensations proves that, though every failure of man is followed by a new trial, with new opportunity he persists in his decline from truth, his compromise with evil, his pursuit of self-interest, his defiance of God, and makes judgment a necessity.

Notwithstanding all this perversity of man, there is a divine progression through the ages and dispensations, never one backward step on

God's part, however many on man's. The prophetic period melts into the priestly; then both blend with the kingly when in one person, Prophet, Priest and King unite to make believers a kingdom of priests unto God. Satan, who, before Christ overcame him was dominant and defiant, in this age of the Spirit is by him restrained or counteracted. In the coming age he is to be bound and finally burned.

Election is also progressive, constantly widening: at first an elect *family* and *nation;* now, an elect *church;* and finally, an elect *kingdom.* The failure is always man's—never God's, and each new failure gets man nearer to the end of himself and nearer the beginning of God, so giving him a new advantage and preparing for the day when, with man's full consent he shall be all in all. Prophets and priests, an oral and then a written law; afterward God's incarnate Word and the Spirit's descent; a New Testament and complete Bible; yet with all these accumulated privileges and opportunities, man proves incapable of self-government or loyalty to God. Evil men and seducers wax worse and worse, deceiving and being deceived; and of our own selves do men arise, speaking perverse things and drawing away disciples after them.

The millennial age—God's last experiment with man, will also be man's last chance. The latter rain on "all *flesh,*" as the "early rain" was on all believers; the binding of Satan and the personal reign of Christ will not together prevent a final disaster—a gigantic revolt such as has not been known since man was created! And all this permitted in God's wisdom, that man may learn that, *save as he stands in God, he can not stand at all*, whatever his privileges; and with all self-confidence wrecked, and all compromise with the world at an end, he will at last utterly LOSE HIMSELF IN GOD, and so GOD WILL BE ALL IN ALL.

Perhaps this is God's way of securing for redeemed man that holy city into which sin will never enter—that man, having learned his lesson that he must *live in God*, shall merge his will so completely in his maker's that there shall be, between him and God, but one thought, desire, or purpose! This is the true solution to the mystery of the ages and the dispensations.

3. The kingdom

Both the ages and the dispensations are inseparable from the *kingdom;* and, as definitions are to the writer what outlines are to the painter, we need to define the kingdom of God. Experience supplies no data, and we must inquire at the holy oracles. Even here deductive methods might tempt us to warp Scripture to fit the crook of some preconception, and the only safe way is the inductive, collating and comparing its testimonies, and seeking that center where all converge as Roman roads at the "golden milestone."

A kingdom—the house or domain of a king—is the realm he rules. Wherever God sways a community or even an individual, there is his kingdom, as every flag that floats over a sailor on the sea or every uniform of a soldier on land indicates a subject of a human ruler.

In the New Testament, the kingdom is represented as related to the "world," the "church," "Israel," the "nations," and the "ages." The English words, not always being true equivalents of the originals, sometimes confuse. "World" is used for the earth, the cosmos, the habitation of man and the age; in a material sense, of the globe; in a social sense, of the race; and in a chronological sense, of an indefinite time. Church means an *out-called* body; Israel is, in prophecy and history, always distinct from both "church" and "kingdom;" and all, from "Gentiles," or nations. Age, or eon, means a period indefinite in length but defined dispensationally, and these ages are to the kingdom its successive periods of preparation or manifestation. They are built up in symmetry and proportion like a great structure, with base blocks, story on story, columns and capitals, spires and pinnacles—all finding termination and consummation in him who is both cornerstone and capstone.

Augustine says: "Distinguish the ages and the Scriptures will harmonize." Their relation to the kingdom we have already indicated, but it is important to observe that when God called out a people of old, it was to establish a *theocracy* or kingdom of God, himself its head. When his people demanded a human king, they disowned him; and this apostasy ripened into division and dispersion. When Christ came, he offered the kingdom to the Jews; but they both rejected the offer and crucified him. This new apostasy brought a longer captivity and a wider dispersion, now already lasting nearly two thousand years. The offer of the kingdom is now in suspense—and this is the age of the church—the out-gathering of the body or bride from all nations—the "times of the Gentiles," during which the offer of the gospel is to be made to all people.

The "church" and "kingdom" are therefore not *convertible terms*. The kingdom is constantly referred to as characteristic of the past and coming ages, but in neither is the *church* found; its history fills the interval between the sufferings of Christ and the glory that shall follow. To confound with the kingdom of God any external organization of believers is a blunder; still worse is to confuse with it the kingdoms of this world, or to trust to that master device of the Devil, a superficial union of church and state, as the kingdom of God. We talk of "Christian nations," forgetting the fatal fallacy lurking in that phrase, since a nation is a political organization incapable of faith, having no conscience, will or personality as such; and in the companion phrase, "the Christian world," we combine what are as mutually hostile as light and darkness.

This age is peculiarly the *dispensation of the Spirit. His* peculiarity is *invisibility.* He is not incarnate. For temporary and special reasons, he appeared in the form of a dove and in tongues of fire; but he has no proper form or body. He is invisibly administering the kingdom instead of the king; and hence, during this age, the kingdom is marked by *invisibility* and *individuality.* Emphasis is laid upon internals, not externals. Unseen of men, the kingdom is "within you" or "among you"—invisibly present in individuals, elective, not collective, marked by intensity, not extensity. The visible church is not, of course, identical with the invisible kingdom, for beside a militant body, contending for the faith, the church contains a termagant section, warring against its peace, and an apostate body, fighting against the truth. God sees in the church the "circumcision," the "concision" and the "excision."

Hence the vice and risk of *statistics.* "Numbering the people" brought to David a choice between plague, famine and war; to count up converts and parade numerical results brings to the church all three at once. During this evil age, evil will permeate and dominate it to the end. Though the Second Man recovered the kingly scepter Adam lost, he waits until he comes again before he sets up his throne on earth. Meanwhile, the usurper is the acknowledged "god of this world," and his claim seems supported by fact, that it is his to give its riches, wisdom, power and honor to whom he will (Luke 4:6). So far as Satan triumphs, for the time, saints are fettered by restraint and restriction; and the church is in the wilderness rather than on the mount of victory.

The phrase "kingdom of the heavens," peculiar to Matthew, seems applicable to this age, while the king is in the heavens, from thence, in the person of the Spirit, his substitute, administering the kingdom. The sheet is now let down from heaven to gather of every kind, to be drawn up again at our Lord's second advent.

As to the *coming* age, it is as peculiarly that of the *Son of Man* as the present is of the *Spirit*. His own marked phraseology, the "Son of Man" and "*his* kingdom" (Matt. 13:41; 16:28), cannot be without meaning. He will come to resume and complete his personal dispensation, interrupted by his ascension, when he gave place to the Spirit.

The peculiarities of this *coming* age are these: first of all, Christ's personal reign, frequently and plainly set forth in Scripture. The kingdom will then be marked by *visibility;* comprehensive, extensive, advancing toward universal dominion. Then all the sheep shall be gathered into one flock under the one shepherd. Then "all Israel shall be saved, born at once" (*paam*, at a beat, or step), the only "nation" of whose conversion the Bible speaks as of a totality. The collective and universal feature will doubtless then be as prominent as the elective and individual is now; organization, conspicuous and world-wide, a compact government of which Jerusalem was, in its best estate, a type (Ps. 122:3).

This coming age is to be one of *conquest*. Now the policy is persuasive, not coercive; witness, not war; the word, not the sword which belongs rather to the kingdom. Both at the beginning and end, there are to be wars of conquest and judgments more or less destructive. Satan's dominion is to be destroyed, and the saints, bound now, are to be *unbound* then; the first resurrection from among the dead will let loose the bodies of "them that sleep" from the bonds of death and the grave, and they, with the living saints, caught up to meet the Lord, will be associated with him in glory. Then shall we understand the full significance of those ten mysterious words which are like bright points in that grand circle of the coming age—"return," "revelation," "refreshing," "restitution," "restoration," "regeneration," "resurrection," "reception," "recompense," "redemption." This coming age is also the age of *completion*, when all things are to "head up" into Christ.

There is an age yet *beyond*, when time shall be no longer—an eternal age (better described by the Greek word *aidios* than *aionios*). This seems distinctively the period of the *"Father's* kingdom." "Then cometh the END, when he delivers up the kingdom to God, even the Father, when he shall have put down all rule and all authority and power. For he must reign till he hath put all enemies under his feet. Death, the last enemy, shall be destroyed. And when all things shall be subdued unto him, then shall the Son also himself be subject unto him that put all things under him, that God may be all in all" (1 Cor. 15:24–28).

These words indicate a still grander END—a close to Christ's proper mediatorial reign, the object thereof being attained, and the consequent delivering of the Son's scepter back into the Father's hands.

Toward this final consummation *all the ages grandly move.* This is the final fulfillment of that prayer, dictated by the Son himself, specifically addressed to the *"Father,"* which refers to an ultimate state of perfection to be reached and realized only in the "Father's kingdom," and therefore in the "eternal" age. The qualifying phrase, "On earth as it is in heaven," which we connect only with the *last* of three petitions, undoubtedly refers to all. "AS IN HEAVEN, SO IN EARTH, let thy name be hallowed, thy kingdom come, thy will be done!" Such construction interprets and lights up the prayer as sunshine transfigures a cathedral window. We are taught to turn our eyes to heaven, toward him whose fatherhood has been disowned, whose benignant paternal rule has been dishonored, whose blessed will has been resisted by his rebellious subjects, and to pray that, once more, the conditions of a celestial state may be restored in the terrestrial sphere; that on earth, as in heaven, that name of Father may be hallowed and worshiped; his kingdom may have universal, undisputed sway, and his fatherly will may be done, with obedience as immediate and implicit, self-surrender as complete and cheerful, here as there. This is a prophecy and forecast of an age beyond even the millennial; for not even during that is predicted any triumph or transformation so complete. This age is militant, marked to its close by a fight for the faith. Even the triumphant age coming is to close with a battle against foes found in the four quarters of the earth "whose number is as the sand of the sea." A prayer that anticipates a triumph over evil so complete that on earth worship shall be as devout, God's sway as absolute, and man's obedience as complete as in heaven itself must refer to a period when the last enemy is destroyed and all foes have been put beneath the feet of the enthroned Son of God. This is also the full and final revelation of the glory of the saints, when the righteous are to "shine forth as the sun in the kingdom of *their Father*" (Matt. 13:43).

Imagine a worldwide empire of a father who associates with him, in equal honors and dignities, a prince and princess royal. The administration of a distant and revolted province is by this father committed to the son during the period of revolt. The son goes there in partial disguise on his mission of reconciliation, revealing himself to certain who repent of their rebellion, receive him, and gather around him as the nucleus of a restored state. Being rejected, insulted and outraged by others, he with-draws, having used no coercive measures, and sends the princess royal to use her singular charms to win back other rebels to their allegiance. Hers is a strictly secret mission; herself always unseen, she prompts messages of love and sends out far and wide her heralds with the good news of amnesty until the whole province is pervaded by the tidings and a large body of loyal subjects has been organized. Then suddenly the prince royal, in all the glory of his father and with a vast army, appears on the scene and leads on his elect host to a final contest and an overwhelming conquest. All enemies who do not voluntarily bow before his power are slain by his sword; and, perfect peace being re-established, he surrenders back the reins of government into the father's hands.

In this study of the ages and the kingdom, the ages are the courts, of which the kingdom is the tabernacle, and we advance from outer court to inner shrine. The present age is the outer court, with its altar of burnt offering and laver, reminding us of the two great truths to be empha-sized and proclaimed, the *"terms* of communion" with God—a new rela-tion by the blood of atonement and a new nature by the Spirit and the Word. Behind the first veil lies the coming age with its ideal *"forms* of communion," the sevenfold lamp of witness, the consecrated offering of self and service, and the incense of heart worship. But, beyond even the second veil is to be realized a perfected ideal—God himself dwelling in the midst of a redeemed and glorified humanity as the Shekinah shone between the wings of the cherubim.

In his remarkable book, *After the Thousand Years*, Mr. George F. Trench has shown conclusively that what we call "the millennial age" cannot meet all the requirements of the prophetic forecast. The kingdom, as described especially in the four Pauline epistles—to the Ephesians, Phi-lippians, Colossians and Hebrews—cannot be the kingdom that closes with a general insurrection against Christ as king, which could only be the outcome of heart-subjection to Satanic rule. Between the end of the millennial and the beginning of the eternal, Mr. Trench contends that there *must intervene* that "dispensation of the fullness of times," when, as heir of all things and undisputed head of the whole creation, the Lord Jesus Christ shall reign with all in absolute and hearty subjection to himself.

This view is so clearly scriptural that the only surprise is that it has not been more definitely and widely held. It adds immeasurably, both to the glory of Christ as the coming king, and of the Father as the former and framer of the ages. It is the period typified by the eighth day of the Mosaic code; the perfect glory of Christ, reserved for "the *morrow after*" the millennial "Sabbath!" And while the millennial period is limited to a thousand years, there are no definite limits to this final age of glory.

That mystic phrase, "fullness of times," suggests a certain overflow, as if past ages were but partial and incomplete: this is a full-time dispensation, and may be also in duration—"to a thousand generations."

But the point is that the glory of the coming king, as revealed only from the mountain summits to which we climb in the four epistles already mentioned, demands something more than a reign in which hostile elements are only held in check, at last to break forth in a monster revolt. Surely our Lord is not to reign simply till he has put all foes under his feet, and then with his conquest just achieved and with no opportunity for the peaceful enjoyment of his victory, surrender up his scepter!

We fully agree with Mr. Trench that all the prophetic conditions are not met until between the last revolt and "the end" we make room for a period, indefinite in length, when, after all enemies are routed, the King of kings and Lord of lords shall peacefully possess his seat of empire and reign over a loyal and loving people, among whom no secret traitors foster their dark designs.[35]

The bearing of this study upon missions is fundamental, vital. To a true disciple the one question is, *"what is my master's will?"* Our great commission is a world's evangelization, and its sphere is this present evil age: now, crucifixion with Christ, fellowship with him in travail; in the coming age coronation with Christ, fellowship with him in triumph. To the end of this age we are at his command to "go into all the world and preach the gospel to every creature," leaving all results with him, and not measuring success by superficial signs.

Now, the kingdom, being invisible, extends its sway in the hearts of disciples one by one. Its conquests, in silence and secrecy, come not "with observation," sounding no loud trumpet as a signal for advance, sending no imperial herald to cry, "lo, here! lo, there!" Sometimes its progress is like that of ocean tides, rising toward a higher flood mark, even while seeming to recede toward a lower level. An invisible Spirit leads on, leaving behind no track traceable by the carnal eye; an unseen Christ assures, "Lo, I am with you always, even unto the end of the age." Why

35 *After the Thousand Years*, George F. Trench.

not be satisfied to do our duty and not attempt to gauge the kingdom by man's measuring rod? Though unseen, the kingdom is as divinely real, the Spirit as divinely mighty, the master as divinely present, as though supernal splendors smote our eyes. To look for a world's complete conquest during this age deludes us with a false hope unaffirmed in prophecy, unconfirmed by history. After many centuries "the offence of the cross" has not ceased; evil still rules this world, and Satan is still its god. Yet, from all nations, the church is surely being out-gathered, though the race is still in rebellion; into one temple the "living stones" are being built, though masses of bedrock lie dead in the quarries.

The church waits for her full salvation, the world for its true transformation, the whole creation for its final redemption, until he comes who maketh "all things new." LET US DO OUR DUTY IN THIS PRESENT EVIL AGE and the kingdom will come now, so far and so fast as God means it shall, in hearts subdued and renewed by the Spirit. Then the king will return, and the kingdom will come in that grander sense and on that grander scale that befit the glory of his new advent and formal assumption of regal dignities. And when that final age shall open, which is the apex of the time-worlds, whose eternal noon knows no shadow of sin or death, then *the kingdom will have come* in splendor, consummate, infinite, eternal. On a new earth, arched by a new heaven, God's name shall be hallowed and God's will shall be done by a redeemed race of humanity, as now before his throne the intelligence of cherubs and the affection of seraphs blend in ceaseless adoration and ecstatic obedience.

4. The two advents

To understand this mystery of history we need a correct biblical idea of the *two advents of Christ and their relation* (diagram 12).

For the illustration of these truths, an ellipse serves better than a circle with but one center, for it has two foci and by the law of this curve the sum of two lines, drawn from any point to the foci, will be the same. This illustrates the relation of the scheme of redemption to *two great events:* Christ's first and second comings. Let this left focus (B) represent his first advent, and the right focus (C) his second advent; the creation of man be represented by the left point (A) where the axis cuts the curve; and the delivering up of the kingdom to God and the Father (D) at its other extremity. Thus the curve outlines the *entire range and scope of Christ's mediatorial work*, backward from his incarnation to the fall of

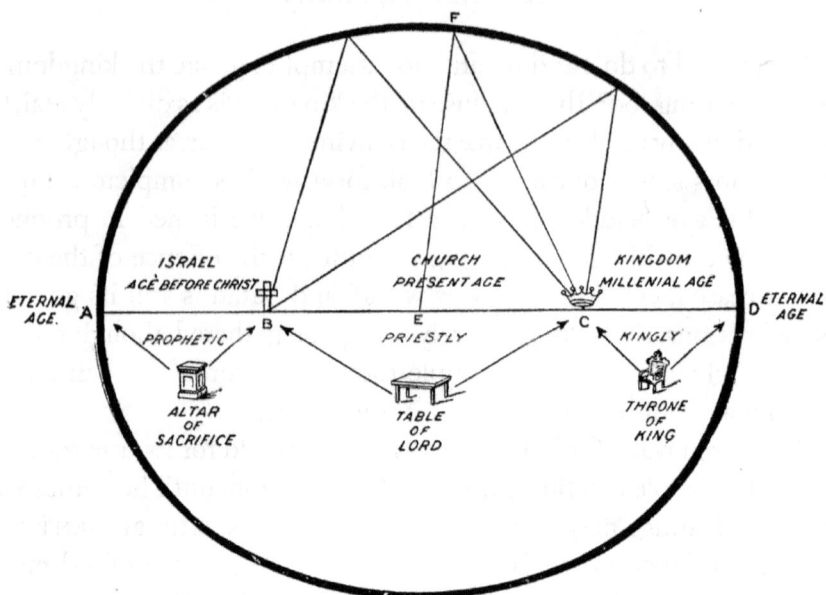

12. The two advents

Adam, and forward to the conclusion of his mediatorial reign.

Between creation and the incarnation there stands conspicuous an altar of sacrifice, and between the two advents the table of the Lord. The altar refers back to the fall and forward to the cross; for every victim that bled upon the altar reminded of sin and pointed forward to one who was to take away sin. Lines are drawn from both directions to the altar to indicate this mutual relationship. Likewise the table of the Lord points backward to the cross and forward to the crown; for, "As often as ye eat this bread and drink this cup ye do *show the Lord's death till he come.*" We therefore unite these also by similar lines.

Between this second coming and the delivering up of the kingdom stands a throne; it points back to the assumption of the kingship at his advent and forward to the delivering up of the kingdom at the end; and hence again connecting lines.

Thus we have a philosophy both of theology and of history, for the ellipse embraces the entire mediatorial work of Christ, from the fall of man to the final surrender of the mediatorial scepter.

Again, there are three offices of Christ—the prophetic, the priestly and the kingly; and three periods of history are embraced within this ellipse: First, the *prophetic,* mainly from the fall to the cross; the *priestly,* from the incarnation to the second coming; the *kingly,* from his coming to "the end." During the prophetic period, there was a forecast of his priesthood in the Levitical offices and sacrifices. During the priestly, a forecast of his kingship in individual surrender of believers to his sway. There is no indication in the Word of God that *Christ has ever yet assumed the kingship;* yet the whole conception of his mediatorial work rests ultimately upon this idea as its basis.

In studying God's scheme of redemption, we must note that the Bible is a blank as to what we call "profane" history, having very little to do with the annals of the *race* as such; it is the history of *God's chosen people.* Accurately to make out the various 490-year periods (in 1 Kings 6 and Dan. 9), we must *leave out the periods of the captivities or apostasies of Israel,* for God does not count in his calendar *time not spent in his service, reckoning only the period of obedience!* To study *"church* history"—the spiritual development of the race—we must look up past the human to the divine chronology and notice how God's clock ticks and strikes for the fullness of time. When the Israelites pressed for a king, God gave them one, but with his own disapprobation; then, when Saul, their choice, was an utter failure, he says, "I have chosen me a man *after mine own heart;* his kingdom shall be a perpetual kingdom; and ... there shall sit on the throne of David a prince in David's line, of whose kingdom there shall be no end." Here, while the Israelitish idea of the kingdom was apparently *adopted* by God—it is rather *adapted*—he transmutes the human conception of kingdom into the *theocratic,* or rather engrafts the latter on the former.

John the Baptist's proclamation was, "the kingdom of heaven is at hand"—"make ready for the coming king." Jesus began his ministry with the same announcement; and so, when he sent forth the seventy and the twelve, they also said, "the kingdom of heaven is come nigh." Zechariah's prophecy: "Behold, thy king cometh unto thee," was fulfilled when Jesus entered Jerusalem, exactly as prophesied, and made the offer of the kingdom to the Jews, as had been foretold, and the people and the children said, "Hosanna! Blessed is the king that cometh in the name of the Lord. Blessed be the kingdom of our father David."

But the rulers and representatives of the people and the members of the Sanhedrim said: "We will not have this man to reign over us." Consequently, the offer of the kingdom was suspended from that time and has never yet been renewed. Hear the words of the Messianic king: "How often would I have gathered thy children together, even as a hen gathereth her brood under her wings, but ye would not;" "ye shall not see me henceforth, until the time come when ye shall say"—as the common people and the little children had said—"blessed is he that cometh in the name of the Lord."

From that time forth there was no more proclamation of the "kingdom." In fact Christ himself says: "The kingdom shall be taken away from you;" and likens himself to "a nobleman that goes into a far country to *receive for himself a kingdom*, and to return."

We find confirmation of this divine philosophy of history in the priestly offices of our Lord. There were *four parts* of the priests' work: first, *sacrifice* at the altar; second, *service* in the holy place; third, *intercession* in the holiest of all; and fourth, what should be made more conspicuous, *the return into the court to bless the congregation.*

In the tabernacle (diagram 8), sacrifice was performed in the outer court, service in the holy place, intercession in the holiest of all, and benediction outside near the brazen altar. These are all noted in the epistle to the Hebrews: "Now when these things were thus ordained, the priests went always into the first tabernacle, accomplishing the *service* of God.... It was therefore necessary that the patterns of things in the heavens should be purified with these; but the heavenly things themselves with better *sacrifices* than these.... For Christ is not entered into the holy places made with hands, which are the figures of the true; but into heaven itself, now *to appear in the presence of God for us.*" That is *intercession.* "So Christ was once offered to bear the sins of many; and unto them that look for him *shall he appear the second time* without sin unto salvation." That corresponds to the high priest's *return and benediction* (Heb. 9:6–28).

The high priest thus took the blood, went into the holy place, and into the holiest of all, for "intercession" at the mercy seat, the people waiting outside for the sign of the completed "atonement." Then he returned, not in the white garments of humiliation with which he went in, but in the garments of glory and beauty; and, standing before the people and lifting his hands, pronounced the Levitical benediction (Num. 6:26), and the ceremonies of the great Day of Atonement were finished.

But they were not complete *until the benediction was pronounced;* nor will the priestly office of the Lord Jesus Christ be until he returns and, with the same pierced hands uplifted in blessing as at his ascension, bestows upon his waiting people the fullness of benediction in a perfected salvation!

The high priest of old *began* with sacrifice because sins—of his own and of the people—must first be atoned for; but the sinless Christ *began with service:* "Wist ye not that I must be about my Father's business?" Then, as one who already in the holy place had given all he had to God, he comes back, as to the brazen altar, and, because no other victim would suffice, became at once *priest and victim*, giving himself for our sins. Now he has gone into the holiest, there to appear in the presence of God for us, thence to come again and appear to those who look for him—not again to be made sin for us, but to bring us the fullness and the glory of salvation, as now reserved in heaven, ready to be revealed in the last time.

This coming of the Lord is complex, involving at least seven other associated facts and truths.

First, his *session at the right hand of God.* If, when he ascended, he took his place *on his own throne*, why does Scripture refer to his kingdom as something yet to come? But when he ascended, the Father said to him, "Come and sit with me on *my* throne." He is not yet enthroned as king in his *own* right but as the expectant heir, seated not on his own throne but his Father's, waiting till his enemies are made his footstool; until as on their necks he mounts to his *own* throne; and hence he says: "To him that overcometh will I grant to sit *with me on my throne*, as I also have overcome and *am set down with my Father on his throne*" (Rev. 3:21).

To evade such plain teaching introduces chaotic confusion into Scripture. A prominent writer, seeking to explain the prophecies about Christ's kingship, without admitting that, though not yet so reigning, he is coming as a king, treats as nonsense all attempts to verify the prophecies about Israel by *literal* facts about their regathering and restoration, and holds that all such forecasts are to be *spiritually* interpreted, *Israel* being equivalent to the church. A little further on he concedes that, "*after the fullness of the Gentiles shall have been gathered in, all Israel shall be saved!*" Israel is at one point the church; and, shortly after, separate from the church, with suspended privileges, not to be saved till after the fullness of the Gentiles has been gathered in. He says, "If these prophecies about the kingship of Christ are to be literally interpreted, then Jesus Christ has never come, for he certainly did not come as an earthly king;" which is as much as to say that if the prophecies indicate that he shall literally be an earthly king, inasmuch as he did not come in the first place as such, he did not come at all.

Of these seven truths, *four* pertain specially to *the church;* and first, that the church is an *out-called body—ecclesia.* The late Dr. A. A. Hodge says, *"ecclesia always implies a minority."* Hence, during this age—the period of the church—it will always remain in the minority—a fatal admission for those who expect a *millennium before Christ comes.* Again, the church is thus called out *to be a witness to the world* and throughout the world until the end of the age. This witnessing includes whatever helps to put before human souls the grandeur, dignity and power of Christ as Savior and Lord. Some have ridiculed this idea of "witness," representing messengers as rushing on horseback into a village, trumpeting forth the message that he who believeth shall be saved and he who believeth not shall be damned, and then hurrying away. Witnessing covers the whole process of calling out of the world a people for God; but we are not to wait till we first *convert* any part of the world before we *evangelize* the whole, "preaching the gospel to every creature" that all men may *hear.*

Again, the church as a whole *will drift into apostasy.* There is to be a falling away. While some will be true to God, many will not hold fast the faith, and an alarming defection is foretold toward the end of the age. Some of us wonder whether this apostasy is not even *now* in progress, when men teach, even in theological schools, who would not have been tolerated at the Lord's table twenty-five years ago, but classed with infidels. Preachers cast contempt on blood atonement, inspiration of Holy Scripture and all that is vital to a supernatural gospel.

The other church-truth is that there is to be a *resurrection of dead saints* out from the general body of the dead when Jesus Christ appears in glory.

Another truth concerns *Israel.* "The gifts and calling of God are without repentance." When the first covenant of God with his own people was made void by their disobedience, he made "a new covenant," in which the Lord Jesus Christ is the contracting party on behalf of men. "Inasmuch as they regarded not my covenant, saith the Lord, I will make a new covenant with the house of Israel after those days. I will put my laws in their minds and in their hearts will I write them, and their sins and iniquities will I remember no more" (Heb. 8:8–13, 10:16–17). Man has broken every covenant he has ever made, and the Lord Jesus Christ now undertakes to be responsible for frail human believers, who cannot keep their promises, and their unfaithfulness and unbelief never can make that new covenant void.

Once more as to *the man of sin*. All systems opposed to God are essentially anti-Christ, but there is probably a *final person* in whom all these will head up. These are the subordinate truths specially connected with the Lord's coming.

Adolph Saphir, in his *Divine Unity of the Scripture*, presents an original view of the connection between the two miracles recorded in the sixth chapter of John: the feeding of the five thousand and the appearing to the disciples, when rowing on a stormy sea, so that the ship was immediately at the land whither they went. The former represents the world hungry for food and satisfied only when Christ feeds them. The disciples, with Christ in the midst of them, bring the loaves and fishes to him; he blesses and breaks, and they distribute them, so that all are fed and filled, and twelve baskets of fragments remain. That miracle represents Christ, co-working with all true disciples in preaching the Word, enabling them to take the barley loaves of the gospel, despised by men because it does not conform to human standards of learning and culture, and is too plain diet for philosophers and sages. Yet disciples, taking the simple message of salvation, which is still foolishness to the Greek and a stumbling-block to the Jew, feed hungry souls the world over. The miracle still goes on and the supply undiminished; nay, as we divide, the Lord multiplies; as we subtract, he adds; as we decrease by distribution, he increases for distribution.

In the other miracle, the world is represented by a restless and tossing sea. It is not now hunger, but *unrest*—opposition to God. The ship in the midst of the sea is the little church of disciples, tossed on the stormy waters, Satan using the winds and waves to blow and beat upon it and seeking to destroy it utterly; Christ, away on the mountain top, communing with the Father, and out of their sight. However they toil in rowing, the ship makes no progress. The world's unrest continues; its hostility abides, and it opposes Christ as much as ever. Though some fancy that the world is growing better, the carnal heart hates him as it always has; and if he were on the earth today would crucify him as in the days of his flesh. Those who are hoping to convert the world keep pulling away at their oars, but they can neither still the sea nor bring the vessel nearer shore; all they can do is to keep it afloat! But in the fourth watch of the night, Jesus will come to them as they toil in rowing; and immediately the ship will be at the land. The sea will be stilled when he appears, and straightway the church will reach her haven.

Is there no significance in those two miracles? The first, the world in its hunger coming to Christ and getting the loaves and the fishes, and being filled in the ministry of the Word; and the second, the world in its unrest and its hostility to Christ, beating away against the little ship of the church and trying to swamp it and sink it, while all that disciples can do is to keep the ship afloat. We cannot still these waves; we cannot give peace instead of this unrest; we cannot abate this antagonism of the world. But just as soon as Jesus comes, now away communing with the Father, there will be peace. The world will be brought to a new state, and the church will be at the shore whither it seeks to go.

"Now of the things that we have spoken this is the sum." We have a high priest who once accomplished a perfect atonement for us—who, through the rent veil, having passed into the holiest of all, has taken his seat on the right hand of the throne of the majesty on high, ruling over his people by reigning in their hearts. He, being the mediator of a new covenant established upon better promises, representing his people before God, and making their service perfect because his own service is identified with it, representing God to his people in bringing down the mighty power of God to control them in their sinful propensities and carnal desires, buoys them up with patience, and gives them encouragement and hope and joy and the assurance of his divine presence. And there he sits, with no "footstool" as yet, but he shall shortly bruise Satan under his own feet and under his *saints'* feet, and then his foes shall be made his footstool. While the church, rowing against wind and tide, seeks to get nearer heaven, making little or no progress, he is watching from the hidden place of communion with the Father; and, when the crisis is greatest, the danger most extreme, the darkness deepest and the distress the most overwhelming, he will suddenly appear in the very midst of the troubled waters, walking on the sea in divine majesty; and immediately when he comes into the ship it will touch the millennial shore, and all the dangers and disasters of church life will be past.

There is mystery in God's Word, for it is his workmanship. The range and the scope of it is terrible, like the wheels Ezekiel saw that reached from earth to heaven; full of eyes before and behind; complicated, wheel within wheel; and yet moving all in one direction, because they fulfilled the purpose of God; but no man can fathom such divine mechanism.

The mystery compels us to bow before it as his Word. But *mystery never once touches duty.* "The secret things belong to the Lord our God, there things revealed belong to us and to our children, even all the words of this law."

When *reason* decides that this is God's Word, then we are prepared for the venture of *faith*. If there remain about the character or nature of God, the awards of the future, the elective purposes of God and their consistency with man's freedom, the immutability of God and its consistency with the doctrine of prayer, much that we cannot understand or reconcile; we must lay it to the weakness of our vision and the obscurity of the medium through which we look, and not attribute it to contradiction in God himself.

We shall stumble over this doctrine of the Lord's second coming if we try to bring down the things of heaven to the low level of earth. When Christ comes again it will be on a scale of grandeur and magnificence for which human experience furnishes no adequate terms. When God would express celestial things he must use a human dialect, necessarily imperfect, because all language intelligible to us must be on our level. We must, therefore, wait for the day itself to unfold and reveal what the Holy Ghost can but partly reveal now because our eyes are inadequate fully to discern spiritual things.

The Lord's coming, being so important as a center of biblical doctrine, must be equally so as center of biblical practice. Again reverting to the ellipse (diagram 13), the middle of the axis (E) may stand for the present viewpoint. Let us bear in mind that every point in the circumference bears a proportionate relation to each of the foci.

If we conceive this ellipse as pertaining to the infinities of God, it will be seen that to the observer (at E), a point in this circumference (F), though moved toward the right or the left, will not vary essentially in its relative *apparent position* on account of its exalted height above the axis, like a remote star in the sky. "One day is with the Lord as a thousand years." The earthly base line may seem broad, but how narrow the angle that line subtends! So, as to the comparative remoteness of our Lord's coming from the time of his incarnation; though the earthly base line may be 2,000 years or more, the angle between the lines that ascend from its extreme points is very acute. The time which seems long to us is nothing to the eternal.

If, then, we draw a line from this supposed position of the observer to a point in this circumference, and another down to the point C, one will represent the upward look of the believer towards Christ, and the other will represent the descent of Christ at his coming.

The Lord's coming, being viewed from the New Testament point, especially, two words that have to do with it need first to be explained: *imminence* and *eminence*. Imminence means *certainty*, as a revealed fact, but *uncertainty* as to time. These together constitute an overhanging event, always liable to occur, and lead the believer to be perpetually looking for and waiting for the coming. If the time had been revealed, there could not, in the nature of the case, be a perpetual looking for it; for interposing his millennial reign between the two advents makes impossible this posture and is enough to condemn it, for all the warnings of Christ touching its imminence, and our watchfulness with reference to it, become absurd and farcical if the Lord's coming is not to *introduce* the millennial reign but *end* it; and we need not be on the constant watch for *the signs* of its approach.

Eminence means prominence, rising above all else. In the New Testament this is the one eminent event that surpasses, in dignity and importance, even his incarnation and the coming of the Holy Spirit. The diagram hints at both imminence and eminence. To the observer looking into infinite heights, Christ appears an exalted object; and his coming must have like eminence by the height to which he is exalted, and will have imminence by the fact that, to the observer, this point is so lofty as to be always in his zenith. No earthly base line alters the relative position of an object, which is so high above as always to seem overhead. So Jesus Christ is the star in the zenith to every true believer; and however long he waits before he comes, he will still be in the zenith.

The eminence of this event also depends upon this, that his coming is the hinge upon which everything else turns. In its *relation to Christian living, it is the practical center.* There are three graces: faith, hope and love; then there is the external conduct, or good works; and the decline of all Christian character, which is apostasy.

If, therefore, this doctrine is expected to have a predominant influence upon holy living, that second advent will be urged as a great incentive. Let us take a representative passage from each of the five epistle writers, beginning with Paul, the apostle of faith. "For the grace of God that bringeth salvation hath appeared to all men, teaching us that, denying ungodliness and worldly lusts, we should live soberly, righteously and godly in this present *age*, looking for that blessed hope, and the epiphany of the glory of the great God and our Savior Jesus Christ, who gave himself for us, that he might redeem us from all iniquity and purify unto himself a peculiar people, zealous of good works" (Titus 2:11–13). The word *epiphany* means a coming out from obscuration, as when in the shipwreck in the Mediterranean "neither sun nor stars in many days appeared"—"had their epiphany." "The grace of God that bringeth salvation to all men" had its epiphany in our Lord's incarnation, teaching us how to live in this present evil age, which is the base line subtending this whole arc, and "looking for that blessed hope and the glorious epiphany of the great God and our Savior Jesus Christ"—that expresses the upward look of the believer toward the descending Christ.

Thus Paul says: the epiphany of grace is past; the epiphany of glory is future; and there is the intermediate evil age. By looking back to this epiphany of grace as the foundation of salvation in the dying and risen Christ; and by looking forward to the epiphany of glory as the consummation of that salvation in the returning Lord, the believer is enabled to live soberly—maintaining holy self control, righteously—honoring all his relations with his fellow men; godly, fulfilling duties and obligations to God. If all motive in holy living is sufficiently supplied by the past revelation of grace, why does he insist that we must look forward to the epiphany of glory in order to the complete incentives to godliness?

Peter, the apostle of hope, writes of "an inheritance incorruptible, undefiled, and that fadeth not away, reserved in heaven for you, who are kept by the power of God through faith unto salvation ready to be revealed in the last time" (1 Peter 1:3, 5). A salvation not already revealed but *ready to be revealed* in the last time. And again "that the trial of your faith … might be found unto praise and honor and glory at the appearing of Jesus Christ. Whom, having not seen, ye love; in whom, though now ye see him not, yet believing, ye rejoice with joy unspeakable and full of glory; receiving the end (the consummation) of your faith, even the salvation of your souls" (verse 7). Not a word about a salvation completed at the cross. Christ's resurrection from the dead only *started* that salvation as our *begetting* unto the living hope, which is fixed on a salvation reserved in heaven for us who are reserved for it. We are to receive the end of our faith, even the salvation of our souls, at the appearing of Jesus Christ. That upward look is prophetic and forecasts and foretastes, even in the present life, that consummated salvation that awaits us when he comes.

Again, "hope to the end for the grace that is to be brought unto you at the (verse 13) *revelation* of Jesus Christ," which implies that his incarnation was rather a *disguise*. He came in humiliation, a king in essential character but robed in humanity; and only once—in his transfiguration—this disguise was laid aside so that the star of empire was clearly seen gleaming on his breast! When he comes again it will be in the glory of his Father with the holy angels, *the true revelation* of Jesus Christ. Moreover "the grace to *be* brought" at such revelation implies as yet only a little *foretaste* of it. Peter evidently thought the Lord's coming a mighty factor in the development of hope.

What has John, the apostle of love, to say about it? "Beloved, now are we the sons of God, and it doth not yet appear what we shall be; but we know that when he shall appear we shall be like him; for we shall see him as he is. And every man that hath this hope in him purifieth himself, even as he is pure" (1 John 3:2). In his opinion nothing helps to the purification of character like this blessed hope! Again, "whosoever shall confess that Jesus is the son of God, God dwelleth in him and he in God. Herein is our love made perfect, that we may have boldness in the day of judgment; because as he is, so are we in this world" (4:15, 19). The believer confesses Christ in the face of an opposing, perhaps persecuting age; and when this world is dissolving, the elements melting with fervent heat, and he seeks a solid standing place, lo, the Son of God appears in his behalf: you "confessed me before a gainsaying world; I confess you before my father and the holy angels." He who with his eye fixed on Christ's second coming has courage to confess him in the face of opposition shall in the day of final judgment have boldness.

What has the apostle of good works to say on the same subject? "Hath not God chosen the poor of this world rich in faith, and heirs of the kingdom which he hath promised to them that love him?" (James 2:15). In those days disciples were, for Christ's sake, taking joyfully the spoiling of their goods. Their gaze again is directed to his coming, when the kingdom is to be set up, and the poor in this world shall inherit the kingdom, and, having shared Christ's humiliation, shall share his exaltation. "Be patient therefore, brethren, unto the coming of the Lord. Behold, the husbandman waiteth for the precious fruit of the earth, and hath long patience for it until he receive the early and latter rain. Be ye also patient, stablish your hearts, for the coming of the Lord draweth nigh" (5:7). Just as when a man steeping his seed in tears plants it, waters it, watches over its germination and growth and waits for the harvest, so the apostle says: "In all your labors be patient. The harvest will not come till he himself comes, so that the Lord's appearing is the day of harvesting."

Jude, the prophet of the apostasy, says: "But ye, beloved, building up yourselves on your most holy faith, praying in the Holy Ghost, keep yourselves in the love of God, looking for the mercy of our Lord Jesus Christ unto eternal life." What is more vital to spiritual life than to keep myself in the love (20, 21) of God, as a plant needs to keep in the sunshine to keep growing?

How do we keep ourselves in the love of God? By building up ourselves on our most holy faith through a growing knowledge of the Holy Scriptures; by praying in the Holy Ghost as the divine element in which we live and breathe; and, associated with the others, as a necessary part of this Christian culture, is "looking for the mercy of our Lord Jesus Christ unto eternal life"—not back to what he did on the cross only, but forward to the mercy to be revealed when he comes. So all these epistle writers present as the preeminent point on which to fix our vision, the coming of the Lord.

Faith, in New Testament usage, means, first, the *acceptance of truth*, and second, the *bond of union* with Christ. By a true conception of his second coming, faith is vitalized, energized, quickened. As an intellectual process of receiving revealed truth, faith depends largely upon *perception*—clear apprehension. What is vague, indistinct, obscure, becomes proportionately difficult to perceive and receive; but when it becomes clear and obvious, because we have a transparent medium through which to look, believing becomes correspondingly easy and satisfactory. Biblical conceptions of the Lord's coming get mists and clouds out of our way, presenting before us something easily apprehended by the faith of a child.

The prophetic, priestly and kingly periods are related to Christ himself. Peter writes, "that the *Spirit of Christ, which was in the prophets*... testified beforehand of the sufferings of Christ and glory that shall follow," so that this prophetic period belongs to his mediatorial work, though he had not yet been manifested as a prophet himself, not yet incarnate—the very spirit of prophecy being the *Spirit of Christ*, forecasting his future.

As to the priesthood, was not he the Lamb of God, slain from the foundation of the world, but manifested in these latter times for those who, by him, do believe in God, who raised him up and gave him the glory, that their faith and hope might be in God? This exhibition of the whole scope of his mediatorial work systematizes the whole subject, relieves it from difficulty, and dissipates the mist so often confounded with mystery. Whoever knows what it is to walk in the light through this truth becomes intensely earnest in its advocacy, from the desire that others should see Scripture teaching in the same luminous aspect.

Many other things are simplified by the scriptural view of the Lord's coming. For instance, there are distinctions of which the New Testament never loses sight, and which help greatly in understanding the Scriptures. Four or five terms are used but never confused: "the whole creation;" "the Gentiles" or "nations," or "the world;" "the Jews," or "Israel," and "the church of God." These terms are never equivalent or interchangeable. The whole creation, the all-embracing term, seems to include even the lower orders of animals and created matter. Paul writes (in 1 Cor. 10:32) "giving none offence, neither to the *Jews* nor to the *Gentiles*, nor to the *church of God.*" If not distinct, why did he carefully distinguish them?

We have already noted the distinction between *matter* worlds and *time* worlds. When "eon" or "age" is translated "world," confusion results, as when we read of "those that have *tasted the powers of the world*"—literally the *"age* to come"—meaning those who, in this age, standing thus between the first and second advents, anticipate the glory of the coming millennial age. Again, Christ "gave himself for our sins that he might deliver us from this present evil *age.*" "I am with you even unto the end of the *age.*" Of the Holy Spirit, Christ says he is to be with disciples *for the age.*

Another distinction is always made *between the three resurrections:* The resurrection of Jesus Christ; the resurrection *from the dead* of the saints at his coming; and the resurrection *of the dead* a thousand years after." As in Adam all die, even so in Christ shall all be made alive. But every man in his own order: Christ the first-fruits; afterwards they that are Christ's at his coming. Then the end, when he shall have delivered up the kingdom to God and the Father" (1 Cor. 15:22). Notice: *"every man in his own order"* or military rank. The two Greek words, *epeita* and *eita,* are correlative, like "now" and "then." If *epeita* covers already nearly 2,000 years between Christ's resurrection and the coming resurrection of the dead saints, why should we find any difficulty in the fact that *eita* covers at least 1,000 years between the rising of those saints and of the rest of the dead? *Eita does* cover that period, for so are we taught in Rev. 20:4–5:

"And they lived and reigned with Christ a thousand years;" "but the *rest of the dead lived* not again until the thousand years were finished." Thus we have the resurrection of Christ as the first-fruits; *epeita*, afterwards, of them that are Christ's at his coming; *eita*, then the end, after the thousand years, when the rest of the dead live again—three resurrections, separated by these intervals of time.

This helps us to understand what Paul means in the epistle to the Philippians (3:10), where he uses a word only found there: "If by any means I might attain to (*ex-anastasis*) *the elect resurrection,*" *out from the general mass of the dead.* When Christ arose it was such an *ex-anastasis*, and Paul counted everything but loss to know the *power of his* resurrection and attain to a like *ex-anastasis*.

He knew that he would *rise;* but he desired to have part in the *first* resurrection of saints, who at Christ's coming rise to have partnership with him in his reign—that "better resurrection" reserved for "those that are Christ's at his coming" and are "counted worthy to attain that world, and the resurrection from among the dead."

With regard to faith *as a bond of union* between ourselves and Jesus Christ, what effect has this blessed hope? The most important phrase in the New Testament is one of two little words: "In Christ," upon which every epistle in the New Testament hinges. What is the idea of being in Christ? By faith the believer enters *into Christ*, becoming a member of his mystical body, so that everything that he did and suffered in his representative life on earth the disciple is reckoned as having done or suffered in him. In his birth through the Holy Spirit, he is born from above; in his circumcision he puts off the sins of the flesh; in his temptation he is victorious; in his crucifixion, crucified; and in his burial, buried; in his resurrection he is counted as having risen; in his ascension as having ascended to the heavenlies; in his session at God's right hand, as seated with him in heaven; and when he comes again he will come with him in glory. Faith means union with Christ, and his coming the consummation of that union. Such an event therefore appeals to faith as the bond of fellowship with the Lord, and he himself looks forward to his advent as his own consummation, because it is the consummation to his saints; and his joy in that day is in part due to his satisfaction in the exaltation and exultation of his saints, whom he presents faultless before the presence of his father.

How does the coming of the Lord affect *hope?*

Hope depends for its inspiration upon, first, a sublime or exalted object; second, the warrant of Scripture promise; and third, the confirmation of experience. Hope centered on the second coming of the Lord in glory has the sublimest object that can engage it—the Savior, glorious in his coronation. Whatever in the prophetic or priestly periods engrossed and absorbed the believer's mind and heart will then have added to it regal glory and dignity, while he himself will be perfected in Christ's likeness. No wonder "the blessed hope" is known in the New Testament as the consummation of all expectation.

This highest hope finds its sanction in the authority of Holy Scripture, inspired by a multitude of promises both in the Old and New Testaments. Does it find confirmation in actual experience?

In Proverbs we are told that "hope deferred maketh the heart sick." There are two phases of teaching as to the office of the church in the world: one is that it is commissioned to *convert the world*—that it is to grow like the mustard seed, spreading its branches far and wide until it covers the globe—that the world is to be assimilated to the church, hid, as in the meal, until the whole lump is leavened. It certainly bears against this view that the dough expands by a process of fermentation, which is a stage of decay, and that leaven is always in the Word of God the symbol of corruption.

The natural result of the acceptance of this theory is that, as the world is *not* converted, we must charge the church with failure and guilt in not pushing the work with sufficient energy; and it must increase in activity, fervor and enthusiasm. If the mission of the church in this dispensation is to convert the world, there must be grievous fault somewhere, as there are no signs of success as yet, and after nineteen hundred years only disastrous failure.

The other view is that the church is in the world to *gather out God's believing body of people from the nations, as a nucleus;* and gather *in* such saved souls, regenerated by the Spirit, into the one mystical body of Christ; that the church's mission is to *bear witness to the world and to every creature;* and as soon as this elect company is fully gathered out from the nations, so that his mystical body becomes complete, the head will appear and the body will be associated with him in glory.

The writer began his ministry fifty years ago, confident that the church is destined to convert the world in this age, and endeavored to do his part in this work, preaching with enthusiasm, ardor and conviction, expecting to see his whole congregation converted. This hope was never realized; here and there a few were gathered out, and so it continued to be through all the years of the half century. Many of us have rejoiced to see God's Spirit working, converting many souls under our preaching; but who has ever yet seen a whole congregation thus brought to Christ, every hearer being also a believer, and a whole community transformed into a true church? If there be any such case, it is sadly exceptional.

The gospel has been preached for nineteen centuries, Mr. George Müller of Bristol solemnly said, "probably not more than ten millions of souls, now living, are regenerate." Meanwhile heathenism and Mohammedanism grow more rapidly by natural births than the church by new births. How sick at heart from hope deferred must they be who, laboring all their lives expecting to see the world converted, are yet compelled to confess that the great proportion of the human race does not even *know about Christ* thus far, and that even the large majority of members of the nominal church have never experienced the regenerating power of the Holy Spirit.

If, on the other hand, the hope which the Word holds up before us in this dispensation is *not* the *conversion* but the *evangelization* of the world; and we are simply, like our Savior, to bear our witness and gather out those whom the Father hath given to Christ, *this hope, the actual facts so far confirm and fulfill, for this is exactly what is being done.* Our hope, being scripturally warranted, is not defeated nor even deferred; our hearts are not made sick, for our hope finds confirmation in actual experience.

When we think we have indulged a scriptural hope, but facts only disappoint us, the consequence is often very serious. We begin to doubt the Holy Scriptures, perhaps even their inspiration and infallibility; or lose confidence that we are ourselves true messengers of Christ because God does not confirm his Word by signs following.

Hope, thus disappointed by actual results, may become a snare and lead to infidelity because, perpetually baffled, it weakens confidence in God and his Word. He who builds on what is believed to be a divine promise, but which is not fulfilled, naturally asks if it is safe to build at all on this Word of God. The apostles went out from the presence of the council and said, "And now, Lord, behold their threatenings, and grant unto thy servants that *with all boldness they may speak thy word, by stretching forth thy hand to heal.*" All workers for God have a like right to challenge him to infuse new courage into their souls by standing by them in the fulfillment of his promises! The only way to keep us bold for his service is to confirm our faith and hope from time to time by appropriate results. The view of Scripture teaching above presented is very precious to those who hold it because it has in them been the birth of a new hope never brought to confusion.

This blessed hope puts *rewards* where they belong, *at his coming*. "Behold I come quickly, and my reward is with me, to give every man according as his work shall be" (Revelation 22:12). His servants and stewards are not to expect their reward till he appears, and then the recompense will be gloriously abundant. "Other foundation can no man lay than that is laid, which is Jesus Christ. Now if any man build upon this foundation gold, silver, precious stones, wood, hay, stubble; every man's work shall be made manifest: for the day shall declare it, because it shall be revealed by fire; and the fire shall try every man's work of what sort it is" (1 Cor. 3:11).

What is the admonition? The believer has built on Jesus Christ. Let him take care what kind of materials he uses in building. Are they gold, silver, precious stones, consistent with the foundation? Will they stand the ordeal of fire? Or, like the wood and hay and stubble, of which those huts or hovels were built in the swamps near the temple of Ephesus, will what we build be swept away in the conflagration of judgment! When the Lord comes, he will try our work as by fire. Those who have built on him as a foundation will be saved, even though, like a man fleeing out of a burning house with the timbers falling around him, they are "saved as by fire;" but if on that foundation has been built material appropriate to it and like unto it, in the ordeal of fire it will stand and glow with luster like precious gems when the light shines upon them and irradiates them with rainbow hues.

Such is the *time of reward*. When Peter said, "Lo, we have left all and followed thee; what shall we have therefore?" Jesus answered, "Ye which have followed me" (in my humiliation) "in the regeneration" (or reconstruction, *notice when*) "when the Son of Man shall sit on the throne of his glory, ye also shall sit on twelve thrones judging the twelve tribes of Israel."

The reward comes when the Lord comes. It is a very small matter to be judged by man's judgment—*in man's day*—(margin); let us study to show ourselves approved unto God and not seek to gather our rewards here—either in compensation to our purse or in honor to our person—but look for his coming, willing to have the crown of life, of righteousness, of glory deferred until he himself is crowned.

How could this hope but have a quickening effect on *love!* Remember what it is to be *in Christ*—that he is coming again to receive you unto himself and cannot himself be satisfied until his bride sits with him on his throne. Was ever bridegroom satisfied with what his bride did not share? Can the head be crowned without the body being also honored, enthroned? Nothing is so fitted to inspire and increase love for the master as that he looks forward to his coming as *our* coronation; that his joy will be to present us faultless, blameless, holy, unreprovable, so that even the omniscient eye shall find in us no relic or remnant of sin!

During the American war for the Union a strange sight was seen in a western city. The day was very dark and the rain had been descending in torrents. But high up on the brow of the mountain that overlooks the city, the national flag was seen waving, bathed in the only beam of sunshine that lighted the whole landscape. The clouds had parted at such a point that this one rift opened the way for the sunbeams to rest directly on the star-spangled banner, and the crowds stood admiring and wondering as they saw the flag of the Republic waving in the breeze and glorified by sunshine. How that flag came there was a mystery. It transpired that an exploring party had gone up for some measurements and had chanced to set the flag there at the precise moment when that solitary rift in the clouds permitted the sunlight to flash radiance upon it. By a curious coincidence, on that very day, Fort Donelson was captured and the war for the Union turned its crisis!

Fellow believers, thick darkness covers the firmament. Despite many clouds and severe storms, there is a rift in the clouds, and God's golden sunbeam rests upon that banner of our hope—the Lord's second coming! Keep your eye on that blessed hope and you will turn the crises of life gloriously—patient in sorrow and suffering, in unrewarded and unrequited toil, in unrecognized and unappreciated service and suffering for humanity. Faith will be quickened, hope transfixed, love glorified. Keep your eye on the Lord's own banner, and pray him to hasten his coming.

Buy online at our website: **www.KingsleyPress.com**
Also available as an eBook for Kindle, Nook and iBooks.

Also from Kingsley Press:

AN ORDERED LIFE

AN AUTOBIOGRAPHY BY G. H. LANG

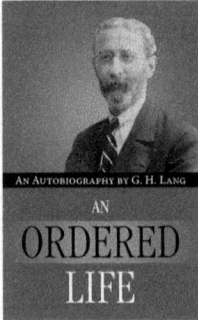

G. H. Lang was a remarkable Bible teacher, preacher and writer of a past generation who should not be forgotten by today's Christians. He inherited the spiritual "mantle" of such giants in the faith as George Müller, Anthony Norris Groves and other notable saints among the early Brethren movement. He traveled all over the world with no fixed means of support other than prayer and faith and no church or other organization to depend on. Like Mr. Müller before him, he told his needs to no one but God. Many times his faith was tried to the limit, as funds for the next part of his journey arrived only at the last minute and from unexpected sources.

This autobiography traces in precise detail the dealings of God with his soul, from the day of his conversion at the tender age of seven, through the twilight years when bodily infirmity restricted most of his former activities. You will be amazed, as you read these pages, to see how quickly and continually a soul can grow in grace and in the knowledge of spiritual things if they will wholly follow the Lord.

Horace Bushnell once wrote that every man's life is a plan of God, and that it's our duty as human beings to find and follow that plan. As Mr. Lang looks back over his long and varied life in the pages of this book, he frequently points out the many times God prepared him in the present for some future work or role. Spiritual life applications abound throughout the book, making it not just a life story but a spiritual training manual of sorts. Preachers will find sermon starters and illustrations in every chapter. Readers of all kinds will benefit from this close-up view of the dealings of God with the soul of one who made it his life's business to follow the Lamb wherever He should lead.

Buy online at our website: **www.KingsleyPress.com**
Also available as an eBook for Kindle, Nook and iBooks.

The Revival We Need

by Oswald J. Smith

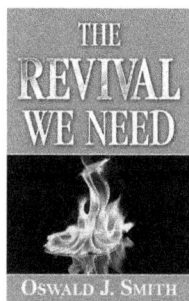

When Oswald J. Smith wrote this book almost a hundred years ago he felt the most pressing need of the worldwide church was true revival—the kind birthed in desperate prayer and accompanied by deep conviction for sin, godly sorrow, and deep repentance, resulting in a living, victorious faith. If he were alive today he would surely conclude that the need has only become more acute with the passing years.

The author relates how there came a time in his own ministry when he became painfully aware that his efforts were not producing spiritual results. His intense study of the New Testament and past revivals only deepened this conviction. The Word of God, which had proved to be a hammer, a fire and a sword in the hands of apostles and revivalists of bygone days, was powerless in his hands. But as he prayed and sought God in dead earnest for the outpouring of the Holy Spirit, things began to change. Souls came under conviction, repented of their sins, and were lastingly changed.

The earlier chapters of the book contain Smith's heart-stirring messages on the need for authentic revival: how to prepare the way for the Spirit's moving, the tell-tale signs that the work is genuine, and the obstacles that can block up the channels of blessing. These chapters are laced with powerful quotations from revivalists and soul-winners of former times, such as David Brainerd, William Bramwell, John Wesley, Charles Finney, Evan Roberts and many others. The latter chapters detail Smith's own quest for the enduement of power, his soul-travail, and the spiritual fruit that followed.

In his foreword to this book, Jonathan Goforth writes, "Mr. Smith's book, *The Revival We Need*, for its size is the most powerful plea for revival I have ever read. He has truly been led by the Spirit of God in preparing it. To his emphasis for the need of a Holy Spirit revival I can give the heartiest amen. What I saw of revival in Korea and in China is in fullest accord with the revival called for in this book."

Buy online at our website: **www.KingsleyPress.com**
Also available as an eBook for Kindle, Nook and iBooks.

Lord, Teach Us to Pray
By Alexander Whyte

Dr. Alexander Whyte (1836-1921) was widely acknowledged to be the greatest Scottish preacher of his day. He was a mighty pulpit orator who thundered against sin, awakening the consciences of his hearers, and then gently leading them to the Savior. He was also a great teacher, who would teach a class of around 500 young men after Sunday night service, instructing them in the way of the Lord more perfectly.

In the later part of Dr. Whyte's ministry, one of his pet topics was prayer. Luke 11:1 was a favorite text and was often used in conjunction with another text as the basis for his sermons on this subject. The sermons printed here represent only a few of the many delivered. But each one is deeply instructive, powerful and convicting.

Nobody else could have preached these sermons; after much reading and re-reading of them that remains the most vivid impression. There can be few more strongly personal documents in the whole literature of the pulpit. . . . When all is said, there is something here that defies analysis—something titanic, something colossal, which makes ordinary preaching seem to lie a long way below such heights as gave the vision in these words, such forces as shaped their appeal. We are driven back on the mystery of a great soul, dealt with in God's secret ways and given more than the ordinary measure of endowment and grace. His hearers have often wondered at his sustained intensity; as Dr. Joseph Parker once wrote of him: "many would have announced the chaining of Satan for a thousand years with less expenditure of vital force" than Dr. Whyte gave to the mere announcing of a hymn. —*From the Preface*

The Way of the Cross
by J. Gregory Mantle

"**D**YING to self is the *one only way* to life in God," writes Dr. Mantle in this classic work on the cross. "The end of self is the one condition of the promised blessing, and he that is not willing to die to things sinful, *yea, and to things lawful,* if they come between the spirit and God, cannot enter that world of light and joy and peace, provided on this side of heaven's gates, where thoughts and wishes, words and works, delivered from the perverting power of self—revolve round Jesus Christ, as the planets revolve around the central sun. . . .

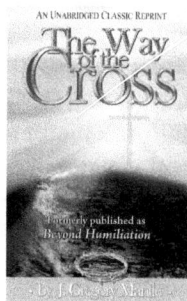

"It is a law of dynamics that two objects cannot occupy the same space at the same time, and if we are ignorant of the crucifixion of the self-life as an experimental experience, we cannot be filled with the Holy Spirit. 'If thy heart,' says Arndt in his *True Christianity*, 'be full of the world, there will be no room for the Spirit of God to enter; for where the one is the other cannot be.' If, on the contrary, we have endorsed our Saviour's work as the destroyer of the works of the devil, and have claimed to the full the benefits of His death and risen life, what hinders the complete and abiding possession of our being by the Holy Spirit but our unbelief?"

Rev. J. Gregory Mantle (1853 - 1925) had a wide and varied ministry in Great Britain, America, and around the world. For many years he was the well-loved Superintendent of the flourishing Central Hall in Deptford, England, as well as a popular speaker at Keswick and other large conventions for the deepening of spiritual life. He spent the last twelve years of his life in America, where he was associated with Dr. A. B. Simpson and the Christian and Missionary Alliance. He traveled extensively, holding missions and conventions all over the States. He was an avid supporter of foreign missions throughout his entire career. He also edited a missionary paper, and wrote several books.

Buy online at our website: **www.KingsleyPress.com**
Also available as an eBook for Kindle, Nook and iBooks.

GIPSY SMITH
HIS LIFE AND WORK

This autobiography of Gipsy Smith (1860-1947) tells the fascinating story of how God's amazing grace reached down into the life of a poor, uneducated gipsy boy and sent him singing and preaching all over Britain and America until he became a household name in many parts and influenced the lives of millions for Christ. He was born and raised in a gipsy tent to parents who made a living selling baskets, tinware and clothes pegs. His father was in and out of jail for various offences, but was gloriously converted during an evangelistic meeting. His mother died when he was only five years old.

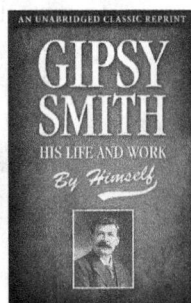

Converted at the age of sixteen, Gipsy taught himself to read and write and began to practice preaching. His beautiful singing voice earned him the nickname "the singing gipsy boy," as he sang hymns to the people he met. At age seventeen he became an evangelist with the Christian Mission (which became the Salvation Army) and began to attract large crowds. Leaving the Salvation Army in 1882, he became an itinerant evangelist working with a variety of organizations. It is said that he never had a meeting without conversions. He was a born orator. One of the Boston papers described him as "the greatest of his kind on earth, a spiritual phenomenon, an intellectual prodigy and a musical and oratorical paragon."

His autobiography is full of anedotes and stories from his preaching experiences in many different places. It's a book you won't want to put down until you're finished!

THE AWAKENING

By Marie Monsen

REVIVAL! It was a long time coming. For twenty long years Marie Monsen prayed for revival in China. She had heard reports of how God's Spirit was being poured out in abundance in other countries, particularly in nearby Korea; so she began praying for funds to be able to travel there in order to bring back some of the glowing coals to her own mission field. But that was not God's way. The still, small voice of God seemed to whisper, "What is happening in Korea can happen in China if you will pay the price in prayer." Marie Monsen took up the challenge and gave her solemn promise: "Then I will pray until I receive."

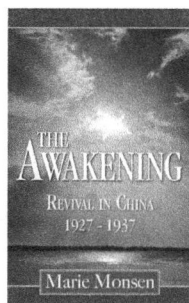

The Awakening is Miss Monsen's own vivid account of the revival that came in answer to prayer. Leslie Lyall calls her the "pioneer" of the revival movement—the handmaiden upon whom the Spirit was first poured out. He writes: "Her surgical skill in exposing the sins hidden within the Church and lurking behind the smiling exterior of many a trusted Christian—even many a trusted Christian leader—and her quiet insistence on a clear-cut experience of the new birth set the pattern for others to follow."

The emphasis in these pages is on the place given to prayer both before and during the revival, as well as on the necessity of self-emptying, confession, and repentance in order to make way for the infilling of the Spirit.

One of the best ways to stir ourselves up to pray for revival in our own generation is to read the accounts of past awakenings, such as those found in the pages of this book. Surely God is looking for those in every generation who will solemnly take up the challenge and say, with Marie Monsen, "I will pray until I receive."

A Present Help
By Marie Monsen

Does your faith in the God of the impossible need reviving? Do you think that stories of walls of fire and hosts of guardian angels protecting God's children are only for Bible times? Then you should read the amazing accounts in this book of how God and His unseen armies protected and guided Marie Monsen, a Norwegian missionary to China, as she traveled through bandit-ridden territory spreading the Gospel of Jesus Christ and standing on the promises of God. You will be amazed as she tells of an invading army of looters who ravaged a whole city, yet were not allowed to come near her mission compound because of angels standing sentry over it. Your heart will thrill as she tells of being held captive on a ship for twenty-three days by pirates whom God did not allow to harm her, but instead were compelled to listen to her message of a loving Savior who died for their sin. As you read the many stories in this small volume your faith will be strengthened by the realization that our God is a living God who can still bring protection and peace in the midst of the storms of distress, confusion and terror—a very present help in trouble.

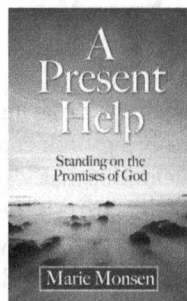

ANTHONY NORRIS GROVES
SAINT AND PIONEER
by G. H. Lang

Although his name is little known in Christian cirlces today, Anthony Norris Groves (1795-1853) was, according to the writer of this book, one of the most influential men of the nineteenth century. He was what might be termed a spiritual pioneer, forging a path through unfamiliar territory in order that others might follow. One of those who followed him was George Müller, known to the world as one who in his lifetime cared for over ten thousand orphans without any appeal for human aid, instead trusting God alone to provide for the daily needs of this large enterprise.

In 1825 Groves wrote a booklet called *Christian Devotedness* in which he encouraged fellow believers and especially Christian workers to take literally Jesus' command not to lay up treasures on earth, but rather to give away their savings and possessions toward the spread of the gospel and to embark on a life of faith in God alone for the necessaries of life. Groves himself took this step of faith: he gave away his fortune, left his lucrative dental practice in England, and went to Baghdad to establish the first Protestant mission to Arabic-speaking Muslims. His going was not in connection with any church denomination or missionary society, as he sought to rely on God alone for needed finances. He later went to India also.

His approach to missions was to simplify the task of churches and missions by returning to the methods of Christ and His apostles, and to help indigenous converts form their own churches without dependence on foreign support. His ideas were considered radical at the time but later became widely accepted in evangelical circles.

Groves was a leading figure in the early days of what Robert Govett would later call the mightiest movement of the Spirit of God since Pentecost—a movement that became known simply as the Brethren. In this book G. H. Lang combines a study of the life and influence of Anthony Norris Groves with a survey of the original principles and practices of the Brethren movement.

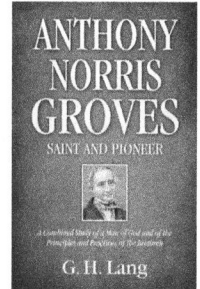

MEMOIRS OF DAVID STONER

EDITED BY
WILLIAM DAWSON & JOHN HANNAH

The name of David Stoner (1794-1826) deserves to be ranked alongside those of Robert Murray McCheyne, David Brainerd and Henry Martyn. Like them, he died at a relatively young age; and like them, his life was marked by a profound hunger and thirst for God and intense passion for souls. Stoner was saved at twelve years of age and from that point until his untimely death twenty years later his soul was continually on full stretch for God.

This book tells the story of his short but amazing life: his godly upgringing, his radical conversion, his call to preach, his amazing success as a Wesleyan Methodist preacher, his patience in tribulation and sickness, and his glorious departure to be with Christ forever. Many pages are devoted to extracts from his personal diary which give an amazing glimpse into the heart of one whose desires were all aflame for more of God.

Oswald J. Smith, in his soul-stirring book, *The Revival We Need*, wrote the following: "Have been reading the diary of David Stoner. How I thank God for it! He is another Brainerd. Have been much helped, but how ashamed and humble I feel as I read it! Oh, how he thirsted and searched after God! How he agonized and travailed! And he died at 32."

You, too can be much helped in your spiritual life as you study the life of this youthful saint of a past generation.

"Be instant and constant in prayer. Study, books, eloquence, fine sermons are all nothing without prayer. Prayer brings the Spirit, the life, the power."
—*David Stoner*

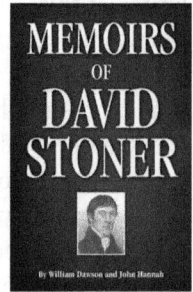

The Christian Hero
A Sketch of the Life of Robert Annan

If you've never heard of Robert Annan of Dundee, otherwise known as "the Christian Hero," prepare to be astounded at the amazing grace of God in his life as you turn the pages of this incredible little biography. Its thrilling story will stir you to the depths and almost certainly drive you to your knees with an increased desire to be used for God's glory.

The record of his beginning years reads much like that of John Newton—a life of wandering far from God in the ways of sin and rebellion. At least once he miraculously escaped death through the overruling providence of God. As time passed, he became thoroughly discontented with his sinful life; but he didn't want anything to do with God or Christianity. He thought he could overcome sin and live a morally good life by his own efforts. He soon discovered, however, that he was no match for sin or Satan; and casting himself entirely on God's grace and mercy in Jesus Christ, he was gloriously saved.

From the very first day of his conversion, he became a tireless seeker of lost souls. He worked during the day time as a stone mason, but his evenings and weekends were spent preaching in the streets or in homes. Frequently he would spend whole nights in secret prayer, pleading at the throne of grace for lost sinners. As he went to his employment in the early mornings, he would often write Scripture verses on the pavement for others to read as they passed by on their way to work or school. Thus he was instant in season and out of season, using every opportunity to present to men the claims of Jesus Christ and the reality of heaven, hell, and the judgment that awaits every human soul.

Read his story and be amazed, remembering that what God did for Robert Annan he can and will do for anyone.

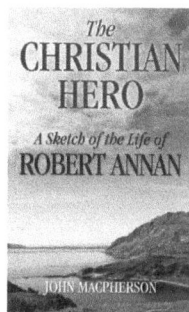

Buy online at our website: **www.KingsleyPress.com**
Also available as an eBook for Kindle, Nook and iBooks.

www.ingramcontent.com/pod-product-compliance
Lightning Source LLC
Chambersburg PA
CBHW071408090426
42737CB00011B/1392